Attaining the Ultimat

Within us all there lies a sacred seed of individual immortality which, if properly germinated and nourished, will grow into something greater than anything existing within Earthly incarnation!

A new edition of a classic work, *Attainment Through Magic* is the authoritative guidebook on creating a Magical Cosmos that will lead you to the Divine Will Within. Originally published as *A Self Made by Magic*, this important work is reprinted in its entirety, with new illustrations and a new introduction by the author.

William G. Gray, an initiated magician in the Western Inner Tradition, has devised a brilliant system of Magic that takes you, step by step, from the darkness of ignorance into infinite Light. Based on the ten principles of the Qabalistic Tree of Life, this system teaches you how to create rituals that allow you to

- harness existing forces to create a Cosmic Circle of living energy around you.
- formulate a magical Name that will summon these energies in an instant.
- create Inner sources of enlightened instruction by means of personified Archangel concepts.
- grow a metaphysical Tree of Life within you that will extend into Infinity.

To Become AS WE WILL, it is necessary to Know Our Selves, and *Attainment Through Magic* presents a means of attaining that Knowledge. By diligently following this plan of perfection represented by the Tree of Life, you will learn to live *wholly*, bringing each part of yourself in line with the Highest Light, thereby entering the state known as *Perfect Peace Profound*.

About the Author

William G. Gray received much of his early training in the Western Inner Tradition from an associate of Papus. This individual was a Qabalistic Rosicrucian, and Gray believes that his writings were profoundly influenced by this person's teachings. Later, Gray became a member of the Society of the Inner Light.

His writing career commenced when he completed two projects that Dion Fortune left unfinished at her death. One manuscript became *The Talking Tree*, and the other, *The Magical Mass* (which later became *The Sangreal Sacrament*). However, Israel Regardie's enthusiastic response to the manuscript published as *The Ladder of Lights* provided the impetus for Gray's works to reach the public.

Since that time, Gray has written several books on Western esoteric ceremonialism, devoting particular attention to what he calls the Sangreal concept.

To Write to the Author

We cannot guarantee that every letter written to the author can be answered, but all will be forwarded. Both the author and the publisher appreciate hearing from readers, learning of your enjoyment and benefit from this book. Llewellyn also publishes a bimonthly news magazine with news and reviews of practical esoteric studies and articles helpful to the student, and some readers' questions and comments to the author may be answered through this magazine's columns if permission to do so is included in the original letter. The author sometimes participates in seminars and workshops, and dates and places are announced in *The Llewellyn New Times*. To write to the author, or to ask a question, write to:

William G. Gray
c/o THE LLEWELLYN NEW TIMES
P.O. Box 64383-298, St. Paul, MN 55164-0383, U.S.A.
Please enclose a self-addressed, stamped envelope for reply, or $1.00 to cover costs.

LLEWELLYN'S NEW WORLD MAGIC SERIES

The European re-discovery of the "New World" was much more than a geographic confirmation of the "Lands to the West."

For the members of various esoteric groups, America was to be the "New Atlantis," a utopia free of ignorance, superstition, fear and prejudice—incarnating a Great Plan for the spiritual evolution of this planet. Central to the political foundations of this *New Order for the Ages* is the intellectual freedom to pursue knowledge and wisdom unrestrained by the dictates of Church and State, and to publish and speak openly that all the people may grow in wisdom and attainment.

At the very core of this vision is the recognition that each person is responsible for his or her own destiny, and to freely pursue this "Happiness" requires that one throw off domination by "personal devils" of psychic nature, just as the American Colonies rebelled against the despotism of the British King.

We must be free of that which hinders our Vision and obstructs the flowering of the Life Force. For each of us that which obstructs is our *inner* personal Evil, and it is the Great Work of the magician to accept responsibility for that Evil and to transmute its powers into personal Good. Therein lies the secret of spiritual growth.

And with personal transformation comes our enhanced Vision and Power to work with magical responsibility in the outer world and to transmute those Evils resultant from human ignorance and fear, superstition and prejudice. We move forward as we perceive such Evils as originating from within ourselves and as we challenge them in their true nature.

We live in perilous times, but a "New Age" is at hand as the techniques of personal magic are used by more and more people to accept responsibility for Evil, and to redeem it for the Good—for individual growth and success, and for the Good of the planetary life within which we have our being.

New World Magic is visionary, recognizing the role of the individual practitioner in the world in which we live, and accepting the promise of a "New Order for the Ages." It is magic that is psychologically sound and spiritually committed. It is magic that builds upon older traditions in the knowledge that within them are our roots, and it is magic that looks to new understanding to ever expand the potential into which we grow.

New World Magic is for all who want to make a *New World*!

Other books by William G. Gray

Evoking the Primal Goddess
Between Good and Evil
Temple Magic
The Ladder of Lights
Magical Ritual Methods
Inner Traditions of Magic
Seasonal Occult Rituals
The Tree of Evil
The Rollright Ritual
An Outlook on Our Inner Western Way
The Talking Tree
Western Inner Workings
The Sangreal Sacrament
Concepts of Qabalah
Sangreal Ceremonies and Rituals

Forthcoming

By Standing Stone & Elder Tree
Sangreal Tarot (tentative)

Llewellyn's New World Magic Series

Attainment Through Magic

Evoking the High Self

(a new edition of *A Self Made by Magic*)

William G. Gray

1990
Llewellyn Publications, Inc.
St. Paul, Minnesota 55164

International Standard Book Number: 0-87542-298-5
Library of Congress Catalog Number: 89-78491

Originally published as *A Self Made by Magic*
by Samuel Weiser, Inc., 1976
First Printing, 1976
Second Edition (published by Llewellyn), 1990
First Printing, 1990

Library of Congress Cataloging-in-Publication Data
Gray, William G.
       [Self made by magic]
       Attainment through magic/by William G. Gray.
       p. cm. — (Llewellyn's new world magic series)
       Reprint, with new introd. Originally published: A self made by magic. York
Beach, Me. : S. Weiser, 1976.
       ISBN 0-87542-298-5
       1. Magic. 2. Self-realization—Miscellanea. I. Title.
II. Series.
BF1611.G69 1990   89-78491
133.4'3—dc20   CIP

Cover Painting by Lissanne Lake

Produced by Llewellyn Publications
Typography and Art property of Llewellyn Worldwide, Ltd.

Published by
LLEWELLYN PUBLICATIONS
A Division of Llewellyn Worldwide, Ltd.
P.O. Box 64383
St. Paul, MN 55164-0383, U.S.A.
Printed in the United States of America

Contents

Introduction . . . . *ix*

Chapter One: Selfsearch 1

Chapter Two: The Self We Search For 33

Chapter Three: The Search System 53

Chapter Four: Cosmo-Commencement 69

Chapter Five: Cosmo-Continuance 97

Chapter Six: An Achievement of Archangels 119

Chapter Seven: In Whose Name 171

Chapter Eight: The Tree Is "Me" 201

Chapter Nine: Self Systems Are For Living With 255

Introduction

Every human being in this world is here for one particular purpose: to find and form the Real Selves we were meant to be by the Originative Power which began our beings. There are endless ways of achieving this end, and the probability is that we will choose different methods in successive incarnations so as to maximize the extent of our evolution as human souls and Selves. For example, in one life an individual might become a doctor, next time a soldier, and following that, a politician possibly succeeded by living as a minister. On the other hand, there might be a preference for some particular following that would be pursued for several incarnations in succession, or several might be selected during one lifetime. We all have our own ways of gaining the eventual Grail which will emancipate us eternally from the necessity of existence as inhabitants of this Earth and the bodies we must endure in order to live on it.

In this book we are going to consider the possibilities of making ourselves by means of Magic, as that word should be understood in our times. That means to say, an esoteric spiritual system based on beliefs and customs derived from our earliest Earth-experiences and cast into mental and spiritual molds that our contemporary consciousness can feel comfortable with. The source material of this study is taken from standard procedures that should be familiar to most students of the Western Inner Tradition. This material is presented with the intention of producing favorable Self-developing effects with the average Occidental individual; or in other words, selective processes that encourage the best of our potentials while diminishing or even eliminating our worst characteristics.

It is highly important to bear this idealistic scheme in mind the whole time these exercises and practices are being followed. They are specially designed to help you become a better and more fulfilled soul along your own natural lines of Inner development. However, if they are to indicate what you should evolve *towards*, they cannot do so adequately without indicating at the same time what you should be evolving *away from*, because these two extremities are coefficients of each other. In order to appreciate the effects and value of what is called White or beneficient Magic, the corresponding dangers and detriments of maleficient or Black Magic have to be apprehended at the same time. Consequently these will also be dealt with in this study.

Nevertheless it is essential to adopt proper perspectives when evaluating the whole picture, so that nothing is seen out of all proportion to its true importance or spiritual significance. Magic is Magic per se, and if defined as "causing change in conformity with will," it may be Black if performed with an evil intention, or White if performed with a good one. It is the causative intention that decides the definition, though not necessarily the results. We should never forget the significance of Goethe's lines from *Faust*, by which Mephistopheles the demon describes his nature: "I am ... part of that power—misunderstood—which always evil wills, yet ever worketh good." We might also consider another and probably better known saying, "The road to

Hell is paved with good intentions." Ultimate effects are usually determined by higher than human authority.

So in the end, every single soul has to take responsibility for its own Self-development along whichever lines may be chosen, though this does not give an automatic right to prevent others from following their peculiar preferences, providing those do not contravene commonly accepted codes of reasonable behavior agreed upon by a majority of their fellow mortals. The principle to uphold was once expressed publicly by whoever was the first to say, "Sir, I entirely disagree with every word you have said, but at the same time I would gladly die defending your legitimate right to say it." Perhaps free choice of consciousness guided by conscience might be an adequate definition. Human history alone affords plenty of proof concerning what happens when this freedom becomes interfered with or suppressed to any serious degree. We have seen in our own times the terrible results produced by those motivated by power and profit who have tried to restrain or regiment the minds and souls of Humankind with narrow, prescribed religious or political boundaries. Although this could not entirely be categorized as Black Magic in one sense of the term, it is certainly descriptive of activity within that field when considered in its broadest meaning.

All sorts of people are liable to be involved in such a sphere of influence, many without accurate knowledge of or complete conscious consent to what they are really doing. Some indeed might well be quite unwitting agents, even if perplexed ones. Such persons cannot fairly be described as true Black Magicians, however much they can be blamed for their indifference, lack of scruples, or disobedience to every rule of ethical behavior. The more influential their positions, the greater will be the liability incurred by deviating so far from the codes of civilized conduct and moral responsibility. Whether these practitioners happen to be ministers of religion, politicians, lawyers, teachers, bureaucrats, or whatever, they are certainly contributing to the funds that help keep the forces of evil flowing around our environment. It is sufficient that we should always be aware of their existence, yet never overestimate their ability to interfere with our unquestionable entitlements to Self-determination, however much they might desire and attempt to do just that.

We should always bear in mind that the only real power any evilworkers can hold over us is precisely what we allow them to have, and that is all, no matter how much greater it may appear. Therefore the best thing to do is refuse all suggestions coming from suspicious sources and remain with whichever reliable spiritual system is being followed, even if results obtained from it may not seem very spectacular. This position may be compared with that of an investor with limited funds who places them all in a low-interest but completely trustworthy corporation that has never failed those who relied on it for a modest and steady income. Suddenly a golden opportunity seems to open up— a new and extremely interesting possibility of making a lot more money that would double, treble, or even quadruple the capital in almost as many months. Glowing accounts are published concerning the prospects, and publicly known names are associated with them. Along with many others, the small investor withdraws his secured savings and hands them over to the profit-promising company, receiving a splendidly printed certificate in return. As might be expected, when the rapidly collected monies have been safely secured beyond the reach of investigators, the inevitable bankruptcy occurs, and all the shareholders are left practically penniless. Again and again with monotonous regularity, this South Sea Bubble has burst over the heads of greedy and stupid humans caught in the trap of their avarice and gullibility sprung by those who know very well how to set it. This entire process can perfectly well be paralleled on Inner levels when people are equally foolish with their spiritual capital for comparable reasons.

For optimum spiritual development, Western types of souls need complete freedom of choice, even if the choices they make may sometimes be wrong so far as they are concerned. Providing such freedom persists, they can subsequently choose a more suitable method for finding their True Selves. Therefore Inner and individual freedom is the most essential factor that we need to safeguard by every possible means. With it we may reach the heights and depths of Deity Itself, but should we ever be deprived of that freedom or prevented from using it to the best advantage, then we might as well live in the worst hell we humans are capable of creating for ourselves. Put in simple terms, no Devil of any sort can deprive us of the noblest gift our God has given us, but nothing prevents that same Satan from trying its utmost to persuade us to abandon or pervert this most priceless possession into wicked and wasteful channels of consciousness. So the entire responsibility for selection and choice of spiritual motives and methodologies is all yours, and YOU alone will have to abide by this until and unless you find sufficient reason for changing your course. The only question remaining is, *what* do you propose doing about it all? I do hope this special study might help in some practical way.

—William G. Gray
1989

Chapter One

Selfsearch

What is of most importance to any living entity, including the all-inclusive entity we call God by various names? If this vital question be answered truthfully, there can be only one reply—the entity Itself, whatever or whoever it is. However we disguise this basic fact of life, it remains fundamental to each and every single one of us. We are all of primal importance to ourselves from first to last of us, and the sooner we realize or admit this essential element of our existence, the better shall we begin to observe the primal and final Law which initiates us into the mysteries of Life: MAN—KNOW THYSELF.

We are intrinsically Self-seekers throughout our whole beings. We seek ourselves by birth, life, and death. We seek ourselves internally and externally as long as we exist. We seek ourselves in others, in events, everywhere and anywhere. We are our own Life-quest. If we ever found ourselves fully, the Cosmos of our Consciousness would be complete, and That would indeed be THAT. Only in Eternal Living Entity is it possible to find oneself finally. In God alone is Humankind fulfilled.

To know what one is looking for is the greatest help in finding it. How many people positively know what they are searching after all their lives? Relatively few. They may suppose they are seeking the obvious objectives of material success, such as money, social status, positions, and so forth, but these things are temporary and relatively ephemeral to the sense of Self-existence behind our beings. At best, they can only last a single human lifetime, and that is insufficient to satisfy a need for Self-becoming that is based on Life-lines extending for far longer periods of progression. It is only when we discover that what we are really looking for in life is actually Ourselves, in the truest sense of the term, that we shall make much sound sense of our lives on this Earth, or continue them with any good purpose. That single and vital piece of knowledge alone will carry us from the beginning of our beings to the end of our existent entities.

Mystics and magi alike concur that the ultimate aim of Humanity should be Divinity. All the major faiths and divergent branches of religion postulate a Deity or Deities with which human beings should attempt some kind of relationship. The various concepts and beliefs we have accepted or followed on this account are beyond any reasonably brief description, yet how often is it made indubitably clear to sincere seekers that their goal is not some abstract or anthropomorphic Divinity of indefinable attributes and remotely beneficent intentions, but THEMSELVES, for whatever they may become in fulfillment of their own BEING? That, and that alone, is truly worth living for.

It must be admitted that we are somewhat hampered in dealing with this topic by the restrictive associations connected with the word *Self* in English. This stands uncompromisingly for the entirety of every entity, making no allowance for the shades of meaning that should distinguish any Self-aspect from the rest, or one type of auto-behavior from another. We are also conditioned by inaccurate implications that "self" is wrong or bad, while "un-selfish-ness" is noble and good, yet no satisfactory explanation seems to be given anywhere for either opposite course of conduct. It is scarcely surprising that we frequently live such confused lives, with one side of ourselves trying to hide from the other, and both ends attempting to avoid the middle.

Some systems have tried to sort out Self-ideas by postulating a Higher Self and a Lower Self, as though one end of us were good and the other bad. This is obviously absurd. No Self is good or bad per se, but it is fair to say that there are auto-intentions and behavior patterns that may well be classified as good or bad relative to a Self-state sharing a common Cosmos with others. Given a standard of Self-existence to work with, our auto-activities either identify or unidentify us with this image of Individuality. Everything depends on the nature of such a standard and how we react to it. Comparatively few humans are completely aware that such standards exist, and remain content to accept conventional codings imposed upon them by the culture or society in which they live. Perhaps, more simply, they follow nothing but their lowest levels of genetic inheritance. How many individuals are capable of setting up their own Self-standards and living in line with these so as to become the best sort of Selves possible for human beings? Obviously, not a great percentage of our Earth's population, yet this process must not only be learned but also put into successful practice by anyone seeking initiated admission to the Holy Mysteries of Light.

In olden times, the basics of this procedure were explained in a very homely way to questing candidates. They had to cut a staff of their own height and make personal marks on it to represent themselves. Then a suitable place was chosen to work at night, and beneath the brilliant stars of heaven, the solitary seeker traced a circle around himself on the ground with one end of the staff. This circle stood for the limits of his comprehension around himself as a conscious living creature. The staff was then planted upright in the center of the circle, and there was the simplest of practical diagrams demonstrating the fundamentals of Self-existence. The surface of the Earth itself represented the lowest level of the Self in question. The entire Heaven showed the ultimate height which that same Self could reach. The staff signified whatever degree of development the Self had arrived at already. Placing one foot forward firmly on Earth, the individual said: "I was thus." Grasping the center of the staff, the statement "I am this" was made. And, finally, the head was raised until vision became fixed at the point of Heaven directly above, and the resolution "I Will be That!" affirmed. So did Humankind once determine its direction toward Divinity. However the elementary beauty of this simplest of rites may appeal to the imagination, there is no substitute for its practical performance, and those able to appreciate ritual procedures will gain much from the experience.

Strictly speaking, Self is our Becoming into what we Will Be, and this may be from Anything to Nothing. From our genetic psychophysical roots, through our environmental existence, both materially and metaphysically, we are faced with the life-task of extending and evolving our entities into the sort of Selves with which we are seeking Identity. All of us have this in common, as we ultimately aim toward the single Self of the Supreme Cosmic Life-Spirit. Individually, however, this universal work (or Magnum Opus as it used to be called) may be done well or badly, depending on whether or not it accords with what might be termed the Inherent Initiating Identity or cosmic constituent of every Self. Since this may be a strange concept for many to grasp, some detailed explanation seems needed.

Just as our material genetics are determined by what

are known as chromosomes, so our metaphysical or spiritual genesis is Life-linked through what might well be termed "psychosomes"—or basal characteristics of differentiated conscious energy which amount to our Self-hood as distinct from other Selves of our species, yet still connected fundamentally to the Life-Spirit of Cosmos which so many mortals call God. Every distinct Self bears within its spiritual basis a sort of program pattern of the Identity intended for it by its original Cosmic Creative Consciousness. Deep inside each of us is a built-in blueprint of the sort of Self we ought to become if we faithfully followed the Will or Intention within the Creative Word at the very back of our Initial Origin, and may therefore be considered as the most inherent part of our Identity. This initiated us into life at our cosmic commencement, and indeed continues to initiate us through all the lives we shall ever lead in search of whatever the Ultimate means to us. It is thus our Inherent Initiating Identity, sometimes called the "real" or True Self, Divine Will Within, Immortal Identity, or similar terms.

Though originating from a Single Source, every Self is unique insofar as it exists particularly for the purpose implanted in it initially by its Divine Decider. We are all distinct and different from each other in that respect, and most certainly *not* "all equal in the eyes of God," since we each have some specific and especial Intention in us that can only be fulfilled through our Selfhood in the best and truest sense of the word. Whatever carries that Intention correctly through its cosmic courses we may consider beneficial to us, and whatsoever impedes or impairs such an action can only be detrimental to our deepest interests.

Granted all this, why do we remain such imperfect people living in a world so full of our spiritual failures? Here is where our legendary "Fall" comes in. Once Humanity lost conscious contact with its Primal Purpose and sought Self through biological processes of Earth existence, we automatically limited ourselves by the laws governing these relatively minor conditions of Cosmos, and "came down" in Life as it were, into very restricted areas of awareness from which we may only emerge again by eventual evolvement, or individual Initiation. To adequately express the fulfilling forces of an Inherent Initiating Identity through a purely human personal incarnation is a virtual impossibility, and this may only be expected to a maximum degree of practicality. This means that only a partial projection of any Self is possible as a human mortal on Earth, and merely fractional and proportional energies of our Inner potentials operate through us. Whether to a major or minor degree, we are Selves very much scaled down to fit our present framework in the physical dimensions of this planet.

As an outcome of prolonged projection into conditions of incarnation, there developed an entire species of "semi-Selves" whose life-interests became more and more absorbed with affairs of this world for their own sakes. Where these tended to clash with wider cosmic issues, preference was given to the "Earth-side" consideration of Self, and gradually a separative effect throughout the Earth-based life-stream of Selves produced Humankind in its present condition: semi-Selves of limited initiative, confining their consciousness between birth-death boundaries of flesh-forms for the sake of maintaining their mortality for various reasons entirely connected with their Earth-dependent entities.

Such are the "selves" so many millions of humanized lives accept as their whole beings for indefinite cycles of incarnation. Pieces of themselves posing as entire entities, and attempting to set up an artificial state of autonomy in imitation of the Immortal Identity that should rightfully be theirs. Between our Initial Intentional Identity and our personified partial projections of it into humanized flesh-formations has grown up this apparently independent

Pseudo-Self demanding recognition in its own right and insisting upon its dictates being accepted as authoritative throughout its sphere of influence. It is inevitable that this should be so in the course of our development as cosmic creatures, and if only our evolving Earth-selves were correctly related with our other extensions into Existence as a whole, we should have no serious problems or troubles to deal with on any life-level. As we know to our cost, such a state of affairs certainly does not exist on this Earth to any noticeable degree, yet we may scarcely expect true peace and worthwhile prosperity on this planet until we become ourselves in the best sense of the term.

How do we know what we are? We originate from Spirit as individual Divine Sparks, each with its own Inherent Intention. Then we fall into materialized flesh-formation, and our consciousness becomes narrowed and circumscribed to the levels of cellular life which we come to accept as "ourselves" because of confinement thereto. This becomes a sort of Self on its own, and has been termed "Body." Inter-reaction produces "Soul," which feels, and "Mind," which reasons, as other Self-categories of consciousness. Though these nonphysical components of ourselves survive bodily death in their own way, that is not true immortality—which is a condition of Spirit alone—and until we become fully functioning Entities in that category of consciousness, we shall not be really *Eternal Individuals*.

What has happened in the case of Humanity is that we have gradually built up these almost separate Selves on our own accounts consisting of components from our Body, Mind, and Soul areas of awareness. Over the aeons, we have grown accustomed to accepting these composite constructions of consciousness as our entire Selves—more or less taking for granted an assumption that this is all we may ever be. Moreover, a large proportion of Humanity is content to confine its Self-seeking indefinitely to these relatively artificial Life-limits. The majority of Humankind has little inclination to advance beyond secondary Self-states that satisfy its immediate demands for persistence of projection. Then again, there are humans who feel or know instinctively that their ME make-up is unsatisfactory in some way, and so they struggle around from one incarnation to another in an attempt to set themselves up in some kind of order. A few of them may eventually succeed in drawing the line through themselves that connects their Initial Intentional Identity with their correct cosmic course of completion, and so the circle of initiates of the Living Light increases.

That is the central and principal point of true Self-seeking in its mystical and magical sense: lining up all the projected parts of Self-extensions so that they carry the Initial Intention of our Innermost Identity around the complete cosmic circle of autonomous awareness, thus becoming WHAT IT WILL. In old-fashioned words this is "doing the Divine Will" or, "Thy Will, not mine, be done." In fact, it is simply BEING ONESELF in the deepest meaning of the phrase. To *Be* Oneself it is necessary to *Know* Oneself, as the Mystery Dictum points out, and that is chiefly what this present work is concerned with. Many methods have been employed by human entities in search of themselves, and perhaps the oldest and most instinctive of all is known to us by the generic title of Magic, the "mighty art" through which Humankind dealt directly with Divinity. So we shall continue to make use of this method in the most modern fashions convenient to our current consciousness. If it serves us now as it did once, we shall be rewarded for our choice of a medium through which we may explore the eternal enigma of ME inherent in all of us.

There is one overwhelming reason why Magic is a valid means for such a vital task in this day and age of human Earth-occupation. The "day and age" itself supplies the answer. We are always people of our time, and these times—which extend into the foreseeable future—are particularly perilous times in which to live, from the viewpoint of all who seek their real Identity as a Self in the true meaning of the term. There have always been on this planet those whose personal interests are bound up with preventing others from Self-becoming. Not a very difficult matter in a world where few seem concerned with this to any marked degree. In past times, controls exerted through religious, military, and economic channels affecting the basic fear-greed mainsprings of human conduct proved adequate means for manipulating the masses of Humankind. Though these still apply, recent improvements and discoveries already make them look old-fashioned, and in the future may prove to be the most widespread methods of Humankind management all over the world. Most of these modern "person persuaders" are psychological, but others are chemical and biological with truly frightening possibilities. Never before in this aeon has the human psyche been so probed, pressurized, and scientifically interfered with by specialists in these fields for extremely questionable reasons. The human herd is being rounded up for an odd market, where souls and selves are readily purchasable commodities once they are trimmed to buyers' requirements. The sanctity of Self and the integrity of individualizing entities is threatened almost beyond belief. All this much is ascertainable through material available in any public library. What is not readily forthcoming seems to be encouraging or practical suggestions for Self-salvation and achievement of individual Identity in the face of formidable opposition to the natural rights of every living soul. This is where Magic comes in, because it is full of Self-liberating formulae, and intrinsically individualistic by tradition right down through the ages.

Let us face the problem squarely and sincerely. How many individuals on Earth are, or ever can be, the Selves they truly could be deep down in their basic beings? How much of the apparent Selves we present to everyone else is genuinely and truly "Us," and how much is nothing but a convenient cover or camouflage we have collected around us for various reasons? What do we take into ourselves because we Will or want to, and what gets forced upon us because of what others wish us to do for their benefit rather than ours? Which part of our make-up is really our Selves, and what remainder have we borrowed or had inflicted on us for a lifetime? What prevents the process of our own perfection, and how close can we come to being our actual Selves amid the circumstances and constrictions of our human Earth-lives? All these are very vital and pertinent questions indeed. Self-becoming is the life-purpose of every soul on this planet or anywhere else for that matter. If we are prevented from carrying out this purpose, or deliberately refuse to recognize it, then we are in trouble. The proportion of human ills and afflictions arising from this very cause is almost incalculable. How can we be healthy, happy, or worthwhile humans while our Self-systems are in such a shockingly disordered condition? We are surely justified in using whatever corrective methods may be called for, including Magic, if it seems likely to help sort ourselves out into correct cosmic categories.

Why should Magic be such an ideal means of Self-seeking, and what gives it the slightest significance in the twentieth and twenty-first centuries? The first part of the question is answered by the fact that Magic is first and foremost a personal and individual practice whereby Selves relate with spiritual energies. It is the operation of individual or private intentions, either singly or collectively, brought to bear through circuits of cosmic potencies. Everyone has their own particular abilities and understanding of Magic, and this is something they must do for themselves with their own energies or not at all. The secrets of

Magic are secrets of Self, and its "Initiations" are stages of Individuation intended to reach right back to the Supreme Self of All. For the second part of the question, Magic is an art, and every genuine art adapts itself to its era. Arts do not alter in principle, but in presentation and practice. So with Magic. The magical practices of the twentieth century are naturally enhanced by modern knowledge, techniques, and available accessories, but, *au fond*, the Ancient Art is basically what it always was and will be: Humankind making more of itself through Intentional Inner Activity and through selected circuits of consciousness.

Most significantly of all, perhaps, is that Magic happens to be essentially a secret art extending between its practitioners and their Inner areas of awareness. Other arts are angled between human artists and their equally human appreciators—the single actor or singer and their large audiences, the writer and his readers, the painter and his viewers, the priest and his congregation, are all instances of creative activity flowing through the few to the many on human levels of participation. In the case of Magic the force-flow is rather in the reverse direction through individual magi to participators existing in different dimensions of life than purely physical projections. Magic can never be a public or a paid performance in the usual sense of the words. True, there may exist relatively small associations of practicing ritualists for the sake of mutual assistance in routine or other matters, but if these are genuine, their aim should be the emergence of highly entitized experts in the Art, whose individual abilities will necessarily help others along the single-file Path of Initiation. Where one has gone others may follow, one at a time.

This is why there are not, and never will be, huge magical organizations on Earth with millions of members, even though millions of people may have some interest in Magic. Even the most successful magical groups can only work with very few members, and the more that membership is numerically increased by earthly entrants, the less effective their mutual Magic may be as an interdimensional instrument of art. It is like saying that the broader and blunter any cutting edge of consciousness gets, the less power of penetration or purpose it has. To flatten out the field of Magic so that it becomes common property is to decrease proportionately the extent of its effects. There are certainly many mainstream opportunities for entering the magical arena via published material and various types of group-working, but even the most esoteric of these is only a general fund of information from whence the Self-specializing disciplines and procedures, which constitute the real Magic, may be eventually constructed. Those who are unwilling or unable to Individualize themselves will never become magicians of any kind, though they may become victims of Magic misapplied by others.

This immediately raises the inevitable topic of so-called Black Magic, so relished by sensationalists. It is obvious that any art or activity can be put to beneficial or malicious uses relative to human beings. Magic is no exception. At the same time, most of the viciousness and cruelty which masquerades as Black Magic on the level of yellow journalism is no more than just that: stupid, sadistic, unbalanced, and chaotically disposed creatures, together with their discarnate associates, behaving in accordance with their character. There is sufficient such activity in this world already, without any implications of Magic. To dress up common or garden depravity in the theatrical trappings of stage-set Satanism and call this mess Black Magic is utterly inaccurate to say the least. Real Black Magic consists in the exploitation of such situations for much more deadly purposes by those who are well aware of how to handle evil for their own exclusive interests, which are opposed to the cosmic ends of entitized evolution.

This is the clear dividing line between Black and White Magic. Both are techniques of Self-assertion, but the Black Magician asserts and maintains his own ego at the expense of others, and by preventing their individual evolution as much as possible. This is much the same principle as being wealthy by keeping everybody else poor, or seeming to be clever by preventing others from learning. It is the "control by contrast" method of the big frog in the little pond, which only works for frogs that are able to retard development in tadpoles occupying the same space. In the case of the White Magician, individuation of Self is carried out as a direct act of advancement between the Initiate and his Inherent Cosmic Intention, independent of other Self-activities in any direction. Because such an act is essentially cosmic, however, many other Selves may benefit from it, as for instance someone who gains wealth enriches others, or the cultural attainments of a single soul might influence whole generations of people. Such is the fundamental difference between Black and White Magic. The former inhibits individualization of Selves past the arbitrary limits it imposes for its own purposes, while the latter encourages this process of perfection through its entire field of influence.

It must not be assumed, however, that a White Magician is necessarily a "do-gooder," inflicting unasked benefits upon less able fellow beings. His primary concern is his own personal perfection for the sake of increasing power to serve the single Cosmic Cause that intends the individual evolution of every conscious entity. Accordingly he tries to work this Will within himself, and does not intentionally interfere with its workings in others. By respecting the integrity of other Selves, he enhances the state of his own. Where benevolent activity is called for in the normal course of civilized conduct, this is readily forthcoming, and where defensive measures are needed in support of ethical standards, these are freely applied, but in general the White

Magician is a minder of his own business rather than an intervener in affairs that do not demand his attention. When engaged in ordinary human affairs he uses straightforward human abilities unmixed with Magic in the proper sense of the word. Never does a true White Magician attempt to use his art to inhibit the wills of other individuals, even if those intend evil. In such a case, however, a competent Initiate of Magic could arrange means whereby a projection of ill-intentions would reflect back harmlessly from the objective to the detriment of the sender. No more. Revenge plays no part in White Magic, and the energies used for evil are sufficient to cause their own retribution and equation when transformed and redirected to their intentional transmitter. The Self sought by a genuine White Magician is above injury by the malice of Humankind, however much the lesser sections of the Self closer to personal human presentation in this world may be hurt in the course of ordinary living.

An intentional practitioner of Black Magic has to live in this world like everyone else, and must therefore come within the general framework of conventions, codes, laws and regulations of human behavior customary to human associations on Earth. Consequently, he must make his Magic conform with convenience. He, like his White Magic counterpart, has to use twentieth-century circumstances in which to do his will-working, and if his rewards seem much richer in contrast to past times, so have his risks of failure increased. We must always remember the central aim of Black Magic, which is interference with the Initial Individualizing Intention, and the supplanting of this by the Pseudo-Self, or imitation individuality. This is like an artificial ego developed after many incarnations during which the surviving consciousness operating through a human unit has become more and more attached to mundane matters, and is more deeply involved with the occupation of Earthly power-positions than with the ends of cosmic evolution and subjects of spiritual importance.

During each incarnation we build up what is known as our personality, or Me-mask, which is a compilation of consciousness derived from our reactive experiences with life in this world. When our bodies die, this personality should also come to pieces and its essential energies be absorbed into our surviving spiritual nature so that our living entities may be modified more closely to the Initiating Intention. This is one of the main reasons why the traditions of White Magic are emphatically against attempts to recall the past personalities of dead people. To do so interferes with the natural and beneficial process of Inner integration of that personality with the Identity whose projection it was. Once the personal part of a Self is safely reabsorbed and assimilated on spiritual life-levels, the incarnating side of the Self may seek fresh experiences through Earth-existence, if it so wills, with an improved outlook for fulfilling the Intention behind it. This process might be called "clearing past Karma," "Purgatory," or whatever term seems applicable. It is actually a cosmic corrective course for the realignment of a Self with its individual standard of spiritual integrity, which is set by the Initiating Intention. If this worked as it should, there would be few troubles among the human inhabitants of Earth. But we are still undeniably imperfect people, fully capable of creating calamities for ourselves.

What happens with a high proportion of incarnating entities is that their personal projections into Earth life are not fully absorbed into higher categories of consciousness, but remain as a sort of residual Self-section in a subconscious state composed of multiple accretions of awareness derived from others sharing the same conditions of what can only be described as semi-living. As one incarnation succeeds another, these undigested portions of past personalities take on what amounts to a Pseudo-Self of their own, which survives physical death and may even be capable of sustaining their independence until the cessation of Cosmos. The only hope of extending past that point is some kind of symbiosis with Chaos, which carries the terrible implication of yet another Cosmo-Creation threatened with structural imperfections at its inception, resulting in the imprisonment of the Identity in the Indefinite, rather than release into the Infinite Reality of PERFECT PEACE PROFOUND.

Nevertheless, we must not make the mistake of supposing our Pseudo-Selves to be fundamentally bad, evil, or wrong for what they amount to. While they last, they can and should be like our bodies, a very useful means of mediation between our extensions into Earth-Life and the Selves we truly are as Individual Entities of the Life-Spirit. In fulfilling this function they are serving the cause of Cosmos and the purpose of ultimate perfection throughout its totality. It is only when these Pseudo-Selves of ours refuse absorption into our spiritual systems of regeneration and insist on setting up their antagonistic authority against the Individual Intention of their Overself that they make serious trouble for anyone. Unhappily, this is a common complaint among human beings in general, and with Black Magicians in particular.

In the case of most people, the Pseudo-Self is not especially potent, even though persistent, and taken by and large it averages out more or less to the good in the long run. In the case of the Black Magician, circumstances are very different. The Pseudo-Self becomes increasingly dominant and insistent on its interests being made the principal concern of whatever consciousness passes through the personality projecting it into Earth-existence. This desire for domination is typically characteristic of a Pseudo-Self insurrection, cleverly disguised though it may be. The almost invariable symptom is determination in some way to prevent individualization of others in order to secure its own apparent Self-status. Realizing its limitations, a Pseudo-Self knows its best chance of survival is among those who have not yet developed its degrees of acquisitive authority and status assertion. Therefore it does everything it can to retard or discourage others from advancing past its personal position. This is a common situation among humans who are far from being Black Magicians, and such a designation belongs strictly only to those who make intentional use of essentially magical means to achieve an objective shared with many Pseudo-Self-minded members of Humankind.

The distinguishing feature of true Black Magicians is a conscious knowledge of this Self-situation, a resolution to exploit it for Pseudo-Self ends, and an intentional association with discarnate intelligences of parallel purposes in different dimensions of existence who may be classified as "evil," or not in the best interests of human spiritual evolution. Conversely, a real White Magician is characterized by consciousness of the Self position, determination to set the Pseudo-Self into mediatory service between its Overself and personalized projections into humanity, and willingness to link up with Inner Intelligences dedicated to the cosmic cause of the Life-Spirit. The means by which these relationships are maintained constitutes the kind of Magic employed in either extremity.

Popular ideas of Black Magicians indulging in sex-drug orgies of depravity, or fiendish sado-masochistic revels for the sake of Satanic satisfaction are very far-fetched and incorrect indeed. It is true that such events occur in connection with Black Magical activities, but they are indulged in by the victims rather than by the vice-presidents of what we may call Crime against Cosmos. Such practices degrade the Pseudo-Self, or leave it in a seriously damaged condition which may cause impediments to the Initial Intentions, taking considerable time and trouble to rectify. In effect, the sensory personal practices of so-called Black Magic result in severe spiritual ill-health which may persist over several incarnations and spoil the correct cosmic workings of a Self-system for quite a period of projection. This is exactly what the real Black Magician intends for others rather than his own Pseudo-Self. Realizing only too well the injurious effects of such stupid behavior in terms of weakened will and personal instability, a genuine Black Magician provides full facilities for others to indulge their self-destructive tastes to suit his convenience, but keeps well clear of personal participation or involvement with the direct energy-fields of these ruinous rites or practices. For one reason, he knows he dare not lose control of his Pseudo-Self, and for another, he has no intention of exposing that Pseudo-Self to risks of criminal prosecution or blackmail. Those proceedings are for his clients—not his own Pseudo-Self.

Ostensible Black Magicians soaking in Satanism and wallowing in Witchcraft of the worst sort are somewhat inferior imitations of the authentic article. They are far more likely to appear as pillars of the Church whose beliefs they are betraying, staunch supporters of the society they undermine, or the most law-abiding members of the community they corrupt by cleverly converting courses of consciousness into channels likely to have the worst consequences from a cosmic viewpoint. Not a single illegal or even very immoral action in the customary sense of the word can be laid at the door of an efficient Black Magician. He does not have to break conventional laws and codes of conduct to work his ill-will toward human entities on Earth. With some skill he may have the force of man-made laws behind him and weight of public opinion in his favor. Whatever faults a real Black Magician may have, incompetence is certainly not among them. He is not recognizable for what he is by any ordinary kind of investigation, and his cover would stand the closest screening by the strictest methods of conventional security checks any human authority might devise. There is just one clue to his nature which he can never completely conceal from even moderately sensitive souls: the most terrible Inner feeling of coldness and isolation when in his presence. It is an unmistakable feeling of abandonment and "lostness," as if threatened by a pitiless extinction in some appallingly vast and utterly engulfing Void. In some way or other, there is always an uncanny sense of chill and Inner iciness associated with the aura of intense evil, which no Black Magician can wholly hide, no matter how complete his cover. On the surface his personal presentation may seem pleasant or reasonable enough, but sooner or later this strange sense of chilly isolation should warn those who feel it antipathetically to take protective precautions on their own account.

Fortunately, Black Magicians of this degree are relatively rare, shun publicity, and avoid contacts outside their close circles except through intermediaries if possible. They are unlikely to be met in milieus accessible to average individuals, and they certainly would not attract attention to themselves in connection with Magic, any more than a political agent or spy would advertise his connections with his employers. This puts the claims of imitation or amateur Black Magicians where they belong—in the braggadocio bracket, or false-front field. Who talks loudest usually knows least, says the old saw, and this certainly applies here. Secrecy is even more important to a real Black Magician than a White one, though for entirely opposite reasons.

A noteworthy illustration of this issue is the late Aleister Crowley, whom the popular press exaggerated into a Black Magician of ridiculous proportions—not, it must be admitted, without some deliberate encouragement from Crowley himself. Crowley was all too human and far too fallible to qualify for more than a somewhat murky grey Magic, relieved by flashes of occasional brilliance which revealed what he might have been otherwise. To claim

Crowley as an Adept of Evil, or Magus of Malice, is sheer ignorance of the subject altogether. Leaving aside all Crowley's theatricality and ambitious absurdities, such as deliberate attempts to disgust people in order to attract attention to himself like a naughty child, he had two characteristics in particular that make nonsense of his Black Magical reputation. One was his undoubted sense of humor, unpleasant as it might sometimes have been, and the other was his genuine affection for children. So far as can be ascertained, there seems to be no record of him ever being cruel or mildly unkind to a child. This alone should speak for itself. Had his roots been as deeply implanted in evil as some seem to suppose, the fact would have invariably shown up in his behavior toward children and in an absence of humor toward life. His own childhood accounted for most of his sadly distorted Self. He started incarnation with a definite disadvantage— he had wealthy parents of badly biased religious and sexual opinions. Had he been born of poor and understanding people, his own natural talents would undoubtedly have taken him where he wanted to be without any help from Magic, Black or White.

The genuine expert of evil is a passionless pursuer of his purpose, and Crowley was positively not passion-free. His Pseudo-Self lacked the quality of icy isolationism necessary for focusing the forces of anti-Light effectively against cosmic creation. Just as Light needs the purest possible condition of a lens through which to concentrate energies, so does darkness demand an equivalently suitable medium for intensifying its influence. From an essentially evil viewpoint, any traces of compassion, affection, mercy or inclinations toward feelings for other humans would be serious defects of character, impairing the efficiency of any projection mechanism such as a Pseudo-Self. These must therefore be eliminated as far as possible from the entity being used for such a purpose. Although this greatly increases the performance and efficiency of such a specialized Pseudo-Self, the process has the disadvantage of making the mechanism rather conspicuous in a world full of ordinary humans. Therefore, the more finely finished foci of evil are likely to remain relatively anonymous, influencing others through less efficient but more acceptable media to the general public. A qualified Black Magician is no flamboyant fool, but a coldly competent professional who knows his work to its smallest details. He has to, because if he fails he is finished. Mercy is an entirely meaningless word in his vocabulary, and there is no forgiveness of fools known to his code of conduct. Expediency is everything, and sentiment the worst of sins.

Not that an intelligent Black Magician disapproves of sentiment—in others. It pays him best to operate in a community of docile do-gooders. A cheat makes his largest profits from those who trust him most and question his methods least. A liar is credited mainly by ready believers, and all types of unscrupulous behavior flourish best in atmospheres of willing acceptance. None are more exploitable than those who enjoy or invite exploitation, and a major part of a Black Magician's art is devoted to persuading other people to accept his schemes and comply with his policies. In commercial terms, he has to sell his Pseudo-Self products in a very variable market, but there seems to be no great shortage of customers at the trade-counters.

On the opposite side of the picture, the White Magician sets about constructing his own Self-system of Cosmos. It has many comparable points to those of the Black procedure. As an individualizing entity, the White Initiate of Magic moves away from the levels of mass-Humankind, becoming more and more marked as a Self with every degree of rising. His Pseudo-Self, however, becomes less and less dominant during this changeover of personalizing polarity, and begins to fulfill its useful function of mediation between the Initiating Self-Intention and the presentation of personality as a member of Humankind. Other humans sensing something of this while in contact with the Magician might feel disturbed or even somewhat uncomfortable and awkward, if the influence troubles their Pseudo-Self complacency, or more deeply still, touches what amounts to their "cosmic conscience." Since no threat to their individual Wills exists with a White Magician (as it does with a Black one), no one experiences anything like a lonely, frightening chill or a soul-freezing sensation of impending doom when in his presence. However disturbing an encounter with a White Magician may be, there will always be an impression of light, warmth, and stimulus obtained through the experience.

White Magicians are not delicately disposed creatures of sticky sweetness and lackluster light. They are essentially Selves struggling for consistency and coexistence with the Cosmic Consciousness originating their Initiating Intention. They are souls striving for Selfhood, and minds aiming at an awareness far beyond the boundaries of mortal mentality. In brief, they are Self-Seekers of their own Immortal Identity, and the only reason they might be termed Magicians at all is because of their methods of managing this universal Magnum Opus. Contrary to some popular beliefs, they do not live in a perpetual state of Inner warfare with Black opponents, waging battles of belief that end in temporary triumph for the goodies and disgruntled defeat for the baddies until the next round. That is pure fiction. It is not that any form of nonaggression pact exists between practitioners of Black Magic and White Magic, but simply that an oppositional divergence in their codes of conduct allows coexistence in this mortal world. The guiding principle of a White Magician is noninterference with the will-workings of others unless his own Initial Intention involves itself in the interests of cosmic causes, which is a much rarer eventuality than might be supposed. No experienced White Magician would dream of intervening between Black practitioners and their willing victims, because to do so would be contrary to the wills of both parties and an interference with the laws of Self-determination which the White Magician upholds. If one party intends some evil practice, and the other intends permissive participation therein, such is their prerogative under a common Law of Life which the Supreme Life Spirit Itself cannot abrogate without ceasing Its creative consciousness and ending expressional existence. Since the White Magician is pledged to partnership with Cosmic Law, he can scarcely be expected to break it with casual indifference.

Being bound by no such pledge, the Black Magician is free to coerce others in whatever ways he can, but coercion is not the same as compulsion, and the vast majority of people influenced by Black Magic are quite willing recipients of its terms despite any superficial comments they might make to the contrary. Black Magicians, being fully aware of this, are normally quite satisfied with their situations when these produce high personal profits, providing they confine their attentions to willing victims. No knowledgeable Black Magician ever attempts serious assaults on the true Will proceeding from the Initiating Intention of anyone. This is impractical, effort-wasting, and liable to cause the magician far more trouble and repercussions than is worthwhile. Besides, such an effort is utterly uneconomical while all the ready-made sources of supply await exploitation. A Black Magician may put as much pressure on Pseudo-Selves as they will bear, but once there are any signs of Self-awakening and resistance from higher levels of Identity, pressure will be promptly relaxed or shifted to an altogether different angle. The Black Magician knows just how far to risk his own Pseudo-Self before abandoning a pointless pursuit likely to result in personal detriment of some kind.

This is not to say, however, that if magical methods fail, he might not resort to plain criminal activity or assault. As a rule, though, hired henchmen are the weapons used for such low-level attacks, and their employment is evidence of failure in magical competence, which is seldom clever policy to admit.

A qualified White Magician, therefore, does not deliberately interfere with Black workings unless there is some direct cosmic call to this effect, which is rare, and only likely if an appeal at high level were made for help by some utterly unwilling Self in dire danger from magically directed malicious energy with which it could not cope. Though not impossible, this is definitely most uncommon. Since Black Magic operates mainly through Pseudo-Selves, its effective range of influence is not much higher, serious though this seems to Earth-based people. Nevertheless, as in the case of all energies, there do arise "peak-points" or cyclic concentrations of power having enough intensity to penetrate the protective screening between the different levels of Self-consciousness. In physical terms, we may penetrate the personal perimeter of any individual by (for example) a bullet or projectile that injures or kills him, an injection that saves his life, or anything at all affecting him for good or ill. So in spiritual equivalents, the Self may be occasionally invaded even at a cosmic level, and may need the support of other Selves having similar or superior status for its survival. This is inevitably forthcoming if it is the true Will of that Self to survive in Cosmos. Otherwise its essential energy neutralizes and passes back into the infinite NIL which is behind all Being. This amounts to cessation of that Self, and although another will emerge to take its place, such an interchange, slight as it may be, will prolong by that extent the completion of Cosmos in the Ultimate State of PERFECT PEACE PROFOUND. That, of course, means more time for Pseudo-Selves to enjoy their extended existence, and Black magicians to prolong their period of personal power.

Only when another Self is threatened with such a crisis is a White Magician not only entitled but also obliged to answer a call made on a cosmic level from Selves within his spiritual "degree of kindred." The more highly individualized a Self, the more difficult is its replacement in the procedural plan for cosmic perfection, and therefore the more valuable does it become intrinsically from all viewpoints. If it neutralizes itself by voluntary abnegation of its awareness (which amounts to spiritual suicide), then it breaks up into basic energies which eventually emerge into the area of existence as other Selves. (This is why suicide on even physical levels is so abhorrent to all spiritual systems.) On the other hand, if it Ultimates into the infinity of NIL as its individualized eternal entity, then we all become so much closer to the cosmic closure of creation in Perfect Peace Profound. Thus, the White Magician is actually supporting himself in assisting others of his cosmic category seeking liberation into Light, since their Selfsearch and his coincide in the same Completion. He is not working against, but with, their individualizing Wills unopposed by Pseudo-Self counterclaims. This makes all the vital difference to decisive activity in White Magical matters.

As a mildly amusing illustration of unwise interference in magical activities, an actual incident occurred in which a well-meaning but officiously overzealous magical practitioner prevented a female from being used as "an altar of shame" during some dubious Black Mass affair. Far from gaining her adoring gratitude (as he probably hoped) he was deservedly hurt to the egoic quick by her annoyance and dislike of his action. He had quite a shock when he realized she was regarding him with little but loathing and contempt. One cynical commentator remarked: "Of course she loathed him. He'd ruined her evening of sin!" True if terse. People do hate to have their sins spoiled, especially their sexual entertainments disguised though these may be in Black Magical theatrical trappings. Pseudo-Self-appointed saviors have no place in serious magical practice, where the sensible rule is not to interfere with the vices of others providing these can be contained in their own Pseudo-Self circles. The cosmic way of dealing with such evils is to encircle them with a protective perimeter so that they eventually "eat themselves up" and are neutralized through sheer force-failure. This is actually how the White Magician works in cosmic conjunction with others. They do not tackle evils at ground level, so to speak, but set up circles of containing consciousness that are sufficiently strong to confine the effects of evil of Self high enough to "turn it off at the main" by connecting up channels for the energies of Cosmic Creative Consciousness to flow more freely through Its Initiating Intentions of Individuation.

The most effective way of reducing human proclivities for evil is surely for the majority of Humankind to alter their life-attitudes of their own accord from deep within themselves. This may seem slow over the centuries, but it is also the only sure method productive of peace and progress for all people. To stop the supply of ill-intentioned energies in this world, we must simply eliminate demand. The Black Magician supplies a common demand from many Pseudo-Selves. The White Magician aims at encouraging individualizing entities to cease demanding such commodities and change their type of custom for finer levels of living. Whereas the Black Magician uses every kind of coercion to keep his customers in a queue, the White Magical practitioner seeks no customers at all, but only cosmic companions who have grown into Individual Initiation for themselves as he has. This just about sums up the situation.

None of the foregoing should be taken to imply that a White Magician is a passive permitter of criminal and antisocial activities inflicted on unwilling victims. As an upholder of accepted civil and even religious codes, he is both entitled and enjoined to maintain law and order by any suitable methods. It is simply that he would not employ any form of specifically magical practice in these fields of activity, reserving this for operation on higher Inner levels, from where human affairs must ultimately be influenced. That makes the soundest spiritual sense to an initiated intelligence.

Like every art, Magic has its own particular area of application, and to employ it otherwise would not only indicate an ignorance of its nature, but also be a foolish waste of time and energy. The correct operational area of Magic is within the fields of human consciousness that connect most closely with Inner orders of Intelligence that exist independently of material manifestation. Insofar as these are able to affect our conditions of Earthly living by influencing the courses of our consciousness in any way, it may be said that Magic is workable by Humankind. To demand impossible physical or other phenomena that are totally impractical and outside the limits of life-laws is an absurd abuse of the art altogether. One of the main magical secrets is knowing what may or may not be done with it. For example, a Black Magician attempting to turn someone into a toad would literally be foredoomed to failure. A better-instructed operator would link-in with entities capable of directing "toadified" frequencies of consciousness toward the human target in whatever way seemed most likely to ensure their acceptance. Once this has happened, and the victim continues accepting ideas of "toadiness," his Pseudo-Self will naturally assume some toad-like characteristics. The rest of the process depends largely on circumstances, but all sorts of things may be changed or may occur in mundane events because of such Inner influence. The crux of the issue is whether or not the Pseudo-Self accepts or rejects the initial influence. Most people are scarcely strong enough to resist constant and continued pressures directed at their weakest points. Knowing this, a competent Black Magician keeps hammering away with just the correct insistence until penetration into the Pseudo-Self area of awareness is obtained. After that, the follow-up procedures are switched on. Nevertheless, no sensible Black Magician continues wasting efforts against spiritual surfaces that are not only immune to his usual instruments, but also bounce back his blows so that he only injures himself. Such is the personal protection a White Magician must learn to assume as an armor of Inner living, especially while incarnate in this world.

Both Black and White Magicians employ their art principally for similar purposes—making themselves into what they Will be. Whereas the Black Magician's aim is an artificial entitization of Pseudo-Self centered round a force-focus derived from a power-source inimical to cosmic individuation, the White Magician is concerned with his Individuality becoming WHAT IT WILL through himself, centering upon the natural Nucleus or "Seed of Spirit" that springs into being at his Origination from the Infinite NIL. The difference between Initiates of Light and Initiates of Darkness depends on their type of Self-becoming. This is the significance of Gautama's famous dictum: "In Truth is No-Self, and in Self is No-Truth." Do we center on the NIL (Nirvana) seeking nucleus of Self, which we might term our True Selves, or do we center upon its antithesis in Pseudo-Self, which is relatively unTruthful? That is what we are concerned with discovering and putting into practice by means of magical methods during this present investigation of Inner Identity.

Collaterally, we need to know how to preserve any sort of Self-hood at all in a world where all personality is becoming increasingly processed by modifying media coming more into the control of a "closed-shop" coterie of Pseudo-Self elected entities. We can look back in history with some horror at antievolutionary influences appearing through various mass-controlling concerns such as religious systems, political set-ups, commercial combines, and even particular personages. Even the worst of these was a weak and ineffective effort compared to the coldly calculating caucus that is organizing a complete takeover bid for the future of Humankind on this planet, and possibly further than that if opportunity is ever offered.

It comes to this: Either we learn and practice the secrets of Self-survival toward eventual Individuality, becoming our Selves by Magic or any other means, or else we supinely submit to acceptance of whatever Pseudo-Self substitutes may be deliberately determined for us by the "mind-makers" and "people planners" who are "factory-flooring" our future for their personal profit—a cushioned and comfortable future for the meek who shall inherit the Earth if they are satisfied with spiritual slavery. Contented and satiated slaves are the easiest of all to manage, and the most economical to maintain, since they will support the system that enslaves them almost to the end of their existence. To gain a world, yet lose the Selves we might have been! Who cares enough to count the cost in cosmic coinage?

Many mortals, especially young ones, sense this danger to their developing Individualities from the controlling interests of Pseudo-Self civilization on Earth. Lacking instructed experience, they react wildly and absurdly, driving themselves into the very traps they are trying to avoid. They defy codes of convention, wear ludicrous clothing, cultivate abundant hair growth or assume baldness; they join subversive groups or start their own—all the usual dreary symptoms of defiance that appear century after century among those of each human generation who experience apprehensions about whatever system seems likely to swallow up the Selves they instinctively know are all they truly are as individuals. It never seems to occur to them that their resistance-pattern is not only well known to the "opposition," but carefully calculated and catered to in advance. Their behavior is so stereotyped that it can be fitted in quite profitably with whatever pressure-pattern is intentionally exerted over the human field containing them. They disturb no one in particular except themselves and the relatively harmless fellow members of Humankind. None of their activities along such lines can possibly be classed as magical, and no instructed Initiate of the Art would dream of working in those ways (except perhaps in a nightmare!). The magical establishment of Identity is achieved by quite a different Self-scheme than futile fighting with expert and fully-equipped opponents whose Pseudo-Selves are safely hidden by shadow, yet whose grasp on Earthly environmental factors is firmly enough felt. Besides, our Earth is by no means entirely in the wrong hands, and futile rebellion against one set of controls may also damage others of vital importance to cosmic evolution as a whole. Initiates of real Magic must learn to distinguish which is which in each case, then act in accordance with the Will they believe to be their own.

This, then, shall be the topic of this thesis: the magical Becoming of the Selves we are intended to be by the Will within the Word which began our being. It is the basis of all magic art, for no art can exist without artists, and Magicians are made, not born. That is our project, now as always, even though the search is everlasting. However little we may accomplish of this Opus in a single incarnation, it is at least possible to build up the beginnings of a spiritual Self that will survive all the inimical influences it is likely to encounter among modernizing Humankind. That alone is worth every effort to achieve, because it is something that also survives physical death and proves to be of tremendous advantage when another incarnation is projected into Earthly expression. Ultimately, it will lead us away from such a necessity altogether into far better types of being, but until we are able to lay out our launching-pad properly on this Earth, we shall never achieve enough escape velocity to arrive anywhere else.

Since there has to be some kind of system for Self-making, the system followed here will be the Cosmo-Qabalistic system, which has the master glyphs of the Circle-Cross and the Tree of Life. Apart from obvious reasons, a major motivation for such a choice is that neither Key can possibly be perverted or misused for ill-intentions or employed in any way whatever for Black Magic. The Solar Cosmic Cross cannot be inverted, as the Calvary Cross can. Neither can the Tree of Life be misused, for it is composed of purely cosmic principles related to each other as Beneficent Being. How could any maliciously motivated Magic associate with a ten-point combination consisting of Being, Wisdom, Understanding, Mercy, Discipline, Beauty, Achievement, Honor, Foundation, and Presentation? Who ever heard of a Black Magician with qualities of Mercy and Understanding? Use of the Cosmic Cross and Life-Tree may not automatically save Selves from making all kinds of stupid mistakes and passing on similar trouble to other souls, but these Keys certainly provide the best possible plans for those with fundamentally good intentions to reach Heaven rather than Hell by their efforts. Therefore, these are the Keys we shall insert in this life-lock.

We all seek our Selves, whatever we may call our ultimate cosmic Identity. The God we are looking for is not only within us, but actually IS all the true Self we shall ever achieve. Let us not be deluded into supposing that the principle of Self is something wrong, or that a disapproving Deity demands the disintegration of our Self-Identity in order to enjoy us like some species of spiritual edible during the eternal Banquet of Bliss. We are not here on Earth to lose our Selves, but to gain them and deliver them from evil. In truth, we are our own saviors or our own destroyers. We redeem or ruin the Selves that are all we may truthfully call our own. The rest is nothing but loans from one level of life to another.

We have been told: "Seek and ye shall find, ask and ye shall be answered, knock and it shall be opened." Where shall we seek our Selves, or whom shall we ask about them, and who will open the Doorway of discovery for us? We may call upon the Elements around us with the cry of our Eternal Quest:

Thou sunlit Sea, and airy Sky,
Truthtell me, who on Earth am I?

Yet in the end, we know from the very basis of our being that there is only One able to answer truthfully. The Self Itself. So let us look, listen, and learn how to live with ourSelves in the Light which will lead us ultimately into

PERFECT PEACE PROFOUND.

Chapter Two

The Self
We Search For

Attempting to categorize the human Self into constituent parts is difficult enough to deter even the most illuminated investigators. Without absolute standards for calculation there is scanty hope of arriving at any accuracy. Here, however, it is proposed to take the Cosmo-Qabalistic formula of the famous Tree of Life as a standard, and measure ourselves against that. This should at least give reasonable results for workers of the Western Inner Tradition to follow in their Selfsearch. Others must substitute their equivalent symbolism.

In order to grasp the layout that is being given here it is necessary to have some knowledge or appreciation of the Qabalistic Tree-system. No detailed explanation of this will be gone into now for several reasons. First, because so many works already exist that have covered this ground most adequately, and secondly, because such basic studies ought surely to have been made in some degree by those interested in reading a book of this present description. In any case, there should be no real difficulty in "catching up," since so much information is readily available from previously published material. So we shall plunge straight in at the deep end, and see how the Self sorts out against the background of the Qabalistic Holy Tree of Life.

If we start by taking a Self to mean a connective consciousness of entity between the highest possible apex of Divine Awareness and the least of its mortal manifestations among Humankind, this will cover the entire extent of the Middle Pillar, or "trunk" of the Tree from top to bottom. It is obvious that all this could not possibly incarnate as Itself in a single material mortal, therefore we shall have to accept some intermediary stages of relationship that will account for such "scaling down" until a flesh-formed focus is encountered on Earth. The Tree provides us with two points on its Middle Pillar which fulfill just such a function. Taking the commencing and completion point of a Self to be Kether, the Crown, Summit, or Absolute Apex of the Tree, it crosses the Abyss into Creation marked by Tiphereth, Beautiful Harmony, then descends toward Earthlife via Yesod, the Formative Foundation, finally appearing among Humankind in Malkuth, the Kingdom, as a focalized expression of entity. One Self going through a change of Cosmo-conditions marked with four points of reference appreciable by our limited human capacity for consciousness.

Supposing we develop our ideas about these four Self-stages in the light of esoteric information, and use the cover-code of S.E.L.F. for classification. This gives us an interesting little table to consider:

Self Level	Tree-Sphere	"World"	Cosmo-Level	Element
Spiritual	1. Crown	Origination	Stellar	Air
Evolving	6. Beauty	Creation	Solar	Fire
Living	9. Foundation	Formation	Lunar	Water
Focal	10. Kingdom	Expression	Terrestrial	Earth

Now if we go a bit further and connect in the remaining Sphere-principles of the Tree, these will link up in a most relevant way to show how the Self is stabilized between its

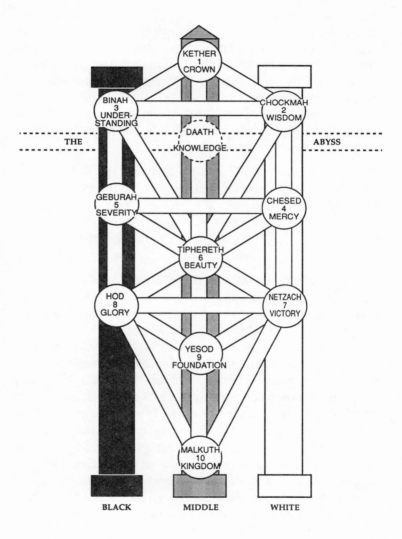

Figure 1 — The Holy Tree of Life

lateral extensions of existence. If we think of a straight "up-and-down" relationship connecting Divinity and Humanity, marked out by the central Tree-Spheres, and the "side-to-side" amount of this relationship determined by the principles of the Outer Pillars, this will make a fair analogy. We might even think of the vertical component of this comparison as "Intensity," and the horizontal plane as "Quantity." An electrical symbology would be roughly voltage and current. At any rate, it seems clear that the Self-levels in order of descent are polarized by:

BLACK PILLAR Principle	MIDDLE PILLAR Self-Level	WHITE PILLAR Principle
Understanding	Spiritual	Wisdom
Severity	Evolving	Mercy
Glory	Living	Victory
	Focal	

This, of course, is the Self-picture of "fallen" or materialized Humankind projected into the flesh-forms we inhabit on this Earth as personalized people of the planet. As and if we change this condition by Knowledge (DAATH) into a state of pure consciousness, we shall achieve the perfection intended in the Primal Plan. Meanwhile, we must take things as they are in order to make them into what they might be. So let us consider each Self-stage with sufficient brevity and clarity to see quite clearly what we are thinking about during our future dealings on these accounts. Above all, we must not make the mistake of supposing that the stages of a Self are like separate Selves within Self. They are all components of the same Self, even though they seem to have independence at their respective levels of life. Even the Pseudo-Self which builds up among them is dependent on their Self-being for its existence, however much it might prefer to ignore such an admission.

From our purely mortal viewpoint, the Self-stages are

distinguishable from each other by their degrees of duration, and the extensions of their energies through finer and finer force-fields until Absolute Awareness Itself is reached as the reality of Total Truth. The Inner equivalents of what we know as Time and Space here on Earth. We might sum this up into two amusing little generalizations which cover the view each way for us.

> Life is finer and stronger
> As Being becomes longer.

> The shorter his span
> The cruder lives Man.

If we look as far and as finely away from our Earth entities as our limited consciousness will allow, we shall perhaps arrive at some idea of:

THE SPIRITUAL SELF-STAGE

This is the highest and remotest part of our reality, yet none of our remainder would exist without it. It is the Divine Spark or truly immortal principle of our being which belongs rightly to Divinity alone, and until we are all-identified with It, we may not really consider ourselves entirely immortal. It exists for the Eternity considered to be the Duration of Divinity, or Life of God, and is ultimately absorbed into the Infinite NIL (AINSOPH of the Tree) whence ALL emanates of its own Intention into Existence, or equates back into Perfect Peace Profound. It is futile to try and imagine this in any terms of our time. So far as we are concerned it means "forever," or indefinitely extended Identity, and that is that.

This Self-stage provides overall extension for the other stages, since it out-exists them all, and should absorb the total of their experiences throughout their various levels of living. Each Self-stage is meant to absorb or "take in" the totality of those below it, so that their whole life-series of experiences combine into single incidents or occurrences in the life-consciousness of the superior Self-stage. For instance, the experiences of a whole evolution undergone by any Self would amount to relatively few impressions in the consciousness of the highest Spiritual Self-stage, yet everything would be completely contained in such summations so that these become interpretable in terms compatible with the type of consciousness functioning normally at that life-level. In the same manner does the Evolutionary Self-stage take up whole ages of Living Self-life and interpret them as individualization incidents, while the Living Self-stage absorbs all the personalized incarnations of any soul in particular, and puts these together as a whole that makes some special sense in its courses of consciousness. Lastly, the Focalized Self-stage has to summate an entire incarnation bit by bit until a human lifetime adds up into a "truth total" ready from passing back along the line of life toward an Ultimate Identity.

So the Spiritual Self-stage is the sum total of whole evolutions and aeons of its other life-levels. Our innumerable human incarnations go into its makeup. It extends Itself across the Great Abyss into evolutionary and biological life-levels. What crosses the life-line of this Self-stage bridges the Abyss and identifies with it attains true immortality. All else must continue evolving and incarnating or be reduced via the Abyss into fundamental forces which eventually become available for the use of other entities.

The power of the Spiritual Self-stage polarizes between the pure principles of Wisdom and Understanding. We only have the remotest reflection of such supernal states of awareness in our Earthly embodiments, but if we do not faithfully foster what we have, we shall never reach the realities they represent. Only the most minute possible proportion of a Spiritual Self-stage projects as far as our focalized human incarnations, and indeed the vital life-contact with it may be severed, while slowly disintegrating souls may go on for several incarnations, just as a limb cut off from its bodily life-supply takes time to die, unless artificially kept going by scientific means. This is what the Christian Church once called mortal sin, **or a** state of severance between the divinely Spiritual Self-stage and the remainder of a Self-hood. Detailed discussion of this is quite outside our present terms of reference, but it may be noted that the human end of the Self had to defiantly deny its divine connections and insist on its own independence in no uncertain way before any real severance occurred. Even so might a leaf on a tree assert its autonomy by falling from its branch, but then it automatically limits its little life to its own small supplies, and the only way back into the tree is through becoming humus to nourish the life-system again. Humankind may indeed live without Self-contact to Divinity—within lessening limits of life or bound into Pseudo-Selfish states of being that offer very little beyond Earth-incarnating existence on a potentially diminishing scale. Those with equivalents of true Wisdom and Understanding in themselves will keep contact with their Spiritual Self-stages by every possible means available, and this, of course, connects through the next immediate level of:

THE EVOLUTIONARY SELF-STAGE

Being on "our side" of the Abyss, this Self-stage has definable limits of life, existing up to the entire extent of a complete evolution. This may not be calculable except as an abstraction in terms of human years, or on the other hand initiated individuals may get through it at "Light-speed" in terms of Inner Illumination. Altogether it means whatever totality of experience and development may be necessary for projecting any living entity right through its course of Cosmic Creation until it reaches the condition of perfection intended for it by its Originating Self-Stage. If and when it reaches this point, there is no further purpose in extending its existence into material manifestation, and it may be "handed over" as a whole into the Spiritual Self to which it rightly belongs. For some beings this may take uncountable millions of our years, and for others a totally different time-rate. All that may be said safely is that an Evolutionary Self-stage is what we need to ensure our perfection as a life-species of individualizing entities. It depends to a very great extent on our own efforts of Will in this direction.

We shall not spend the whole of an evolution as human beings on this planet. That form of living will be far behind us before our evolution can complete itself and we return to purely spiritual conditions of consciousness. All we may do on Earth is evolve up to a perfection point as incarnated creatures of Cosmos, and then pass beyond this stage back into the next living condition of Self. When final development is reached in that condition, an advance is made into purely evolutionary states of existence, and the individualizing process of consciousness continues. Until we have equated ourselves at any one level, however, we cannot fully bring our Focal Self-stage into line with the next level up and live there as a normal means of existence.

The polarity of power at the evolutionary level lies between the pure principles of Mercy and Severity. As we evolve, so shall we direct ourselves more and more by means of these two principles, which together constitute the faculty of Justice, rather than be swayed around by uncontrolled emotions or unstable impulses. In fact, these principles are the main "drives" that effect our evolutionary progress. Only truly evolved beings know how to temper Mercy and Severity in order to arrive at perfect Justice. Our evolution not being confined to this one Earth means that it may be extended into other life-forms and species either in different solar systems or other life-dimensions altogether.

It seems certain that our ideas of Justice on this planet are very far from perfect, but those who reach limits of evolution here need not doubt that opportunities for improvement will certainly be available elsewhere in Cosmos.

A single human incarnation on Earth is unlikely to affect the Evolutionary Self-stage to any great degree, yet nevertheless it makes a more marked impression there than it does upon the Spiritual level. One human life-span in the course of a whole evolution is relatively little, but that is the way we are built up bit by bit so to speak, with each lifetime on Earth being comparable to one brick going toward the "Temple not made with hands."

The Tree-Sphere representing this Self-stage is Tiphereth, or Harmonious Beauty, and that is just what our evolvement amounts to—the harmonious relationship of all our parts toward the Beauty of a single Whole or Individual Identity, everything arriving at proper proportions and correct conditions for the fulfillment of an Original Intention. This is Beauty in the best sense of the word. The higher we evolve the more beautiful we become, and for humans evolution is an essential process of perfection.

Esoteric tradition tells us that certain classifications of entity were expressly created apart from evolutionary circuits of consciousness altogether. These completed productions of the Infinite Intelligence could not become any more than they were by their own efforts, and simply stayed within their specifications until reabsorbed into the Absolute. Though they may seem to be of superior quality as compared with our human status, these Angels and Archangels, as we might call them, must remain as they are placed within the pattern for perfection, fulfilling their particular functions, while we are only able to continue crawling our slow and serpentine ascent up the Tree of Life. It is our evolutionary abilities that make this possible for us, so we should appreciate just what this Self-stage is worth, and we should be glad to contribute toward its continuity from our level of:

THE LIVING SELF-STAGE

This is concerned purely with the possibilities of life upon this planet over the complete course of its continuity. Therefore, it covers every incarnation we shall ever have as humans on Earth, and that is the sum of its existence. Millions of years maybe, but a definably limited life for all that. Not what any reasonably minded individual would consider mortality.

The function of this Self-stage is to absorb the essentials of every Earthlife and bring them to single points of experience in its own terms. In return, it passes down into the incarnated Self-stage whatever it knows of the Originating Intention at the back of its beginnings. Eventually it will be altogether absorbed into the Evolutionary life-level, carrying its total content of consciousness with it. Since this is the Self-stage most directly associated with life on biological levels, it deals with hereditary and genetic factors, and the connective issue of consciousness behind births.

According to one tradition of esoteric teaching, this Self-stage was as far as we were supposed to go as evolving entities. After that point of projection, only animalized creatures should have come on Earth in solid fleshly forms. Legends vary about how the first incidents occurred which caused our ancestral Selves to "fall" into mortal and material bodies. Once this happened, however, the ever widening gates of sexual reproduction invited more and more Selves into incarnational conditions, and our history as Earth-dwelling humans still continues. It is quite senseless to bother about or regret our coming into this Earth-world. Our real problem is how to get out of it again with the greatest advantages in terms of Self-development which will enable us to live in altogether better conditions of being. This cannot be properly done until we have equated out our Earth lives and progressed beyond the necessity for their continuation.

The Living Self-stage is by no means a perfect state of being, though perfectibility is obviously possible by all who reach their *ne plus ultra* point therein. Being immediately behind physical life, it contains all those strange areas of awareness called the subconscious and, of course, provides us with the wherewithal for our excarnatory existence closest to Earth. In that state we undergo the Inner experience of Heaven and Hell, which equates out the energies of our Earth-living into changes of consciousness that enable us to live in finer than physical forms of being. The Christian Church once called this condition Purgatory, or a purgation period for eliminating whatever prevented a soul from rising to higher levels of Selfhood. What the Church did not teach—for reasons of its own—was that failure or refusal to gain such emancipation led back into human incarnation.

The polarizing power of this Self-stage derives from the two "drives" of Hod and Netzach—Glory and Victory—on the Tree of Life. They may not be the noblest of motivations, but they stimulate the Self into activity in no uncertain way. On ordinary human levels they stand for Honor and Achievement, which every normal human alive aims for, in one way or another. We need to make something of our-Selves. That is an Achievement. To do so for the sake of our Immortal Identity is an Honor. What a pity our Pseudo-Selves confuse Honor with adulation on Earth, and Achievement with amassing of world-wealth. Yet without the fundamentals of Glory and Victory, even so little could not have been accomplished.

There is quite a noticeable proportion of the Living Self-stage projected into our incarnational foci. It provides the materials from which our minds and souls grow up around the Self, helping us ascend the Ladder of Light and

Life until ultimate immortality may be reached. Insofar as this Self-stage is guidable by the higher principles of Wisdom, Understanding, Mercy and Severity above it, we may come into better and better conditions of incarnation. If the influence of these is overridden by the exigencies of Glory and Victory, which rule this life-level, we may still incarnate well enough by Earth standards, and yet lack sufficient spiritual and evolutionary influences to develop the Self very far toward Divinity.

Because the Living Self-stage receives Enlightenment from the Solar Evolutionary stage behind it, and reflects this into the incarnating Self-focus, it is likened to Luna, the Moon of Humankind. Our Moon is traditionally associated with Earthbirth, fecundity, and all the Inner affairs of life that lie beyond the borders of our purely physical framework. Humankind seems to have known instinctively that the Moon has always been the first step toward the stars, and it is also true that as Selves we must "land up" in the equivalent Self-stage before we may fare further toward our fulfillment. This will only be reached effectively when we are able to perfect and outgrow the need for:

THE FOCAL SELF-STAGE

This state is our ordinary incarnated Selfhood on Earth. Its extent is but a single lifetime, during which it has to interchange energies between its Earthly existence and the stages of its superphysical antecedents. If it functioned as it should, it would act purely as a connective consciousness linking Earthlife conditions directly with the Living Self-stage operating behind it, and at the death of the physical body would be rapidly and completely absorbed into that life-level, so that another fresh projection of personality might be made at the most convenient opportunity when occasion arose. The double task of our Focal Self-stages is to keep us fully informed at living-level concerning Earthlife, and also to influence the cosmic courses of that Earthlife by means of the consciousness penetrating to our personalities from higher stages of our Selves. Since we are upon this Earth, we have to act as agents for its alteration in conformity with the Cosmic Intention that began our being. The fact that we are imperfect or inadequate agents for this purpose, or that possibly we ought not to have been here at all, does not absolve us from the responsibilities we incur as humans incarnate upon this planet.

Since our embodied entities depend on brain-based cycles of consciousness, these are extremely limited in scope or range. We have only a very narrow field of awareness on Earth indeed. Our physical senses only operate along a very small section of the energy-spectrum which covers the consciousness we need to extend our existence through nonphysical dimensions of living. There is a fair proportion of our Living Self-stage operating through our Focal physical point, but this is still only fractional and far from faultless, since both our Focal and Living Self-stages are still in the process of evolution. While we live in a body, we do our thinking with its brain, and our feeling with its senses, rather than employ the much wider range of thinking by mind and feeling by soul as we have to on Living levels of life. This cuts us off from a considerable amount of the consciousness we ought to be using in other areas of awareness. As we develop our Selves from one incarnation to another, however, the situation is improved by sheer weight of experience (Daath on the Tree), and the influence of mind and soul begins to predominate over bodily based impulses. Not that this development lessens our troubles. It simply raises them to different degrees, though at the same time our means of dealing with them also alters accordingly. All changes of consciousness have their own problems and compensations bound up together.

Theoretically and ideally, the Focalized part of our

Selves which we extend into Earthly embodiment should be entirely equated and absorbed into the Living Self-stage after the physical death of the body. That is why most Inner traditions are so firmly set against spiritualism as systems which attempt to recall human souls in their past forms of personality or relationship with other incarnate people. We make a tremendous amount of trouble for ourselves by deliberately hanging on to our past personalities rather than allowing them to die off decently as we re-issue new and improved modifications of their structural patterns. By trying to reestablish links with deceased humans in terms of their past personal projections we are only interfering with their Inner progress to some degree, and most certainly acting against their best spiritual interests, which lie in the opposite direction entirely. This does not mean that we should not make Inner contacts with discarnate souls at all. To seek them as we should, we must learn how to advance our consciousness into their conditions of actuality and encounter them as they exist in their Living Self-stage. To keep thinking of or dealing with deceased humans as they appeared and behaved while on Earth is both unkind and impractical. What is the use of cremating or burying a worn-out body if we preserve mental corpses of those same people in our minds?

For all these reasons, the old practice of summarizing the main events of the past day and extracting their overall essentials as a truth-total just before going to sleep at night is a very valuable habit. It accustoms the user to doing each day what has to be done proportionately at the end of each incarnation, and so the perfection of a relatively small practice makes the greater one far easier and more profitable. If we get our Focal Self-stages to faithfully carry out this commendable little ritual as attention is being withdrawn from Earthly environments, it will help considerably to establish courses of consciousness throughout our Self-stages, which are most likely to take us where we Will at all levels of life.

Our Focal Self-stage, therefore, which so many of us suppose to be the be-all and end-all of our entire beings, is actually the end link in a complete chain of consciousness reaching from the remotest state of spiritual Selfhood to the point of personal presentation in this material world. A very important link when seen in the right light and used to the best advantage. Most of the techniques employed in Magic, or learned during the processes of being initiated into the Mysteries, are concerned with gaining control of our Self-foci and relating them with the remainder of our Self-stages. The Focal stage of Self is certainly the Key-point we have to work with in order to make the rest of our Selves amount to What we Will in the end, so most of our detailed studies and exercises will be directed mainly thereto. Lastly at present, however, we have to formulate some ideas about:

THE PSEUDO-SELF

This really amounts to all our Self-proportions on the different levels that remain unequated and unabsorbed into the principal life-stream connecting the apex of awareness in spiritual Selfhood with the Focal Self-point incarnate in Earth existence; or whatever in fact lies outside the direct Light-Life line drawn between Divinity and Humanity in anyone. It should be easy to appreciate that the more evolved we become, the greater degree of Pseudo-Self we are likely to have, though this is no asset as regards our ultimate advancement toward total Truth.

The bulk of Pseudo-Self will diminish in proportion to ascent of the Self-scale, and it is very doubtful if any of it actually crosses the Abyss. Its mass is built up from unequated portions of past personalities occurring between the Living and Focal life-stages. On top of this, there is a gradual buildup from the Living to the Evolutionary stage which accounts for quite a considerable section of its more enduring qualities. By and large, the cruder and less sophisticated parts of Pseudo-Self tend to remain at the bottom of its being closest to physical manifestation, while its more refined and developed characteristics associate toward the Evolutionary end of its existence.

There is nothing particularly wrong or evil about the existence of Pseudo-Self per se. Made up as we are out of what we have become, it is inevitable that Pseudo-Self has developed into what it amounts to, and will most probably continue with increasing influence on our affairs into the unforeseeable future. The determining point of issue concerning right or wrong use of Pseudo-Self is whether it is directed toward or away from the Initiating Intention behind each being. Do we use Pseudo-Self as a means of achieving Identity with our Selves at divine level, or do we push it away from that point into a state of relatively artificial egoic existence for the sake of whatever may be gained or contained in such a state of consciousness? Are we setting up in conjunction with, or in opposition to, the Creative Cosmic Consciousness out of which we originated as individualizing entities? That is the whole crux of the matter, and the point where Black and White Magic divide from one another. Which way do we go? Cosmo-Selfward or Pseudo-Selfward? It is of vital importance to distinguish between the two different directions and decide where our personal paths lie.

Such is the distinction usually applicable to what is loosely and inaccurately labeled "selfish" or "unselfish" behavior. It all depends on how we employ our Pseudo-Selves, relative to our Initiating Intentions. There is really no such thing as "unselfishness" at all, except in the sense of Pseudo-Self equation into the Light-Life line connecting each end of our entities together in the cosmic circle of total

Truth. Insofar as we make our Pseudo-Selves line up with this standard of Self-identification, we might be called "un-Pseudo-Selfish," but no more than that. In reality, we are becoming increasingly Selfish as we lessen the limits of our Pseudo-Selves proportionately to those of our Ideal Identity.

The typical picture of a so-called Selfish person is actually that of someone who is pushing his Pseudo-Selfhood deliberately into a state of artificial and apparent autonomy apart from his Individuality. Reasons for this action are various, but are principally because of an instinctive knowledge that confinement of energy within calculable circles enables power to be maintained therein while its relative condition of resonance continues. The effect of this is that a Pseudo-Self can "loop-out" energies that ought to have been equated away along the Light-Life line, and form up a small force-field which exerts an intensification of personalized power over a limited area for the duration of its persistence. This effect may be increased and extended if suitably processed energies are available from other Self-sources. A successfully Pseudo-Selfish person, therefore, is one who metaphorically prefers living as the big fish of a small pool, sustained by the minnows which swim into its ever open mouth. Perhaps the pool may dry up if it becomes separated from the River of Life altogether, but the greed of the big fish and stupidity of the small ones are inadequate to save the Selves of either category. All will be reduced to their fundamental constituents which help to activate the next life-wave washing that way.

A genuine Black Magician is one who, being consciously aware of this metaphysical fact, exploits it for personal purposes of Pseudo-Self gain by magical means. Either single-handed in minor ways, or in combination with others in larger ventures, an experienced Black Magician "rings round" available sections of other Pseudo-Selves in such a manner that these will supply most of the power needed for the purpose intended. If intelligently done, this may well ensure adequate quantities of energy for quite prolonged periods. It should be noted that even the Blackest of magicians does not hold anyone captive in their circles indefinitely against the true Self-Will of those people. Besides, why employ the crudities of compulsion, when clever coercion is so much cleaner and cheaper and more profitable?

The instructed Initiate of White Magic also makes circles out of Pseudo-Self, but for an opposite purpose and with a different design. In the first place, he does not intentionally include within it any part of another person's Pseudo-Self, or anything properly belonging to their Self-spheres of interest which they mean to retain for themselves. Secondly, having formed his circle from suitable forces, he does not hold it in a state of Pseudo-Self, but when it reaches peak resonance, he promptly equates it back into balanced proportions with his Spiritual Self-status. It should thus be seen that a White Magician virtually increases his Self-stature by regulating his Pseudo-Self into harmonious relationship with the cosmic Self-components. A Black Magician conversely increases the area and scope of his Pseudo-Self without reference to his Spiritual structure, and at the expense of all who contribute toward the upkeep of his egoic establishment.

Power over others and payment for that privilege is the first demand of a Black Magician and the last intention of a White one. Responsibility for the care of such souls that may be temporarily committed to the competence of a White Magician acting in some authoritative capacity does not constitute personal power over such people insofar as their necessity is the governing factor involved in the issue, and when such necessity terminates, so does the authority especially set up to deal with it. A White Magician is not precluded from service in positions of responsibility concerning other souls, but above all he realizes that without adequate control of his own Inner Self-Cosmos, he is quite unfitted to assume authority on behalf of other beings. His first responsibility is definitely to the Self he IS initially, into the Mysteries of which he is being Initiated, and with Whom he seeks ultimate identification as an Individual, before passing to PERFECT PEACE PROFOUND.

Now at least we know what we ought to be looking for. A system of Self-survival and individualization of our integrity at a life-level where Pseudo-Self not only preponderates, but is increasing in influence and organization at a very disconcerting rate. We need knowledge of how to live and Focalize ourSelves in the very midst of all this manipulated muddle without being adversely affected by any of it or contributing to its confusion. If magical methods will help us here, then they are not only valid, but also incredibly valuable to whosoever is able to use them. Only those who know their own value to themSelves can possibly appreciate this.

Let us see what assistance Magic has to offer in making the assessment of Self-importance for an individualizing human entity.

Chapter Three

The Search System

Before we begin to use Magic in seeking for our Selves, it is advisable to make sure we have a satisfactory system of working to this end. How shall we know which technique to apply for what purpose, or which to avoid altogether? How, in fact, are we to sort out the rights from the wrongs in the magical makings of a real "Me"? Techniques are techniques, pure and simple, and may be generally used for good or ill reasons. In the case of Magic it is often the overriding motivation alone which decides the purpose of any particular procedure, and this is especially so with systems devised for Self-seeking. To know Black from White, and then follow the thin Gold Line of Light in the middle is obviously the best magical method of "Me-making," and that is exactly what the pattern of the Life-Tree tells us, so this is what we shall take for a guide.

To appreciate the right use of anything, we have to realize its wrong applications, and there are many glaring examples that present themselves immediately. Most of them are to be found in narrowly exclusive sectarian groupings, where they are brought to very fine points indeed. First the group declares a divine mandate for its existence, and secondly consigns to perdition all nonbelievers in its tenets or offenders against its ordinances. It offers bribes of Heavenly rewards, while it inflicts what punishments it dares upon Earthly recalcitrants within its ranks. It is authoritarian, and imposes all sorts of disciplines and injunctions upon its members which are calculated to make them feel dependent upon their group-membership for ultimate spiritual salvation. In particular, it usually postulates a Supreme Deity who is so personally related to human beings that this incredible Entity may be affronted, angered, or otherwise react remarkably in response to the vagaries of human behavior.

Anyone who seriously believes that his Earthly attitudes and actions, of even the worst description, could possibly produce equivalents of emotional disturbance in the Eternal Equilibrium has exaggerated notions of his Pseudo-Self importance. To be big enough to upset God in a Supreme sense is beyond mortal capacity, but not beyond the wildly inflated opinions of many religious egomaniacs. For one small Pseudo-Self to pride itself that it possesses enough personal power to affect the Absolute adversely is no more than cosmic comedy at best, or wastage of living energy at worst. It is ludicrous or lamentable depending on viewpoint. Nevertheless, this is the theme around which so much Pseudo-Self sense of personal importance is built up in the name of organized religious beliefs. To assume the inevitable damnation of most humans while the specially selected alone are saved by divine decree gives a fantastically magnified and distorted picture of personal power in the hands of a mere mortal. Small wonder, really, that so many of us become enthusiastic about it for perhaps several incarnations, until we realize that we are alive on very much larger Self-scales of existence altogether and begin to arrange our Selves accordingly.

In order to work this "I'm saved, the rest are damned, so I'm more important to God than anybody else" scheme, it is necessary to create a suitable God-concept which fits into the picture at focalized life-levels. On each of our life-levels we experience the Eternal Entity in terms of that particular class of consciousness. This means that on Focal levels as people of this planet, we consciously contact personalized projections of the Energy behind our beings which come so far with us into Cosmos. These are our "Gods," and they are relative to the sort of Selves we have reached at this stage of our Selfhood. They are not false, but they are fractional and representative of the Inner Realities they mediate for Humankind. They are also of enormous importance in all magical work once we recognize them for what they amount to—telesmic images of Truth translated into human terms of focalized force. The righteous Pseudo-Self religionist instinctively grabs a share of these and looks for his reflection therein, which he finds in the shape of a God who saves him, damns all the rest, and in fact appears to do everything he would do himself if he were a ruling Deity. This makes him feel mighty when he is merely experiencing a degree of metaphysical megalomania.

There is a crude but workable analogy which can be used to illustrate this point with the aid of some intelligently handled imagination. First, a sheet or surface of rubber or some such material having an indefinite area must be taken to represent the surface of consciousness applied to unknown matters in order to apprehend them. Since they will be invisible through this covering, let a pair of hands symbolize the sensors with which we attempt to translate our findings into terms of touch. Now let us suppose a hypothetical investigator has felt something of interest with the exploring fingers of the left hand and has made a rapid attempt to grasp the reality behind the contacting surface and lift this away from its position. Actually, the reality stays where it is, and what the hand grasps happens to be a sort of ballooning sphere of the elastic fabric with nothing in it except air and atmosphere. The tighter and closer the grasp of the left hand, the more the bubble swells, and the more solid it seems to the touch of the right hand on its exterior surface. It feels globular, appreciably real, and seems like a good handful of something which may be quite valuable. There are three possible outcomes of this imagination situation. First, the holder of such an empty possession may continue for quite a while hanging on to it proudly enough while the pressure is maintained. Secondly, the pressure may leak rapidly away so that the holder feels rather flatly let down, but will then make fresh efforts to find better and closer contacts with the area of exploration being covered. Third, the bulging sphere of surface may be so tightly and graspingly clutched that it pressurizes to a point beyond its bearing and breaks with explosive force. This third possibility says in blunt and forceful terms, "If you try and grab an exclusive handful of Truth (or God) it will probably blow up in your face."

That is metaphorically what happens in the case of those who attempt to "corner" shares of spiritual actualities for their own Pseudo-Self satisfaction. It is also one of the major mistakes which the genuine Initiate of Magic tries to avoid in every way possible. Working along with the preceding analogy, for instance, no attempt at grasping personal handfuls of pressure would be made. Instead, there would be efforts at understanding and exploring the underlying areas of actuality by digital interpretation of what was felt, and movement of the hands over a sufficient surface to make accurate estimations possible in reasonable degrees. The closer such contact can be maintained and continued, the more translucent should become the intervening film of fabric until in the end it becomes transparent to Inner Light, revealing the reality it covers to the spiritual sense corresponding to sight on physical levels. Ultimately, of course, it dissolves altogether as the "Ineffable Union" is attained.

It is very easy to make magical mistakes comparable to the egoic inflations of even the most rabidly Pseudo-Self important religionist. A would-be Magician who supposes that the private possession of spells, invocations, or other occult arcana will make him a Master of potent and intelligent Inner agents who must automatically obey his whims and carry out his most irresponsible commands is no less ludicrous or dangerous than the fiercest fanatic in religious history. It is moreover a very stupid misuse of otherwise valid symbolic material. Therefore, so far as we possibly can, we must avoid the misuse of techniques in our Self-search which are likely to have any such side effects. At least we now have some kind of general criterion with which to test our workings as they progress. This is a kind of triangular relationship between our Selves at one point, Divinity at another, and Humanity completing the circuit. Equilibrium between the points must be maintained for best results all around. If we begin to feel that we have grabbed enough of God to decide the destiny of other humans, then we are overbalancing to a dangerous degree. If, conversely, we are becoming convinced that Humanity is everything and Divinity is a delusion, we are simply making the opposite error. If, again, we start developing a notion that neither Divinity nor Humanity have any special significance, and we can afford to be independent of both, this constitutes the third margin of error in the direction of Pseudo-Selfishness. Any of these more serious symptoms indicate that we ought to check up on procedure and discover where the discrepancy is distorting our balance of being.

This is only a rough and ready, but fairly reliable, means of indicating that something is going wrong with our Self-seeking system. We also need a comparable method of assuring our Selves that the system is running smoothly along the right lines. Again this is shown by our Self-

Divinity-Humanity relationship. All three factors should balance out into a sense of harmonious unison and interaction, giving the unique experience of "belonging to one another" in an inseparable pattern of partnership. The "Me-point" of Self (not Pseudo-Self) must be recognized as the mediating link between Divinity and Humanity in both individual and collective conscious life. As a simple basic in childlike terms, anyone might say, "I meet God in Humanity, reach Humanity through God, and both come together in Me." By the term "Humanity" it should be clearly understood that all other individualizing entities in similar Self-categories are meant. There are many other orders of life to be considered in degrees of cosmic relationship to us as our consciousness opens inclusively toward them, but for practical purposes on Earth, a satisfactory Human-God-Me balance is about the soundest base for Self-seeking to start. Once this seems right, the rest of everything will begin fitting into the pattern of progress where it belongs, and so we shall try and arrange our magical technicalities to produce such an end effect. The result should be a strange sense of true Self-importance deriving from these realizations:

1. Divinity is important to my Humanity.
2. My Humanity is important to Divinity.
3. I am important to Humanity as a life-link with Divinity.
4. I am important to Divinity as a life-link with Humanity.

Once a workable degree of this Entity-equation is experienced, the magical making of a Me is obviously proceeding on a correct cosmic course, and should be continued in accordance with the program being pursued.

In order to relate our Selves to Divinity from these Focal levels of life, it is necessary to find Focalized or personalized projections of the all-inclusive Entity of Existence with which to form relationships. It is of no practical use at all offering impersonal abstractions of a disinterested Divinity for human beings with which to focus themSelves at this stage of living. Our basic need for beliefs in Inner actualities are mainly God-images in our own likeness at this life-level through which we may contact the more arcane archetypes on other and higher stages of our Self-hood. Humanity knows this instinctively, hence the an-thropomorphic pantheons and personifications of divine power all down the ages. The Gods changed over the cen-turies as people progressed and their ideas of Individual-ization improved. Rough and crude God images served rough and crude cultures best, evolving with their par-ticular people toward perfection. By their Gods do humans make themSelves. As tempting as a digression on this point with reference to modern conditions of civilization may be, we must resist being seduced from the subject at hand.

One observation may be made. Our current God-images (where these are still in action) are too indefinite and reduced to recondite rarities for practical application among the less sensitive and selective masses of Human-kind. The old ideas of a thundering, revengeful, but also rewarding and recompensing Deity, with a potently per-sonal interest in their affairs appealed to them. Now that this God is dead they feel neglected and see no reason for caring about a Cosmos which has no concern with them. The Jesus-Christ image of the Sacred King, which once gave Humanity hopes of establishing communion with Divinity, has been emasculated and demythologized almost into obsolescence and obscurity. The calculated, clinical and computerized Christ-concept offered in exchange by priestly pundits has no attraction for the masses of hope-hungry humanity. It does not look right, sound right, smell right, taste right, or feel right to those who rely on their senses alone for information about their Inner Identities. They cannot identify themselves with sexless, sinless, and Self-less Jesus, who seems so utterly remote from the only world they recognize as being real for them. So they accept presentations invented for them by commercial purveyors of pop culture and other suppliers of identification imagery. What else can they do if alternatives are not available?

An Initiate of Magic at least knows where and what to look for in the way of workable God-images or Telesmics. He uses the Focalized or personalized presentations of whatever spiritual scheme, system, or power-plan he follows with faith in the fulfillment of his Self-search. If rightly approached and correctly contacted, these will lead through to their equivalents of Living levels, and so on back to the basis of Being and toward achievement of true Inner Identity. In the case of the practical Qabalistically trained Initiate, the God-images used are naturally those of the Tree. They form as perfect a symbolic synthesis of archetypes linking Humanity with Divinity as may be found anywhere among us on this planet. We shall deal with them in detail presently, for they are major Keys in the process of individualizing our Selves by these magical methods, and as such are an indispensable part of the system we shall be studying.

The answer to the old question, Is there a personal God or not? is plainly, Proportionately to the extent each individual entity is a person themselves. This means that if we are looking for Divinity on personal levels, we may only expect to find It personalized in other Focalized creations, including fellow humans, our own personalities, or else in our formalized concepts of consciousness in response to Inner divine energies which constitute the God-images themselves. Seeking Divinity in external natural forces and forms is a fascinating quest. Seeking It in other humans can be most disheartening or bewildering, but it is an obligation on all who hope to progress past material manifestations as mortals on this Earth. Tracing the appearance of Divinity in one's Self is a vitally necessary but extremely exacting process. Making contact with the Divine Image concepts which come within the reach of our reasonably extended Focal point of consciousness may be fairly termed a magical work of Will which is most worthwhile, because in addition to linking us with other levels, it also includes and improves our ability to experience equivalent contacts via the remaining means of Nature, Humanity, and one's own personal projection.

This is the great advantage of God-images, that they enable users to reach their Inner realities in all other terms of transformation. Being based on pure principles, they are universally applicable through all types of force-field. Through them, we may reach what they represent in other humans, our Selves, any category of natural creation, and the Inner actualities they personify as aspects of divine power. Once their practical purpose is realized, we can carry on using them with a perfectly clear conscience and increasing spiritual skill. As mere idols they have little value, but as Ideals they have infinite possibilities. They are not to be worshipped, but worked with. That makes all the difference. Correctly contacted, they will interchange energies between our Focal personality points and the other stages of Self we are seeking, and that is their magical significance.

To establish the identity of anything in this Focalized world, we name it, and a Name is a very potent magical device indeed. There is an old magical tradition that those who know the secret names of the Gods always have access to those Gods. The principle involved is entirely correct, but the secret names of the Gods are only to be learned directly from those Beings by each soul for themSelves. There is no other genuine way. The same applies to one's own magical or "Self-name," which is an identifying code of consciousness for the True as distinct from the Pseudo-Self.

We must discover by some magical means what to call our Selves when we invoke the deepest levels of our lives closest to Divinity. Nor must any other except our Selves and those Inner levels of intelligence become familiar with it. Our Inner Identity has to remain uniquely our own, unshared by any other Self except at the apex point where all Selves unite in One.

A Self should be truly the most private property in anyone's possession, exclusive of everything and everyone unsuited to the purpose of its primal Initiating Intention. This emphatically does not mean that a magical Initiate ought to be antisocial, but it does imply that discrimination and selectivity are of extreme importance in Self-seeking. We have to learn how to build up protective circles around our points of personal projection which will only allow favorable forces to pass its perimeter in either direction. So far as possible, nothing inimical should reach our Inner reality from our external fields of force, nor should anything emerge from our Self-state which is likely to injure others. This means that our special Self-circles have to be a sort of two-way force-filter system tuned into selected frequencies of acceptance and rejection all around. That is a real Magic Circle, and we have to work our ways of constructing it properly for our Selves if we intend ever to stand therein upon our own grounds, in our own right, for what we really and truly ARE as Individuals.

Let us understand quite clearly that Self-selection by magical means is a responsible act of Inner autocracy which calls for some considerable degree of "cosmic adulthood." It has been described as a long and lonely path toward perfection, but this is mostly how it seems to those in the consciously commencing stages of its adoption at Focal levels. There are so many changes in personal procedures to be made, alterations in outlook to achieve, and resolutions to be taken firmly, that a sense of isolation is virtually inevitable until a positive perception of Inner Self-surroundings and other entities sharing these life-levels becomes possible. With each major alteration of our Self-status we experience an isolation of our Selves in contrast to whatever state of being we are entering which will contain our next expansion of consciousness. We are isolated in our mothers' wombs prior to entry into this world. We feel some relative degree of isolation at the inception of any new venture in life—a new school, a new job, change of circumstances, physical incapacity or death—anything whatsoever that compels us to fall back upon our Self-resources and *survive* for all we are worth as Selves existing independently of environments. Isolation and Initiation go together, and no soul afraid of solitude during certain stages of Self-search should seek such an Inner path of progress until entirely prepared to walk its way apparently alone.

It takes supreme spiritual courage to set up a magical Self-Circle, saying in effect: "Here stand I! Nothing enters or leaves this Circle without my Will being concerned. Whatever I accept or reject within this consecrated area is entirely due to my own decision based on conclusions I reach by means of my enlightened Inner consciousness. This is the ME I am making by Magic in the Here-Now which points to what I Will Be in the There-Then. In all, I AM!" Yet this essential action is expected of every worthy magical Initiate. To KNOW how to be a Self. To DARE to stand as a candidate for Cosmic Companionship. To WILL the entire process throughout, and above all to KEEP COUNSEL concerning everything connected with the Magnum Opus of becoming a magical ME. Those are the rules which have governed the personal procedures of Magic for its Initiates since the art began, and they are still to be observed by whoever follows in their footsteps at the present time.

In order to make up any kind of Me by Magic or any

other means at all, it is obvious there must be some supply of basic "Me-material" or "Self-substance" with and from which we may construct our Selves consciously. This is the elemental energy of life itself, and it is classifiable into four categories, which are symbolized by Air, Fire, Water, and Earth in physically recognizable phenomena, being related to each other by the inclusive Element of Truth. In whatever way we relate ourSelves to life at any level, these living Elements are bound to be involved in some combination of consciousness. Therefore, if we are able to exercise degrees of control over them we should be able to alter or develop our Selves accordingly AS WE WILL. Whoever controls the basic Elements of anything in existence will automatically gain control of the whole concern. To control our own states of Self-Cosmos, we need conscious control over the basic Elements of Self-life. In Magic, this is tackled by intentional direction of the Symbols linked with those Elements through a patterned process which is closely connected with the associated purpose motivating the action.

Out of all these past considerations, we should be able to assemble some sort of magical system for Self-seeking. By the look of things, its general outline is likely to consist of an intentional identification of the True Self by means of a magical Name, and setting up and operating a Self-Circle or "Cosmic Compass" which will relate us to the essential elemental energies of life through all angles of awareness, and will codify our consciousness according to the specifications of ten God concepts which cover the whole of Cosmos from end to end of Existence. Quite a work of Will, or a Magnum Opus of ME! What, however, happens to Pseudo-Self in the course of all this constructive development?

Pseudo-Self can only take one of two courses: either try to sabotage the scheme for its own reasons, or join in with the system for the sake of its advantage along other lines. The alternatives are clear-cut and definite. Pseudo-

Self has the option of identifying with the True Self which ultimately identifies with the Supreme Self, or of attempting to separate out on its own and stay in conscious circulation as best it can. Either it seeks absorption into the True Self to attain its Infinite Identity, or opts out for a separate state of limited living in a lesser life-style, which seems of greater importance from a materially profitable angle. Between these two opposing courses, Pseudo-Self has nothing except a neutral line of nonacceptance-nonassertion to follow, which amounts to a policy of strict nonintervention in affairs that concern its own fate, and that are normally quite foreign and alien to its intrinsic nature.

This is the idea behind "dispassion, uninvolvement," and "impersonality," which sets a recurrent theme in most Oriental philosophies. The assumption is that if the Pseudo-Self can be persuaded not to interfere with or influence the courses of cosmic living, this will give the True Self a chance to become as it ought to be in conformity with its Originating Intention. Pseudo-Self is somehow considered an enemy of the Eternal Entity, and the sooner it can be induced to lie down and die decently, the better life will be for those released from the necessity of physical incarnation. Theoretically this may be perfectly possible, but practically speaking, it is seldom a sensible proposition for workers of the Western Inner Tradition. It leads to unnecessary divergences and disagreements between Self and Pseudo-Self, deliberately widening and deepening a division of the Self-states which is already far too marked for cosmic comfort. This is why Initiates of the magical path usually prefer to employ methods which are calculated to encourage the cooperation of Pseudo-Self as an active partner in the system of Self-search being followed. There is no sense in provoking Pseudo-Self into pointless enmity when it may be invited into a mutually profitable alliance with the inner Reality it is misrepresenting on Earth—once it gains adequate motives for accepting the offer.

Therefore, our magical Self-search system will have to accommodate some means of allowing Pseudo-Self to work out its salvation along the lines of its own necessities, which will ultimately bring it into unison with the Self it rightly belongs with as a whole Identity. No intelligent Initiate of any system would expect this miraculous merger to eventuate only during a single incarnation of conscious effort. It is essentially a process of growth and natural achievement which must be carried out at the proper rate to ensure its correct conclusion. Quite a number of incarnations may be needed to align True Self and Pseudo-Self so that they blend into a single Self-state of being. There is no point in speculating on how many lives this vital task may take, but it is reputed that an almost impossibly low minimum is three. The main thing is not to be concerned about cosmic time-terms, but to carry on with the job conscientiously in the certainty that if it is being done according to the best available Inner individual ability, all is bound to become as it should during the course of Cosmos.

A major mistake of several systems, notably the Christian and other monotheistic faiths, was to identify Pseudo-Self with evil, wickedness, sin and every kind of opprobrium which could possibly be applied to "unregenerate Man." Humans were castigated for their clumsy Self-seeking conduct, and compared to brutes, animals and other quite uncomplimentary beasts of creation. Little by little, humans were taught to make enemies of their own natures, and the harder they were urged to fight inside their own Self-Circles, the easier it became to make them fight each other in the world they shared outside those limits. None are more violently opposed to their fellow humans than those whose Inner state is one of conflict between their own Self-levels. By fostering false feelings of guilt among humans, the Churches became guilty of encouraging unnecessary enmity on Earth, which they were perfectly willing to exploit for their own particular purposes. Only when we learn how to promote peace in the Circles of our Selves are we likely to have any peace worthy of the name in this world.

In our magical Self-search system, therefore, we must find ways of incorporating and absorbing the activities of Pseudo-Self so that it will eventually identify with our True Selves, as these should intend achieving ultimate Identity in Universal Being. Pseudo-Self must be successfully convinced that there are right and wrong methods of Self-seeking, some helpful and others harmful. Somehow or other, the overall longterm advantage has to be discovered by seeking harmonious unity with Self in its own correct cosmic Circle, rather than rushing around inviting other ill-defended Self-Circles, or being helplessly drawn into them because of malicious motivations on their part whether this is actually Black Magic or not. Altogether, Pseudo-Self must be adequately invited back where it rightly belongs, into its own magical Circle, where it will play its proper part in the plan for Perfection, which involves every True Individual.

This is not to say that humans do not commit wrong actions with the worst of intentions. They most certainly do, and sheer Self-defense evokes countermeasures from other mortals. It is the association of God-guilt with unsatisfactory human conduct which causes so much spiritual trouble and conflict. Sooner or later, Humankind must grow to realize that we do not suffer *for* our sins but *by* them. No one injures us because of our iniquities except ourSelves. Nor may we hurt our fellow beings without repercussions eventually affecting us. It is literally true that what we do to the least and littlest Self alive, we do unto the greater ME of its inclusive Identity. Only when the majority of Humankind really appreciates and understands the extent of the Inner injuries they are inflicting on themSelves, and are completely convinced of the benefits obtainable by better courses of cosmic conduct, is human behavior likely to improve greatly on Earth and elsewhere. For this, each one of us is directly responsible to our own True Selves linking with Divinity, with which we seek our ultimate identification. All this should be taken into account when making up our magical Self-seeking system, so that we do not falsify our feelings of guilt before any God, but concern our Selves with the consequences of our misconduct in relation to Cosmos. That is far more than the practical point at issue here.

Surmounting all these considerations is the necessity that our magical Self-seeking system must be one which fits in with modern living and conditions, being applicable in the NOW of our cosmic circumstances, yet bridging past traditions through our present point far into the future. Unless these specifications are met, the system is bound to fail. There is no use trying to scrap everything which has been proved valuable in the past and substitute something so startlingly modern and "with it" that this becomes boringly or revoltingly out of date in less than a decade, so that fresh rubbish is hastily shoveled on top of its corpse to hide the horror. Nor is there any sense in keeping medieval formularies going which have no validity in present practice or recognition. Altogether we must manage to strike some sort of balance by bringing forward from the past what still lives with us now and linking this with what we Will our Selves to eventually become. Providing we can synthesize all the various points we have been talking about into a satisfactory system of Self-search operated by magical means, we should find something very well worth working for. We can at least attempt such an achievement.

Chapter Four

Cosmo-Commencement

The picture of our Self-seeking system should now be fairly clear. Taking our evolving entity of individuality as the center of its own Cosmos constantly extending its existence out of its Nil-nucleus, we have to systematize an arrangement of everything pertaining to that Primal Point around it in balanced harmony, similar to an atomic structure or a solar system. The units from which we shall construct this Cosmos are the four Life-Elements and their connecting tie of Truth, the ten principles or "Spheres" of the Life-Tree, and the associations which bind these together.

There has to be a beginning of everything and everyone somehow and somewhere. The beginning of making a magical Cosmos is the establishment of an Identity at its exact center, and calculated extensions from thence along definable angles of awareness. This forms the true Magic Circle within which all wise magical Initiates live. Nor will they ever go outside it if they value their lives as they should. If they can increase the area of their circles to include what they seek, well and good. Otherwise, they should only deal with externals to their personal perimeters via the properly appointed channels of consciousness, each of which ought to have its special guardian device to prevent injurious influences from entering the entity so surrounded for its own safety.

This ancient pattern of a magician working in a consecrated Circle which no external evils may enter is an absolutely valid process founded on psychological fact and the soundest spiritual principles. As a purely superstitious practice for raising supposed demons and other "slaves of the Ring" to execute capricious commands for instant anything, a Magic Circle is a sheer waste of effort; but as a practical application of Self-servicing power-principles, it is a most commendable custom. To cast metaphorically a complete Self-limiting Circle of consciousness around one's Self, which can only be penetrated through specially conditioned channels determined by Will, is an act of the highest Magic indeed. In this world we all have to build some sort of a protective barrier around us in order to survive with even moderate sanity. Sheer Self-defense drives most of us into this course one way or another. Every ego erects some kind of barrier between itself and other entities for the sake of creating conditions inside its Circle favorable to its continuance. This is a natural procedure, but it may be done well or badly, depending on the hows and whats of its accomplishments.

Everything depends on the materials used to build up the walls of this "Cosmic Castle" around us. Many people, for instance, use a mixture of antipathy for all which is not to their personal liking, and greed for whatever they want to possess for their own aggrandizement. This certainly works for them, though it cannot possibly produce a central Self-status of any spiritual value worth considering. Besides this, such a Self-screen is easily demolished by contra-conditions brought to bear against it by other factors of life. The barriers we build around us for protection against aggression from other areas are frequently very feeble affairs, collapsing under the slightest assault. Other types of protection are rigid and impregnable enough on lower levels, but useless against adversities directed from higher flows of force. What we really need is an all-around "spiritual skin" of elastic energy, serving much the same purpose as our physical skins, which adapt us to the atmosphere and conditions of this planet. In like manner, our spiritual skins should act as adaptive organs which only allow communication between external and internal living through specialized channels of contact, comparable again to our physical senses and systems of adjusting our organisms to suit our necessities of Earth existence. Just as we have to grow these physical skins correctly around the delicate life-material of our bodies, so must we grow their spiritual equivalents around our Self-projections while we are expected to live under present conditions of Cosmos. Anybody can and must develop such a skin in various ways, but the Magical Circle method is concerned with growing a very highly specialized type of spiritual skin. It is meant to adjust itself automatically in conformity with whatever conditions of cosmic life the Self concerned may be associated with. That is what makes it especially Magic. If we think of our spiritual skins as the personal limits of our Cosmic Circles, through which the elemental energies of life are exchanged between internal and external existence, and the Spheres of the Tree of Life as the spiritual equivalents of our physical organs keeping us in good cosmic condition, we shall have a useful analogy to work with. The principle of all this is that we have to construct around our central Self-points a sort of globular spiritual periphery enclosing the personal Tree of Life which will extend our existence as it grows toward the state of its perfection. That is the rough outline of the general plan, and it is interesting to think this was also the scheme of our fabled Garden of Paradise. A circular area with four main channels, the magical Trees of Life and Knowledge in the middle, polarized Man-Woman living here and there, a

"Good Spirit" above, and the "Baddie" below, while Angels guarded the entrances and exits. That is the mythical version of the conditions we shall have to reconstruct around us if we are ever to regain Paradise and redeem our lost Selves. At least if we know, or can remember its pattern, this should give us a head-start with the rebuilding program.

The construction of this magical Cosmic Circle can only develop through efforts of intentionally directed conscious energies having formularies of force in accordance with the structural scheme which covers the entirety of the Entity being made as a Microcosm. From a purely mundane angle, this means that anyone intending to create such a Cosmic Circle around himself must be prepared to devote whatever time, space, events, efforts and energies may be necessary toward this task. Without such a Will, the Work cannot be accomplished. As in the case of all Cosmation, the initiating stages are the most difficult. Once the Circle has been properly cast, balanced, set in motion and is picking up its magical momentum, everything is progressively easier, providing all continues along its appointed lines. Getting started is always the worst part, but only in the sense of heavy expenditure for very slight returns, as with all capital investments. No one in his right mind would put capital into any scheme unless there was some certainty of production and marketing facilities as well. Similarly, before investing the complete capital of Self-integrity into a spiritual scheme for Individuation, we should at least assure ourselves that we shall be able to continue with what we must commence by sinking our capitalized Self-consciousness into. No one can answer this except the Selves concerned, but assuming that factors of ability and available facilities are favorable, a start to the process may be made very simply.

At first, one prerequisite is essential, apart from competence of consciousness: a place of privacy wherein personal practice of a magical and meditational nature may be exercised for a sufficient period to effect their purpose. Later when such practices become a normal part of the living process, they may be extended into ordinary life in ways acceptable to all, but in their beginning an isolated state comparable to womb-conditions is needed for maturing them until they are ready for emergence into everyday expressions of energy. The only physical adjuncts needed for this first part of the program are whatever will simulate womb-conditions of warm, comfortable darkness. A conventional method is a full wraparound cloak and hood, giving a sense of isolated individuality and secure insulation from external interference. It is very important that every possible precaution should be taken against actual physical disturbance during these primal exercises in contemplation. They need not be of long duration—ten minutes or so will suffice at first—but traumatic interference during these delicate Inner rearrangements and realizations of Identity can cause considerable spiritual shock. Should such an event occur, the only sensible thing to do is cease operations for a period until complete Inner calm becomes possible once more, then go back over the beginning again with a series of recaps till the break-off point is reached, and continue normally from there.

What we are trying to do is catch up consciously with our own Origins and simulate symbolically the emergence of our individual entities into existence out of the unknowable Universal Nil which emanates All into Life as we recognize the term. So the initial contemplations of our Cosmos must be concerned with this Primal Point alone. No more. There is no denying the extreme difficulty of reaching such a realization, especially in the case of modern Western people involved in competitive courses of civilized living, but unless some degree of this awareness is achieved, there is no use in continuing with more complicated developments of cosmo-design. Everything we will become has to emerge through this Single Source of our being. Get relationships between our Self-source and all else right, and we shall work out well enough on every life-level. Hence the supreme importance of correct contemplative procedure at this initial stage of our symbolic exercises in constructing our own Cosmos.

The actual program of these primary contemplations is simple enough to describe in principle. It is analogous with both a human birth-process and the mythical Genesis of God at the beginning of the Bible. Originally there is the Unbeing of Perfect Peace Profound—the Omnipotency, Omniscience and Omnipresence of Absolute Zooic Zero. This is symbolized by the cipher, or zero (0). Then comes the selection of Self, or impulse to Individuality. If we symbolize this by a straightforward "I," and superimpose it on the cipher, we shall have ⓪ or 10, the Divine Decade of the Sephiroth. Also, we shall have the initial division or "mitosis" of the living cells which began our bodies. If we consider our "I" as extending from its center outward and at right angles to itself, this will produce the solid Cosmic Cross and the Three Rings of Cosmos, Time, Space and Events. The

Figure 2 — The Cosmic Cross

intersections of these Rings will determine our relationships with the whole of Cosmos through the general headings of Divinity, Humanity (inclusive of every life-type) and the four Life-Elements symbolized by the concepts of Air, Fire, Water and Earth. It will also take into account the containing and conjoining Element of Truth which links all together as an entirety of Existence. Once the force-frame of this Cosmos is completed, we may start growing our Trees of Life inside it and making our Selves by Magic as we Will.

This all sounds so simple to say, but the difficulty in doing it can only be appreciated by those who attempt the task. It has been written about from various angles in other works, so the general layout will probably be quite familiar already. The main difference here lies in approach and buildup as a system evolving from the most recondite depths of Inner Entity to a practical point where it may be projected into the Containing Cosmos of "Other-than-I" in order to make magical relationships therewith. Since everything has to commence from and out of Nothing, that is where we must begin.

To suggest making the mind a blank and thinking Nothing is an impossibility. We cannot be conscious of Nothing, but we can come to consciousness *as* nothing. That makes the whole difference. Strictly speaking, there is no such state as "unconsciousness," but only a condition of universal undifferentiation, which means that all awareness is at Zero potential over its entire extent. Only Nothing can contain All as an absolutely exact Equation. Wherever there emerges the slightest degree of variation in what we might call this Ultimate Verity, an "I" of some sort begins its being out of the Nil-nucleus forming this first focus of force. It may or may not continue in a course of Cosmos. Here we are concerned with the state of spiritual immanence immediately behind the beginning of our individualities.

It would obviously be a supreme stupidity to expect

any kind of verbalized instructions for attaining experience of Unegoic Existence at almost Zooic Zero. Everyone must find this for himself by backtracking along his particular line of Light until it merges into the mightiest Me of All. In any case, we can only achieve a relative and symbolic appreciation of such a pre-cosmic condition while we are yet Earth-evolving entities. To approximate even so much is far more than the vast majority of mortals are likely to learn for a very great many lives. One definite lead may put us in the right direction. This is that we must reverse entirely the ordinary viewpoint of Nothing as being a condition of total insignificance, unimportance, and nonentity to be avoided at all costs. Our Nil-concept must also be our Ultimate in value.

Nor must we ever confuse Nil with Chaos. To the contrary, it is a condition of ultra-Cosmos in which Chaos would be impossible, because Chaos signifies disorder, and in Nil there is Nothing to be disordered. While we are synonymous with our Nil of Zooic Zero, we might be literally anyone, anywhere, or anything whatever. At the very inception of Individuality through a Nil-nucleus, however, we are committed to that Identity for the entire completion of its Cosmos or other cause of its conclusion. This is the Self we should become. Normally we emerge from Nil into a state of Cosmos which has already emerged from another state of Nil in its own scale of being. We must remember that though Nil is an incalculable condition of uncommitted ultra-Cosmos, it nucleates proportionately to whatever is produced from it. Whether a nebula that eventually turns into solar systems, or the nuclear center of a single living cell, the principle is the same. We all go back to nothing.

Hence our contemplative commencement of our Self-Cosmos *as* a Nil-condition. Of course we are aware of our human bodies sitting comfortably wrapped up in the dark to symbolize our aim. For a brief instant at least, we should try to put them in a position of Zero importance, which means they are no more nor less to us than all the rest of our entity. If they ceased, we would be unchanged, and should others appear in their place we would still remain unaltered. Our bodies have no more existence for us than anything else. Everyone and everything else is of equal import to us. Every life has the same significance. There is more difference between dimensions. This is not a rejection of everything except our Selves from the Zero-circle, but an entire equation of absolutely everything containable in us until we have absorbed our All into our Nil, and Zeroed out into Perfect Peace Profound!

Those are a few generalized thoughts guiding toward what Nil should mean to contemplatives dealing with this system. It is, in fact, what the much misunderstood "Nirvana" symbolized—the opposite of extinction, the reverse of life-rejection. Perhaps we might consider it the outgrowing of everything into a totality of truth. Far from being an indifference and utter unconcern entirely unconnected with anything, Nil is the exact antithesis of such an unnatural condition of Cosmos. It is conclusiveness of consciousness to Infinity, and the perfection of peace. What separates therefrom as Self to the least degree must part from that peace forthwith into personification along its own lines of initiative until its Cosmic Circle completes, and its Equation is solved eternally into the spiritual Nil-state behind its Being.

Thus with this system, we do not attempt a Nil-realization by exclusion of everything from our Self-Circles while we try to maintain a sort of defiant defense of our integrity in the middle. Nor do we attempt to make peace terms with the Infinite while remaining at war with all else. We simply take whatever we have inside our Selves, and coming to one conclusion with all, equate the whole lot into Nil, so far as we are symbolically able. The end product is not a Self with Nothing in it, but a state of Nil in which all Self is superseded.

Coping with the Nil-concept is an indescribable process. Intellect or reasoning are hopeless tools for the job. So is emotion and feeling. No amount of argument will explain it, or do more than direct conscious attention thereto. All the words in the world cannot tell the story or do anything except occupy our minds with various ideas upon the issue. The only practical course for contemplatives concerned with the Nil-concept to adopt is to absorb themselves with it until they themselves become absorbed by it and mutual acceptance occurs. Altogether it is a personal process which can only be carried out by reaching up inside one's Self as high as possible, and confiding the Self completely into the care of the Cosmic Spirit containing our Individualities from Whose Nil-state we emerged. Many mystics would term this "The unqualified surrender of Self to God," but it is really a surrender of Pseudo-Self into Spiritual Self to whatever degree the Initiating Intention is accepted. This at least is a good step in the right direction toward Divinity.

Time after time, therefore, we must attempt this same exercise until we realize our readiness to initiate the next step, which will also be taken in silent and dark physical externals. Two practical points need mentioning. For those keeping any sort of a magical diary, no notes, remarks or references of any kind should be kept of these particular contemplations. If there is some insistence upon record-taking which appears valid, a plain cypher (0) is all that's needed to indicate that contemplation has indeed been attempted in that instance. Since the contemplations are to be without words or any recognizable symbols at all, they should not be represented in descriptive terms. The other point is that our exercises ought to be carried out while we are physically seated in ceremonial style, and not just lying in our warm beds, tempting though this idea undoubtedly is. The reason for this is because of our bed-associations with abandonment of awareness, indolence, and other pleasing pastimes. In the case of these contemplations we are not abandoning consciousness at all, but trying to reach a symbolic state of its highest condition, awareness *AS* Nil, in NOTHING. Bed symbolizes the death-state of burial in the covering clothes, and we need the symbology of being suspended in a womb awaiting Life. We are increasing our awareness, not decreasing it. Therefore we ought to be clothed and arranged symbolically as the occasion demands.

The whole of the first step corresponds with the "brooding" of the Divine Spirit before identifying itself by Name. The second step, when we are ready for it, consists of "calling one's Self into being as Light." This is the equivalent of the Divine Spark arising in the Darkness (which comprehended it Not), and the Spark of Life being kindled within the Womb. Symbolically we "utter our Word of Will," which establishes our true Identity for the entirety of an Existence and—I AM. We becomes our Selves.

Here, our contemplation commences with a rapid evocation of our Nil-condition. Then we "emerge as Entity" by means of an awareness that "Otherness" IS. Not more than that at first. Most certainly not an objective awareness of any especial condition whatever, but only "Anotherness." About the only paradoxical description possible here is of a Nil-state being aware within another Nil. A double Zero, one inside the other. Two Nothings making a Something! This starts the Nil-nucleus going out of which all that each I AM becomes will emerge into existence. In that sense, it is the "critical point of Cosmos" so far as each entity is concerned, being the exact "Secret Center" through which the entire Energy behind everyone's being derives directly from what we term Divinity.

When our consciousness is accustomed to coping with this concept, we may safely allow the "First Formula" of I . . . AM to appear. If the magical Identity Name is already known, the Formula can certainly be I . . . AM . . . X . . . , though it is really preferable to commence with no more than just I . . . AM. The magical Name may be developed a little later. At this point, there should be no special emphasis on who, what, or how I . . . AM but simply a single insistence on Identity and no more. This Identity emerges via its Nil-nucleus as a particle of spiritual energy symbolized by Light as we appreciate the phenomena from our physical viewpoint. Therefore, in our contemplations we attempt being conscious of our Selves *as* Light, in the sense of radiant Energy. Our Divine Spark.

The difficulty here lies in being conscious *as* Light *in* Darkness. It should be remembered that Light itself is invisible, and we can only see objectively whatever reflects Light to us. Since Darkness does not reflect Light, how do we realize the existence of Darkness? Only because we are now experiencing the difference between I and non-I. If the non-I is the ambient Darkness, then the I has to be its Otherness— Light. It might be supposed that we should here conceive the most brilliant, intense and incredible kind of Divine Light blazing forth behind our being as a kind of cosmic ultra-illumination. This is precisely what we must NOT do. To the contrary, we should begin by contemplating our Originating Light as the least theoretical degree of Light necessary to make distinction between Light and Darkness possible. This is very important.

Qabalists will recognize this stage as being that of the Pure-Point of Light or Identity emerging at the absolute apex of Kether the Crown, where it meets with the unidentifiable infinity of Boundless Being as Ainsoph, the Nil. It might otherwise be considered as the controlled commencement of a chain-reaction of energy issuing from a Nil-nucleus. However we consider it symbolically, we must certainly realize that we our Selves must happen that way magically if we want to make the most of our Cosmos. To be properly processed, we should try to avoid all sudden shocks, blinding flashes, or bewildering blazes of inner illumination. These are not good for us at all, only injuring the intelligence and scarring the soul quite needlessly. What we should aim for is a slowly and steadily increasing area of luminous awareness extending out of our Primal Points into a comfortable coverage for our consciousness. We should seek no violent and terrifying visions of Truth in terms of Light which we are utterly unable to bear. No Inner equivalents of an atomic explosion—only the natural awakening of our awareness to a golden light gently dawning through our deepest Self-source, which will always be at the center of the Cosmos containing our complete consciousness.

It may be useful to realize that we have a rough comparison for this type of Light in our ordinary physical bodies. This is the invisibly shining radiation of our living flesh at the infrared end of the spectrum. It may not be optically perceptible, but is nevertheless our Life-Light on material levels. We are doing no more here than trying to trace its counterpart at our highest level of life. We ought also to note that this physical phenomenon has to be kept within limits for the sake of our well-being as mortals. A few degrees of rise or fall in temperature result in disablement or death. The same rule applies to Light-Life on higher levels also. It must be regulated to the correct rate for the Cosmos in which we mean to live, even through relative symbology. That is why we should never suppose that "opening up to Inner Light" with irresponsible abandon would be a solution to all spiritual problems. We dare only intensify that Light by whatever corresponding degree we have enabled our Cosmos to absorb safely. Hence the importance of commencing our Inner Self-radiance "lowly and slowly."

Concurrent with our emergence into Entity as Light comes the First-Force frequency symbolized by Sound. Actually it is the same Energy recognized from another angle of awareness. Spiritually, this Sound is our individual frequency or Truth Name which constantly "utters" our Identity at a height where it is inaudible except to the "Holy Ears" alone. Echoes of its penetrating to lower levels may be picked up by other spiritual sensors, and we might even reconstruct some symbolic resemblance to it in our magical Names, which we are charged to treat with such caution. This Sound of Self is our Will-word by which we come into being, as it was reputed the Divine Spirit uttered Its ineffable Name at the commencement of our Greater Cosmos. We all have our own particular "Name-notes," or fundamental frequencies which distinguish us from each other to those able to hear the music of the Spheres. They and our special Sparks go together.

Therefore, in addition to contemplating our Selves as originating of and as Light, we must also take Sound into consideration. This ought not to be taken as something separate to Light but synonymous with it. Perhaps "Singing Light" might be a poetic simile. It may be necessary to cheat our struggling consciousness a shade and actually listen to the Light within us resonating the Word as I . . . AM, unless there is preference for the AUM of the Buddhists, the AMEN of Hebrews and Egyptians, the AWN (AUOON) of Druids, HOO of Sufis, or any other "Mother mantra." At this stage, however, the Word is not to be uttered in any ordinary audible way whatever. Only issued as a silent sonic from the most recondite level of our beings we can manage to reach during these contemplations. It should preferably not be visualized as any form of written word, or imagined at first as an audible sound heard by physical ears.

This may seem difficult, but an approximation may be made by sounding off the Word consciously in the mind, then steadily silencing it while continuing to focus its force from the contemplative control level. Should this be too much during early practices, the Word may be consciously resonated as if it were almost inaudible, and only by straining the attention to the utmost could it be caught—the "still small Voice," in fact.

So there we have an outline of our secondary stage of Self-contemplation. Realization of our Selves as entities energizing into radiance and rhythm. Out of this is obviously to come much more, but we must confine our consciousness to our Self-stages in strict sequence. The actuality we are symbolizing is, of course, a cosmic constant in continual operation, but we are compelled to deal with it bit by bit because of our perceptual limitations as human beings. So we go on building up each exercise in contemplation until we are ready to extend it into a subsequent stage.

How shall we know when to start on another extension of our exercises? This is really something we can only discover as a result of our previous practices. In very general terms, however, anyone is usually ready for a fresh contemplative step when the last one can be readily reviewed and recalled at will so that an Inner sense of actually existing in such conditions may be experienced at least to a symbolic degree. Furthermore, it ought to be possible with as few artificial aids as may be indispensable because of human inadequacy. We must progress from the cloaked silence procedure until it becomes possible to seclude and separate our Selves at will among quite ordinary mundane living conditions—within reason, of course.

The overall idea of these exercises is to initiate them in relatively ideal conditions of consciousness encouraged and facilitated by the magical temple or similar environments, then gradually condense and strengthen them over a series of experimental developments until their principles can be carried through into any life-level, even those of our Earth-lives. If they can be constructed to cope with our Earth-living conditions, they will be of good service almost anywhere in existence. They are actually natural life-processes symbolized synthetically; and the Magic lies in the art of conceiving, arranging, and augmenting them along the right lines in proper order so that they will have a maximum effect in the most concise cosmic manner possible. By controlling the entire operation through a collection of symbolic Keys to the energy exchanges of consciousness involved, we are working this Magic with Will, which is exactly what is needed to assert the Intentions of the Identities we are seeking.

Thus it is impossible to calculate in terms of our human time how long each stage of these contemplations should be continued. The only sensible dictum is until they come right. In one sense they never cease, because our cosmic creation is a constant process, and our conscious recognition of it must eventually cover the entire area. Moreover, each successive stage of contemplation should always commence from the Nil-state, then rapidly follow through up to the point being pondered in that instance. A complete "flash-recap" from the very beginning in Zero with every exercise. This is symbolized by the "lightning flash" from top to bottom of the Tree connecting each Sphere in turn. Metaphorically we should do the same with our Cosmos contemplations on each occasion. Far from being an unnecessary addition, this re-Zeroing is an invaluable technical trick which provides an increasingly potent linkage with the Power stemming from our Life-Source. A few seconds or less of our Earth-time should suffice for this flash, and once the habit is formed of commencing with it in every instance, its effects will be readily appreciated by all contemplatives.

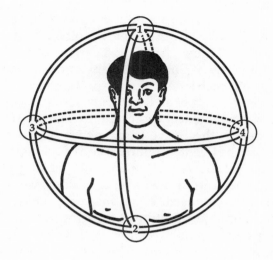

Figure 3 — The Individual Within the Cosmic Cross

The next change to take place in our symbolized consciousness as Cosmos is the introduction of the stress-axis
which will determine the three main Cosmic Circles of
Time-Space-Events, which must contain the whole Awareness of a Self within their compass. These axes extend from
the central Self-Point at right angles to each other so that if
they were solid they would be a three-dimensional equi-
lateral cross. They are not to be considered as solid, however,
but are to be experienced as if we were pushing our Selves
apart along these lines with a distinct impression of also
being pulled in the same directions by some unknown
Power containing us somewhere beyond the limits of our
comprehension. Not unlike the relationship between the
babe in a womb and the outside world of its mother's normal consciousness.

These axes under construction determine the extremities of our awareness throughout the Three Circles of Cosmos. One, extending from our Now-point, tells us of Time through past and future. Another, diverging from our Here-point, informs us of Space from anywhere to anywhere. The last, going each side of our So-point, connects us with the This's and That's of all the Events in our existence. For the sake of convenience, we accept the Time-Circle round us horizontally, the Space-Circle above and beneath us laterally, and the Event-Circle over and under us from front to back. As yet, however, we are only making the three Magical Medians around which the Cosmos we shall construct will be condensed. When these are ready, we must commence our objectification of consciousness by projecting power-particles out of our central Nil-nucleus, which will orbit around us and reflect the Light we are radiating in recognizable terms according to the Way we Will.

This is an extremely interesting and somewhat more intricate process. It may be done with external physical illumination, but preferably at first with closed eyes so as not to superimpose unwanted images on top of our Inner concepts. From our central Nil-nucleus we release a steady stream of Universal Energy along our axial lines which will polarize and be modified according to the confining concepts it meets, which cause it to be deflected into a circulating Cosmic Ring around us. To grasp the fundamentals of this scheme, it may be necessary to recapitulate some of the information previously put forward.

First, it must be accepted that life and all cosmic creation stems from a single Source of Energy emanating into our state of existence via what is to us the Nil or Zero condition of consciousness. We do not know the hows and wherefores of this by any intellectual means, and are simply symbol-stimulating in order to relate our Selves to the process by even the smallest proportion. This Universal Energy, whatever It may be, differentiates into all its various frequencies and categories by means of modifications imposed on it by the Intentions or Wills of the Entities through which, or in association with whom, it enters any distinct set of cosmic dimensions. As far as we are concerned in our human Self-states, we are existent within the Cosmos of some Superconsciousness we term Divinity, and this Encompassing Entity has already modified our common Universal Energy according to Its Will. We may do the same for our Selves in our smaller but similar ways, and are currently engaged in that very exercise.

Going back, therefore, to our central Nil-nucleus, we open up a force-flow of Universal Energy through our Selves along the axes of our commencing Cosmos. The whole action is simultaneous but may be considered sequentially for the sake of explanation. With each axis, the force-flow extends from the center outwardly, as it were, into a polarized extension of Energy until this reaches the restraining Ring of the Greater Cosmos, which contains our Lesser Cosmoses. This is like our Inner awareness suddenly coming into contact with the outer world in which we have to survive. As an initial experience it may be compared with physical birth. At the edge of our Self-Cosmos these extended energies become reacted into rectilinear arcs causing a complete circulation of force around us, which typifies in accordance with the Intention imposed.

For example, in the case of our upright axis we project from the Nil-nucleus an emission of Energy polarized by our ideas of Divinity at the top, and Humanity (inclusive of all lesser life-types) at the bottom. As our Divinity-seeking end of energy meets its complementary match in our Greater Containing Cosmos, it gets reactively bent to an accommodating angle. The same thing happens at the bottom end of the same axis in the opposite direction because of a reaction with Humanity and below. If we can imagine this in physical shape as a centrally pivoted pipe with angled jets at the end powered by steam, for instance, it will be easy to grasp the principles of its rotation. An electric motor also works analogously.

The same principles apply to our other two axes. As the first Circle outlined a Cosmos of Events for us between the extremities of Divinity and Humanity, so the remaining four points of polarity where the Circles cross each other are determined by our relationship with the Life-Elements symbolized by their similarity with what we recognize physically as Air, Fire, Water, and Earth. If we locate these at their traditional stations, our front-to-back polarization of Air-Water will spin our Cosmic Time-Circle for us, and the side-to-side polarity of Fire-Earth will revolve our Space-Circle. Thus do we cover with our consciousness a complete Cosmos emerging from our Selves and engaging with all else in Existence. Once we get this going dependably, all we have to do is fill in the rest for our Selves.

What we are in fact doing is to build up the metaphysical basis of our beings into a sort of spiritual body enabling us to exist as living entities in states of nonmaterial Selfhood. Nevertheless, the same Life-principles behind our physical bodies also apply to our "corpus of consciousness" along rather different levels of application. Just as we must take in food and drink physically, for instance, so must we assimilate their equivalents in terms of Inner aliments. Even as our bodies metabolize these supplies into the energies that keep us alive physically, and excrete their incompatible residue in order to maintain our bodies in a healthy condition, so should our spiritual structures follow the same cycles of eating, energy expending and excretion. Whatever our ordinary bodies do, our Inner anatomies will do better and with much more meaning for our spiritual Self-state.

Although most people grasp the idea of assimilation along spiritual lines, and we find countless references to "feeding on the Body of God," "Eat and drink Me," "not by bread alone," "food for thought," etc., the vitally necessary concomitant of excretion is generally most shamefully ignored or neglected. How can we possibly live in a healthy Inner condition of consciousness if our equivalents of an excretory system are not functioning properly? This topic is really of sufficient importance to deal with separately under the heading of Spiritual Sanitation, but only bare outlines will be given here in order to introduce the idea into our Self-systematization.

We excrete physically in four major ways corresponding to the Elements. The two "subtle" Elements of Fire and Air we release from our bodies in the forms of infrared rays and gases via the surface of our skins and the pores therein. The other two "gross" Elements of Water and Earth are reduced to urine and feces dischargeable via their respective channels. Be it noted that our excretion of heat and vapor is a relatively rapid and continual process, while our rejection of liquids and solids culminates into slower and more static occasions.

Similarly, we should excrete spiritual residuals from our Self-systems by comparable means, once we have extracted the energies we need from our Inner intakes to maintain us in good cosmic health. A well-kept spiritual skin will radiate away from its surface our unneeded equivalents of heat and vapor amounting to our used Elements of Fire and Air. The heavier or "weightier" Elements of Water and Earth have to be dealt with more slowly and filtered down through our Self-systems until we are ready to release their residues through the Inner channels we have to provide for that purpose.

This is a perfectly natural process, applying both physically and spiritually. For instance, we can take in a great proportion of our Inner supplies, react with them fairly rapidly and expel our unrequirements as heat or Fire.

A further proportion we need to retain a little longer and then vaporize what we reject as Air. The next proportion we have to keep in our systems longer still in order to filter out our necessities and subsequently release what remains as Water. After that, we retain the rest until we have reduced what we require into states of spiritual solidity, then evacuate the residue as Earth. Nor is this the final clearance we must make to maintain sound spiritual health. There should eventually follow an evacuation according to the fifth Element of Truth, during which whatever we finally conclude ought to have no place in the Cosmos we are constructing must be expelled altogether. This is a far less frequent occurrence than the other eliminations, but an ultimately inevitable one if we are to stay alive in a state of spiritual wholesomeness. Sooner or later we must bring our Selves to exclude from their systems whatever we can no longer accept as absolute and fundamental truth. This equivalent of a "Last Judgment," or ultimate rejection of all unfitted for inclusion in Absolute Identity, is something taking place on a minor scale in each Self seeking its own Ultimation into Light-Life.

Physically, the release mechanisms of our excretory facilities, which place the function under control of our wills for the sake of convenience, are the anal and urethral sphincters which we can open and shut as we intend. Spiritually, we have to construct equivalents of consciousness for similar reasons. This amounts to a conditioned Inner reflex consisting of an intention to discharge worked-out metaphysical matter from our Self-systems, coupled with some suitable symbolic release-formula. Once the correct combination of factors are made, we can evacuate all effete accumulations from our spiritual Self-areas quite sensibly and safely. For example, the average social customs of Humanity call for special circumstances in connection with eliminative procedures before these become practical. These may include seclusion, some satisfactory sanitation, or whatever other facilities are considered essential to an evacuation act. Though all of these are physical and practicable, they are also symbolic and psychological. We can make use of their principles magically.

In point of fact, the most logical thing to do is to combine our physical and metaphysical evacuations into a common procedure. This makes for simplicity and convenience always. Whenever we connect our bodies to an ordinary sewage system for our functions of nature, we should also consider our spiritual Self-systems connected with the equivalent absorption and purification capabilities of our Inner Life-Elements. Our rejected fluids in both senses flow back into oceanic water and our solids return to terrestrial Earth. We are only sending back spent superfluities from our Self-systems to their rightful Elemental categories. Therefore, as we relieve our physical bodies, we should also act likewise on Inner levels of living.

Very broadly speaking, our residual Inner fluids are more or less all the exhausted and detrimental thoughts we ought to get out of our Self-systems, while our Inner solid detritus consists mostly of outworn and useless feelings, best cleared out of us altogether. So we should make determined and intentional efforts to free our Selves from these in relative ways to our material waste-disposal methods. Because we realize that thoughts and feelings reduced to such a condition will poison our minds and souls if we do not eliminate them like their physical counterparts, we might phrase our discharge formula in this fashion:

Fluids
Toxic thinking—Go!
Like clearest Water flow.

Solids
Foul feelings—Forth!
Return to cleanest Earth.

Whatever formula is used, the wording is best kept simple, forceful, direct, and definite. The formula must become to our consciousness what muscular sphincter-release is to our bodies. That is to say, it must act as an ejector-mechanism for expelling our Inner excretions. With practice and effort, these formulae may be made most effective. They should, of course, be entirely confined to suitable occasions and circumstances. No normal person deliberately voids urine and excrement in the close social presence of others, or in fact anywhere except in some suitable spot. Similar rules should apply along spiritual levels. To pour our internal nonmaterial excremental ejections so that these effluents endanger human Inner health is a most antisocial practice indeed. When we become as deeply concerned about spiritual contaminants as we are about waking up to the dangers of chemical pollution, our human world might be a cleaner place in which to live. The beginnings of spiritual sanitation lie with correct "Inner toilet training" for each Self taking its early steps to Individual adulthood.

Although this subject is of such importance in the formation of a Self-system, it obviously cannot be dealt with in the detail it deserves in a work of this nature. Before we leave it for the time being, however, a mention of how it applies to the Tree of Life pattern should be made. This is really simple enough, once the secret is known. Life-material for digestion, assimilation and ultimate disposal is metaphorically put down the Abyss via Daath, which is Knowledge, or experience of living. We "chew over" all we learn in life, and should get rid of the remains, which are useless to us but still valuable as fertilizer for other cycles of creation on which our own living depends. So how is this ejected from the Tree-system?

To discover the exit point, it is only necessary to set up a Tree-plan as follows. First draw the centerline from top to bottom as a definite measurement, say six inches. Next

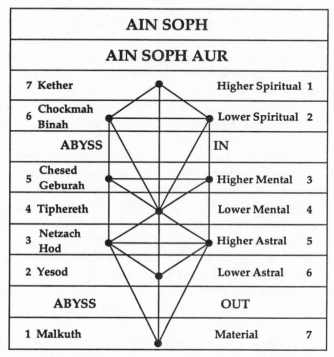

AIN

AIN SOPH
AIN SOPH AUR

The Spheres		The 7 Levels of Life	
7	Kether	Higher Spiritual	1
6	Chockmah Binah	Lower Spiritual	2
	ABYSS	IN	
5	Chesed Geburah	Higher Mental	3
4	Tiphereth	Lower Mental	4
3	Netzach Hod	Higher Astral	5
2	Yesod	Lower Astral	6
	ABYSS	OUT	
1	Malkuth	Material	7

Figure 4 — The "Other" Abyss on the Tree of Life

mark the Sphere centers as dots in their exact places and join the external pairs by three horizontal lines (see Figure 4). Now make a division of the Tree-scale by taking the distance from top (Kether, the Crown) to the Chokmah-Binah (Wisdom and Understanding) level as a unit of measurement, and mark off this in regular lines all down the Tree. A two- or three-color scheme may help. The result of this shows a somewhat remarkable issue. It reveals not one Abyss on the Tree, but two, or rather the other end of the Great Abyss always shown between the first three Supernal Spheres and the remainder. Here we clearly observe how an Abyss also occurs between Malkuth (our Kingdom of Matter) and Yesod (the Foundation of Life) on Inner levels. Just where we might expect to find such a thing once we look for it. The presence of an Abyss is shown up by this method because Spheres of the Tree appear in all other divisions except these two.

Great though the implications of this discovery are, we cannot stop now for further discussion beyond pointing out that no life-scheme could possibly be complete without some kind of expulsive orifice, and here is that very necessity upon the Tree. All that comes out of it may be considered as good fertilizer for the roots of life, just as it would in the case of humus or common useful dung. Re-grading our rejections back into the life-scheme is a vital part of our Inner or Outer activities, and if we are to become real Initiates of the Holy Mysteries, then we must learn how to do this appropriately to our spiritual status.

Returning to our constructions of the Three Cosmic Circles around our Self-Center, there is always a natural query as to how far these should be considered to extend in terms of a physical framework. Theoretically, of course, the Circles of Cosmos extend to Infinity, but for practical purposes we shall probably find that a few feet more than the body area seems most normally comfortable for an average consciousness. It must be remembered, though, that the Circles have to expand or contract together. They are interdependent, and have to be worked as a whole. We cannot alter one without affecting the others. Cosmos has its own laws, and we simply are unable to alter these fundamentally, no matter how we may play around with their effects.

Some workers take a traditional standpoint of legs apart and arms to match above head, then calculate their Cosmic Circles as if these just touched at finger and toe perimeter. This is quite a good symbol for putting into magical practice, since it forms the Circle-Cross design. There is no use leaping ahead into more picturesque practices until these preliminary contemplations and clearances have been persisted in time and time again and are producing results in terms of seeming more essential as parts of our life-schemes. It may seem dull doing little more than staying still physically while encouraging Inner activity, but that is how all life-Magic begins. Babies in the womb probably get very bored while waiting to grow legs to rush through life with. Without womb-work, however, there could be no joys of jumping ahead, and that is how we should look at our present spiritual situation. To make our Magical Cosmos rightly, it has to be started in this Self-stabilizing way in the beginning, or it will only collapse later on and we shall have to start all over again. In order to grow our Tree of Life properly, its "Seed" must be planted and germinated in the silent depths of our beings from whence it will emerge into life-light and eventual fruition. Only when we have got our Magical Cosmos organized reliably will it be ready to raise a Life-Tree within it, so the sooner this is accomplished, the better for us. One major reason why so few people out of the many who are drawn to Magic really get something out of it for themselves is because enthusiasts will persist in trying to start at the showy stages of dramatic ritual while ignoring the plodding prosaic processes which alone make movements of Magic possible. Those who avoid such an error are most likely to succeed in the magical Magnum Opus.

Assuming that satisfactory results have been achieved with constructing our Self-system so far, let us see where the next few exercises may take us. Now we can stop sitting down so much and get on with some of the ritual procedures helping us form Inner forces into patterns of power we can live and work with. As we develop these, everything will seem to take on a new depth of meaning, and we should feel our Selves living much more certainly than before. The question, What do I mean to my Self? becomes somewhat closer to an eventual answer.

Chapter Five

Cosmo-Continuance

The next stage in our proceedings consists in building up clearly defined concepts at the crossing points of our Cosmic Circles and putting them into practical courses of consciousness. The traditional magical way of doing this is by making these into Archangelic personifications that are composed of simple basic symbols.

To try to argue the existence or nonexistence of Archangels and their exact nature is a purely academic pastime. In the sense that Archangels might be people or persons in some way like us, but magnified to X million degrees, they are nonexistent. For that matter, they would be useless to us if such were the case. As concentrations of categorized consciousness, Archangels can and do exist as entitized energies of whatever we care to call our Initiating Cosmic Intelligence. We can and should make Archangels for our Selves by a relatively similar process.

Suppose, for instance, we guided all our ideas, instincts, information and intentions concerning the single concept of "Uprightness" into one channel, brought everything to as high a degree of perfection as we could conceive, personified the whole into a representative Identity, then summed it all up into the evocative control-symbol of a

Rod. We would then have what amounts to a personal appearance of Archangel Michael. Initially this would be only an imaginative image limited to the Cosmos of its creator, but fundamentally it would link up with its archetype in the Overall Awareness, and connect with its fellow force-frequencies along universally used chains of consciousness. True, each Archangel-image will only be effective to the degree of its creator's cosmic capabilities, but being energy-exchangers, they can be used for enhancing the cosmic condition of whomever employs them as adaptors of Self-life on all levels.

The process is basically as simple as that. If we make for ourselves conscious concepts of what are aptly termed the eternal verities, or universally recognized principles, these personal concepts must join up along deep Inner lines with all others of such a category through our cosmic continuum. The only factors of limitation or failure lie with the Self-consciousness concerned. Those verities and principles exist for whatever their values amount to in the Containing Cosmic Consciousness. Whether or not we can translate them into acceptable terms for our Selves depends only upon our determination and ability, both of which are improvable and increasable qualities, and such desirable alterations result mainly from our contacts with Cosmos made through the concepts we have intentionally invoked. This is the Magic involved in the whole operation.

There are seven of these major Archangel-concepts concerned with our Circle-Cosmos.

Name	Position	Designation	Symbol
1 Metatron	Above	"Near thy Throne"	Special Crown
2 Sandalaphon	Below	"Co-Brother"	Special Cube
3 Raphael	Front E	"Healer of God"	Sword-Arrow
4 Michael	Right S	"Like God"	Rod-Lance
5 Jivrael	Rear W	"Virility of God"	Cup
6 Auriel	Left N	"Light of God"	Shield
7 Savaviel	Around	"Circler of God"	Cord

By means of these Archangelic concepts, a Self may be aligned with anything whatever existing in the entirety of Inner or Outer Cosmos. They are not only the Angels, but also the *angles* of Universal Awareness. Once properly placed at the extremities of our individual Self-existence, they will mediate both Macrocosm and Microcosm into a state of mutual significance. That is their purpose, and this is the work proposed at present.

Although an enormous amount has already been written about most of these Archangels, it may prove profitable here to make their literary acquaintance again with a special view to dealing with points that may have been obscure or inadequately covered in previous descriptions, particularly if we look with our present purpose entirely in mind. Meeting the Archangels briefly in order, we learn:

METATRON (Name means "Near Thy Throne") is the "Archangel of the Presence," whose task it is to make us aware of Divinity, and Divinity to recognize us. He (or It) is the means whereby every Self first suspects and then experiences the existence of Supreme Spirit. Thus, Metatron leads us as our Selves into the Only Self. Legend says that he was once human, and has reached the greatest heights possible for any Self to reach short of Ultimation. This, Metatron does not yet achieve because he is willingly fulfilling the function of providing the last linkage in a chain of consciousness connecting every separate life with Infinite Light. Tradition tells us that if Metatron did not intervene between Divinity and the remainder of Cosmic Life, we should long ago have been consumed and dissipated back to the dust we reputedly arose from.

Metatron is the leading Throne Archangel with a host of other names. He means to anyone whatever directs their consciousness toward Divinity, so he may be seen in almost any form imaginable to attain this end. His special symbol is the Crown of Consciousness. This can be seen in a variety of ways, providing it is fundamentally a four-barred crown rising hemispherically from a circlet with a central point of Light. If we think of it as being on our heads, it will mark the crossing of our Space-Event Cosmic Circles. Metatron is not so much visualized as *felt* in the form of two hands securing the crown, one on each side of our heads. There is a link between this idea and the hands of an *accoucheur* carefully guiding the head of a baby being born. So does Metatron deliver us into other states of life. He is for "holding up our heads" so that we face life the right way. This is precisely what a basic faith in Divinity should do for us, and such is Metatron's mediation on our behalf.

Being also the Throne Angel, Metatron is supposed to make us feel correctly seated or "enthroned" at the controls of our "Cosmic Chariot." Whoever comes to accept confidently that Cosmos has indeed a Controlling King, and that they themSelves are also occupying a proportional position of rulership in their own individual Cosmos, will realize what Metatron means. It is through his means they realize the responsibility of ruling their lesser lives by adaptations of the same spiritual standards applied by Divinity throughout the extent of Its existence. Metatron mediates these matters for us mortals.

Thus, Metatron must be considered as a conceptual personification of all that "uplifts" us to whatever we believe is, or ought to be, Divinity Itself. He holds our heads to Heaven, and crowns our consciousness with the highest ideals we may possibly reach. No matter how high we ever go, Metatron is just that much above us, indicating another apex of awareness to be attained. We may think of him as holding a Cosmic Crown fractionally away from our heads, so that constantly we must rise to remain in touch with it. It is he (or *It*) that keeps us in contact with our fundamental faith that somehow, somewhere, there has to be a Someone above us all, with Whom or Which we are personally and individually linked. Divinity is the highest concept of Humanity. Metatron is the mediating link between our two extremities of Life.

Instinctively, Humankind thinks of Divinity in some way "up there," or spatially overhead, in addition to being an Inner Presence. This most likely traces back to an inherent awareness of our origins from elsewhere than Earthly environments. Humanity has always felt its soul to belong among the stars, and its Heaven to be located entirely away from this pathetic little planet. This instinct is cosmically correct, and calculably the time will come when the last human being must leave the uninhabitable atmosphere of this wrecked world, and seek continuance elsewhere in Cosmos. Physically, this may be along other biological lines in quite different planetary arrangements. Spiritually, the same laws must hold good, and the equivalent of Metatron must continue to lead us in ever evolving upward cycles toward the crown of whatever Creation we are concerned with. The better we get to know and appreciate him in our "here-now," the more he is likely to do for and with us in the "there-then." Metatron is a life-leader everywhere, and where he can live, so may we.

SANDALAPHON (Co-Brother) is Metatron's other half, and "Angel of the Footstool" beneath us. This means he keeps our feet on the ground firmly enough to establish our existence wherever we are, and more important, puts us in contact with all other types of life. It is he that gives us a sense of "family" or brotherhood with creatures of all kinds. Not just other humans, but animals, plants, or life to any degree of manifestation. If Metatron makes us feel we might eventually become one with Divinity, Sandalaphon tells us about our fellowship with other life-forms. Together, these Archangels are the pivots on which our whole cosmic construction turns, and so they are rightly placed in relation to the head and feet of our balanced being. They are also the

Archangels at the top and bottom of the Tree of Life which we shall grow within our Cosmos eventually, so they are correctly located at the commencement of our magical exercises.

Sandalaphon is reputed to be an Archangel tall enough to reach Heaven from Earth, and is thus typical of evolutionary life rising from lowest to highest levels. He is said to determine the sex of embryos, and also to make garlands from the prayers of Humanity and hand these up to the All-High. Again these legends show an Archangel-concept concerned with a life-cycle extending from the most primitive to the most perfect levels of living throughout a continuity of consciousness. The prayers and aspirations of those beneath the divine footstool reach the Throne itself by mediation of Sandalaphon.

The symbol of Sandalaphon is very interesting. Outwardly it appears like a cubic Stone or altar, symbolizing the basis or "rockbottom" of being, or the "rough ashlar" of Masonry. Inside this solid symbol, it is actually a double Pyramid of four sides, one being positive, and the other a hollow negative. These fit together so smoothly that they only give the external appearance of a cube. If we visualize our Selves as standing with our feet on this strange Cube, we shall be in the unique position of being both on the top and the bottom of a Pyramid simultaneously. This should provide a great deal of symbolism for meditative mediation. It is really the Crown of Metatron squared, so the "Squared Circle" of Cosmos can be considered as our linkage with Divinity throughout the whole of life.

Sandalaphon is another Archangel whom we recognize by feel rather than appearance. It is he that "sets our feet in the right way," when we realize our kinship with all other kingdoms of life, even extending to the so-called inanimate realms of rocks, minerals, and the barest bones of being. If we bear in mind what the office of "Footstool holder" amounted to in ancient times, the function of Sandalaphon will become much clearer to us. In principle, a king or ruler was always supposedly higher than those he ruled. His throne set him physically above his people when he acted in his official capacity, yet he could not at all times literally occupy a throne. Therefore, as he went around on foot, his footstool bearer accompanied him in the event of royal pronouncements or rulings being made. These were deemed to be authoritative when issued by the king while standing on the footstool, which raised him even a foot above others, symbolizing his pseudo-divine stature. The footstool was thus a sort of Earth-throne—easily portable, and convenient for asserting authority at any moment. In modern paraphrasing, the stool was in fact a "mini-mountain," signifying the Holy Height from which a king was supposed to speak. We might say literally that it gave him a lift, and this is just what Sandalaphon should do for us.

Somehow, every Self ought to feel in some degree superior to others, as though it were something very special and important as an Identity. No matter how obviously other Selves may seem far more advanced in all kinds of ways, everyone should have a unique sense of Self-confidence in their own Cosmos which elevates them into Kingship of their Inner domains beyond any possibility of doubt. That is Sandalaphon putting them on his strange pyramid-pedestal of a footstool, and raising them in their own estimation until they are able to look at life from an authoritative angle. Such is his special function for us all, mainly so for those who cooperate consciously with their "co-brother."

We should always see Sandalaphon and Metatron working in harmony together like opposite polarities of the same Power. Between them their mission to mortals is to awake and assist a realization of responsible rulership in us, so that we tend to become Self-governing Individuals controlling the courses of consciousness which will ultimately determine our conditions of Cosmos. We can and should all become Kings and Priests after the Order of Melchizadek, and Sandalaphon with Metatron are our Archangelic sponsors for this greatest initiation into the Mysteries of our Living Identity. Taking life in general at its average angles with which we have to deal, we shall meet the Four Great Archangels of the Quarters through whom we adapt our Selves to everything else. Reading around our compass they are:

RAPHAEL (Healer of God). He is so called because he heals the hurts we experience through our encounters with life. Suitably enough, he "seals" the crossing of our Time and Event Cosmic Circles. Raphael equates with Hermes, the "soul-leader" and the Dawn arising in the East bringing us a first Light on life. We can come to very personal terms with Raphael. He typifies youth with enthusiastic energy and keen perceptions determined to make life mean an absolute maximum. Raphael *arouses* us, alerts us, directs our attention ahead and probes into possibilities. He is resourceful and resilient, just as skilled in avoiding dangers adroitly as he is in anticipating them. None are better than he as look-out for the various liabilities our lives must necessarily bring to us, so Raphael is properly placed immediately in front of us as we stand in our Cosmic Circles.

The symbol of Raphael is the Sword and Arrow. He has all the attributes of a Sword as regards brightness, keenness, flexibility, purposeful pointing, skillful defense and every such association. Like an Arrow, he aims ahead at a mark and directs an intention specifically to some particular point. He is mobile rather than static, always impelling activity on account of some life contact likely to influence the Self away from its centralized stability. By himself, Raphael would over-activate us, but in combination with his correct Archangelic Cosmic companions, he can only keep us going at a reasonable rate to ensure our forward progress along the Line of Light connecting the human and divine ends of our Entity.

Raphael's Element is Air—atmosphere, aspiration, and whatever we might associate with freedom of movement in material or mental dimensions. Being the patron of travel, he inclines us to go places and see things for ourselves with a kind of cosmic curiosity and a hope of enhancing our experience so that we shall grow into greater and finer types of soul and Self.

We may visualize Raphael clearly enough if we keep to the convention of hair, eye, and complexion coloring which distinguishes the Archangels from each other. They should be seen as ambisexual beings who might be either, both, or of neither gender. As far as possible, their clothing should be timeless, but they may be considered of successive age-groupings to cover a cosmic lifetime. There is no need for imagining any wings or abnormal attachments. Raphael is usually seen as young and fresh with light brown hair and grey eyes. His robes are often blue-grey in tone. His Sword flashes light, and it makes the Circle-Cross emblem by being presented horizontally as a bar, upright as an edge, around as a perimeter, and centrally as a point. All these positions have special meanings which have to be learned from Raphael in the course of our acquaintance together. The signals we receive or transmit through the Archangel-concepts will keep us in communion with Cosmos in all directions. It is a question of discovering the codes, and these can only be taught by the Archangels themselves.

MICHAEL (like God), is the Archangel normally on our right in the South position of Noon with the Element of Fire. He closes one crossing of our Time-Space Cosmic Circles. He should scarcely need description. It is Michael who gives us our ideas of *rightness*, and upholds the standard by which we must measure our Selves against life and act accordingly. Traditionally, Michael is Archangel of the Balance, said to preside at the Last Judgment. In other words, he is whatever determines our decisions as to what is right or wrong on any occasion, and once we have committed our Selves into any course of action, we must abide by the issue. Raphael may urge us to act, but Michael advises us to judge and decide on the nature and extent of our activities. Raphael looks at life with the dawning Light of awakening and sharply perceptive awareness, but Michael shines the Light of noon on all problems, revealing them in full clarity and perspective. Although this may show everything up in considerable detail, it can also overpower very many subtler meanings and values by eliminating delicacy of shading. These, however, will appear at other Light angles of our Cosmos, so we shall not be the losers if we wait for other opportunities of observation.

Michael's symbol is the Rod or Lance. He signals with it much like Raphael. Horizontally it is a barrier to prevent us going the wrong way. Vertically it is a support to uphold our progress. Circling, it is an indicator of whatever needs attending to, and with extended end it offers guidance to whoever holds on to it. Raphael may prod us into action with a sword point, but Michael leads us along our proper path with his Lance of Light. Used on our behalf, this Lance defends us against evils which might otherwise enter our Cosmos. It is also the Rod of Rulership, with which we are expected to govern our Selves in a royal and responsible manner.

Michael is often represented as wearing quasi-Roman armor as he spears the Old Dragon of Evil. However, there is no need to visualize him as always in military fashion. His robes are frequently scarlet and golden, his complexion healthily tanned, his hair golden, his eyes piercing blue. When he speaks, his voice is authoritative and firm, as distinct from the lighter and more youthful tones of Raphael. Michael is considered in a somewhat older age group than Raphael, though still young and at the prime of power. He is firmness and steadfastness personified, resolutely guiding us toward whatever way might be best for our ultimate good as a spiritual Self-entity. Michael speaks to us with the voice of conscience, which is likely to advise quite different course of conduct than our Pseudo-Selfish inclinations might suggest. We justify ourselves before God and Humanity alike by means of Michael.

JIVRAEL (or Gabriel, the Virile One of God) is behind us in the Western Quarter of Dusk and Sunset. This is the Archangel of Love and Compassion in all senses He personifies all that is loving and lovable in our whole world, teaching us how to be in love with life by every possible means. Jivrael shows us that we need not confine our loving and compassion to other humans alone, but may extend this wonderful experience in different degrees throughout the whole of Creation. He represents fertility in every way, not only of body, but of mind and soul also. He can help us put two ideas together and breed them just as if they were biological specimens producing offspring. Jivrael looks at life with a kindly sense of kinship and a maximum intention of being on the best possible terms with everyone and everything. He makes our experiences enjoyable if he can, and endurable if no more is possible. It is from his Quarter that we may expect happiness in the usual meaning of the word, or solace and consolation should we need this. Jivrael does not indulge us in Self-pity, but offers an assurance of love and compassion on behalf of a far greater Self than ours. He also inclines us to extend such qualities from within our Selves through him toward other Selves in need.

The symbol of Jivrael is the Cup. This may be of horn to link up with primitive practices, but is normally of a more sophisticated shape, being of gold in the form of a hemi-sphere mounted above a pyramidal square base. This Cup is often seen ornamented with precious stones, especially blood-red rubies, though sometimes there are four prin-cipal gems of red, yellow, green, and blue coloring. The contents of the Cup vary with circumstances of our need. They will consist of whatever we lack which might make us love our fellow beings, or conversely with whatsoever we try and love our fellow beings. We should not forget that our Archangels are two-way officiants. Not only do they communicate to us offerings and information from our Outer or Containing Cosmos, but they pass out from us what we have to contribute in return or on our own initia-tive. It is Jivrael who offers and receives Compassion on our account. He carries the Circle-Cross pattern by the figura-tion of Light caught within an otherwise empty Cup.

Jivrael is normally seen as a mature personification, with deep auburn or chestnut hair, amber eyes, and thrill-ingly sympathetic voice. Often his robes are green and blue with some gold tracery. His Element is Water, and his occa-sion sunset, when all is seen with splendid and spectacular colors, glowing in the most hopeful Light imaginable. Jiv-rael always tries to make the best of everything, as he aligns our Time and Event Cosmic Circle-crossing. He is apt to be overoptimistic, of course, but without hope how could any-one bear to be alive in this world at all? Besides, we should always take the other Archangels into account as well before coming to any definite conclusions in our Cosmos. So far, Raphael has alerted and interested us, Michael has advised and upheld us, now Jivrael is trying to motivate us with what was once called "lovingkindness." This is all part of a process in which we are participating in order to make our lives mean what they should in cosmic values. To complete our Cycle of the Quarters, we must contact one more Archangel. This is:

AURIEL (Light of God), who is on our left hand, and mediates the position of North and Night, associated with the Element of Earth. Auriel is frequently linked with the Polar Star, or Heavenly point by which we map out our course on Earth. He is essentially the Archangel of Experience and Reflection, counselling us to be cautious and consider everything very carefully before committing ourselves to the smallest action. We should now be able to perceive his purpose on our perimeters at a Time-Space crossing. He completes the cycle of consciousness commencing with Raphael. First we have our interest or attention aroused. Secondly we have to justify our dealings with whatever it is, then come considerations of compassion which must modify our attitude accordingly. Now, at the last stage, we have to reflect very deeply in the light of all experience upon our further course of consciousness and activity. Shall we, or shall we not commit our Selves to this or that particular Path? Auriel would advise us if possible to "sleep on it" so that we might make contact with our remote levels of Being for further consideration and consultation. Where this is not practical, he tries his best to restrain impulsiveness and persuade us to think and evaluate as far as we can before releasing energies into channels beyond our immediate control. Auriel is always attempting to save us from our own stupidities.

The symbol of Auriel is the Shield, which is also a reflector, or species of Magic Mirror. With this symbol, Auriel tries to shield us from the worst we might meet with from outside our Selves, and also shield others from the worst we might inflict on them, this last for our sake as much as theirs. By means of the Reflector, Auriel attempts to show things to us in their most accurate light by contrasting the best with the worst, and reflecting a reasonable average. Using the Shield as a selective screen, Auriel presents us to other Selves as favorably as he can, and gives a good image of us to all who contact his Quarter of our Cosmos. He also seeks to give us a good opinion of our fellow-beings. The Circle-Cross symbol appears on his Shield, where it displays our cosmic coat of arms, or proclamation of our personal Selfhood, in the method of our Magical Motto, or Sigil.

Auriel is usually seen as an elder with dark hair silvering, dark eyes, and a deep deliberate voice. His robes are reminiscent of starlight brilliance, and perhaps he twinkles a little to show that he has profound good humor beneath his somewhat serious mien. He is caution personified, a natural adviser against any action that is not thoroughly thought out and calculated for consequences. It is he who advocates discretion and silence in magical matters, suggesting what should be kept confidential, and what is safe to be open with. Altogether Auriel might be summed up as cosmic common sense employed by enlightened entities.

SAVAVIEL (Circler of God) is the last Archangel in this series. He is another Archangel somewhat beyond our visual range of imagination because of his elusiveness. His Element is Truth, and he ties all our Cosmic Circles together so that they have unified meaning. To gain some ideas of his function, we might try using his symbol, the Cord, in the following way.

Taking an end of any cord a few feet long, let this be wound up steadily to make a ball, as for example, with knitting wool. Each complete turn should be as near a right angle with the last as possible, and as we wind, the turns should be thought of as Time, Space, and Events, in a repetitious continuity. This illustrates how our Cosmos is "wound up" into an ever-increasing mass of those three factors, while yet being only one line of life. Savaviel is the Archangel who winds up our affairs in a relatable manner so that they have a single thread of continuity running through them from one end to the other. Hence the Cord symbol. With Savaviel, we reach into the past or future, for he ties these in with the present to make life plausible for us. Whether we travel in small or large Circles, Savaviel is capable of connecting them together.

Savaviel is the Archangel who links ideas and impressions for us so that chains of consciousness will join almost any points in our lives or memories to make sensible meanings. We have to learn the secret of holding one end of his Cord while he takes the other in search of what we ask about, so that he may signal us back along the line held between us. If we like to think of it as a telephone or TV cable, there is no objection to fitting modern metaphors over ancient fundamentals. The principle is the same. An Archangel of Truth communicating with us through lines of linkage conjoining points of our conscious Cosmos. It makes a useful magical exercise in connection with Savaviel to devise a sort of color-code for whatever Cord he may be using on our behalf. Suppose, for instance, we should be seeking some kind of Saturnian contact. For this, we might visualize ourselves holding a black Cord while Savaviel circles away with the other end. The Sphere colors of the Tree all apply here. Then there are combinations of color which may be coded for any purpose whatever. It all depends on what we associate colors with, and how they are given significance.

If Savaviel is seen as anything, he is an iridescent being with silver and gold garments, shining strangely and mysteriously as he makes his momentary appearances all around our Cosmos. He does not make his presence felt nearly as much as our Great Four do, and he is more difficult to contact than they are. Moreover, he may be very disconcerting when he arrives unexpectedly for an instant at our focal point of consciousness bearing some undeniable message we would much rather ignore. Nevertheless, we must learn to live with Savaviel, because life without him would not amount to a great deal of meaning.

These, then, are the Seven Archangels with whom we must make up our Magical Cosmos. There is no use speculating about their natures and expecting them to demonstrate any sort of objective reality as if they lived only within our material set of dimensions. We may look upon them whatever way we will, so long as we work with them as "attitudes of awareness." Personifying and making people of them in our minds is a perfectly permissible method of condensing their abstract actualities into force-forms we can cope consciously with. Providing we know what we are doing and why we are doing it, this magical procedure will prove invaluable.

Consider, for a start, the difference it would make to any human Self, if every energy of consciousness entering or leaving the Self-Circle were infallibly and consistently channelled around the whole Archangelic Cycle and processed accordingly prior to release along external or internal lines. Say that any kind of conscious energy whatever is directed toward some particular Self-Circle. If this is not a properly constructed Magical Cosmos, or other type of protective perimeter, almost any reaction may occur, and the Self be influenced, perhaps in an adverse manner. In the case of a Magical Cosmos, the entering energy is detected and picked up by Raphael, assessed and weighed against acceptable standards by Michael, converted compassionately by Jivrael, then finally screened and considered in depth by Auriel. Only when this process is completed will the energy be transmuted into terms admissible into a Sacred Self-Circle guarded by the Great Four.

Again, suppose a Self could be inclined to release wrong energies outside its Circle. Immediately the Guardians fulfill their functions. Raphael at once points out the dangerous nature of the issue, Michael judges its unworthiness of the Self, Jivrael discerns its unhappy outcome, and

Auriel brings reflective common sense to bear. If we allow the Archangels to do their appointed duties for us, they will so process our energy that it will either alter into a force fit to send outside our Self-Circle in the Name of our Identity, or else be neutralized harmlessly and returned to the Nil-nucleus of the Cosmos we are sharing with our Archangelic auxiliaries. Savaviel is the agent of connection here. However much Time, Space, and Events have rolled around us, Savaviel still pays out the Magic Cord that accompanies us from our initial inception until our Ultimation. This amounts to the genetic life-line leading back along our ancestry to the beginning of our being, not only in one incarnation, but throughout all. It was once symbolized by the clue of thread laid in a labyrinth to lead an entering Initiate safely around its convolutions from center to circumference. If we follow it faithfully, we shall fare well enough. We might also remember the magic ball of twine or wool conventionally given to some worthy aspirant about to enter a dangerous area. This unwound by itself all the way ahead, and if followed conscientiously, guided the hero right up to the intended objective. Mythical instances such as these illustrate Savaviel in action. Providing we also follow the Golden Thread running through our lives one after another, we too will find what we have been looking for all the time—our own Identity, or True Selves.

Constructing the Archangels at the nodal points of our Magical Cosmos is a matter of conscious effort aided by all the ritual procedures likely to be of service. We not only have to think *of* and *about* them, but, more important, *at* them and *with* them. They must be realized in the sense of making them real for our Selves. This is no affair of half-hearted semi-belief, but calls for a sustained and practical program persisted in, one way or another, as long as we live. Archangels are constants of consciousness to be lived with toward an immortal Identity, and if we are systematizing our Selves with them, then we must expect to use the three constituents of our Cosmos, Time, Space, and Events, for building up the Archangelic Archetypes at the Equatorial edges of our existence.

At first, of course, it will need considerable concentrations of consciousness and perhaps even elaborate little ceremonies to evoke the Archangels so that they seem sensible and practical propositions to us rather than flimsy or foolish figments of fantasy. With progress, this process will become easier at every effort, until eventually there is a constant and continuous sense of living in the company of these Cosmic Companions, not in the least as aliens of any kind, but essentially as part and parcel of our Selves.

It is most important to understand that our Archangels are home-grown products, and not foreign infiltrators from some strange Outer or Inner Space, surrounding us into helpless confinement. Our Archangels cannot compel us to do anything against our determining Will, though being automatically linked with sources of conscious energy other than ours, according to their categories, they may well advocate modifications of our intentions for the sake of mutual comfort in the Cosmic concerned. If we prefer to ignore this intelligence and disregard what our spiritual specialists say, then we must obviously accept whatever consequences come to us without complaining, and that is all there is to the matter. Our Archangels are first and foremost essential parts of our Selves. Then they are linked with all of their kind otherwise. Thus do they mediate us to others, and others unto us. So should we work with them, if we intend them to work for us.

Before we start invoking Archangels and expecting them to appear in answer like some summoned creature responding to a whistle, it is just as well to know precisely what we are doing. In effect, we are deliberately objectifying parts of our own consciousness which are usually subjective, putting these into personalized and identifiable terms, and through them relating our central Selves with everything and everyone else in existence. When talking to our Archangels, we are not just talking to our Selves at all, but communicating through categories of our consciousness with linked lines of awareness leading to attuned life and lives on other levels. With each Archangel, we are literally evoking a representative fraction of our whole conscious Cosmos, and focusing this into a manageable Concept with which to relate our Selves proportionately with the remainder of Creation. This is what "raising an Archangel" means.

The Magic of "making an Archangel" out of our consciousness is an advanced form of the Art, for it is indeed Art in the true sense of the term. If an artist used some material medium for forming an Archangel, such as stone, wood, or canvas, it would be recognized by observers as a work of art, and appreciated accordingly. A practicing Magician has to use his own consciousness as a medium, and so work with this that an Archangel (or any other Concept) is created even more surely than an inanimate representation arranged out of inert and unresponsible materials. The Magician's Archangels must live initially out of his own life-force, and then with the energy they attract from their Archetypal and other Cosmic Companions. That is why a competent Magician is an artist of a very high order. The fact that his artwork cannot be displayed physically for sense-sharing by other Selves makes no difference to the quality or reality of his productions. Art is essentially Art, and art appreciation is entirely a reactive process among those aware of examples and principles. A true Magician does not work his art for the edification or astonishment of other Selves, but essentially as an exercise of his own Entity relative to the remainder of Cosmic Life. The art of Magic is the art of living with the spiritual structures of Consciousness, and making these into the media of Willwork.

When invoking Archangels, therefore, we may assure our Selves that we are dealing with metaphysical realities. Say we are invoking the Archangel Raphael. Is he real? How real is Time? Space? Events? How real is our consciousness, or for that matter the consciousness of everyone else on Earth? Raphael is as real as all that consciousness to X degrees can make him. If we can bring our Selves to believe in individual and universal awareness, then we may believe in Raphael as a Concept thereof, which makes him (or It) a creation of incredible power, capable of extending influence through the whole Circle of the Cosmos covered.

For practical purposes while dealing with these Concepts, however, we shall make use of summative symbols. These may be physically present during our dramatic rites of relationship with their Inner realities, because in this way they help to focus the force of our concentrative consciousness. An ignorant viewer, watching a robed human addressing a Sword as if it were an intelligent being, might be forgiven for assuming insanity in the actor, or at least for being struck by the absurdity of such an apparently pointless procedure. To uninitiated spectators, magical rituals and ceremonies are often either boring and time-wasting affairs, or ludicrously laughable antics by otherwise ordinary enough people. Other considerations apart, this is a good enough reason why no uninitiated, or inadequately initiated, person ought ever to be allowed access to even the slightest magical ceremony. Their presence helps no one and harms all, invalidating the whole action by the degree of disharmony aroused among them. Only those who understand and are capable of dealing with the concepts and symbols concerned should handle them literally or figuratively.

An instructed Magician uses solid symbols made of actual matter for the same reason that an instructed mathematician puts his sets of symbols on paper or otherwise objectifies the abstracts in his awareness: in order to make conscious relationships with concepts having expressible energies in material and metaphysical terms of life. By means of their symbols, both Magicians and mathematicians alike produce arrangements and patterns of consciousness calculated to make their purposes practical on various life-levels, including that of our mundane world. There is an important difference between their respective symbolism, however. The mathematician's symbols stand for purely intellectual evaluations of quantitative cosmic constants and their modifications. The Magician's symbols signify spiritual estimations of the same constants relative to sentient and evolutionary life. Faced with the Tree of Life symbol, for instance, a mathematician appreciates its numerations, and a Magician its nominations. The mathematician isolates laws as distinct from life, but a Magician acknowledges Life as the fundamental principle of existence around which laws arise in the course of Cosmos. Mathematician and Magician have this much in common agreement together: they confidently expect to find solutions to their problems by means of their symbology.

There is nothing really very strange, therefore, in the magical usage of solid, sonic, and other types of sensual symbolism. Once esoteric employment is grasped in principle, the practice will follow perfectly naturally, and this is what we shall encounter during our next steps of Magical Self-Cosmos, when we must make the Archangels come true for our Selves by directing and controlling our emergent energies by a systematic use of the appropriate symbols for this purpose.

Chapter Six

An Achievement
of Archangels

For this practical part of our Cosmo-program, the use of some place which may be treated as a Temple is a very great advantage indeed. Personal privacy is an essential need for the development of these magical practices. Once they have been made into an established part of the Self concerned, they may be extended into ordinary fields of living in perfectly natural ways, but their inception, as with all else in a state of gestation, calls for secure seclusion and all that assists their initial arrangements. Somehow or other, means must be found for at least a few minutes of privacy preferably each day, secluded in sufficient space to set up some symbolic representation of the Cosmic Compass.

The minimum requirements are recognition symbols of the Quarters by which we are aligning the axes of our awareness. If reduced to the very least vestiges of these which are likely to prove practical, four cards with the Instruments drawn on them together with all appropriate Names, data, and other relevant details will serve. These may be laid out on the floor, propped up on furniture, or placed in any convenient way in order to form the Quarters of a Self-conscious Cosmos with the Individuant in center. Should robes be neither possible nor practical, the Cord alone may be assumed either visibly or concealed by ordinary clothing. There are many ways of wearing a Cord, each of which has some special significance, as does the color of the Cord itself. For these exercises, a plain white Cord tied with a reef knot around the waist, or simply hung around the neck like a stole will serve adequately. Thus we have five of the symbols at our doors so to speak, and the other two—the Crown and Cubic Pyramid—may be imagined.

If more elaborate conditions are possible, so much the better if abilities match facilities. For present purposes it will be assumed that exercises are being worked in a minimal Temple, which consists of a small square or rectangular room, its walls suggestive of the Quarters or Seasons, its floor somehow representing Earth, and its ceiling Heaven. The symbolic Instruments are at their appropriate points, and Lights are also placed so that maximum is at South, minimum at North, and about equal levels at East and West. Underfoot there is a floorcloth with a Circle-Cross design showing the Archangelic Names, Elements, etc. The practitioner, or Individuant, is plainly robed in habit and girdle, the hood being down. For these particular rites no central altar is needed, because the Individuant *is* the altar, and therefore occupies its proper position. As extra refinements, a flat square of some hardboard material with suitably painted diagonals may be stood on to represent the top of the Cubic Pyramid, and a skullcap with Circle-Cross pattern worn to signify the Crown. All able to make these accessories should be encouraged to do so for the sake of appreciating their meanings as much as possible.

However much or little may have been possible in the production of a Temple, we shall suppose its proprietor ready and prepared to practice. The outlines of his Time-Space-Event Cosmic Circles have been rapidly evoked from their Nil-nucleus by means of the preliminary exercises, which by now ought only to consume seconds of

Earth-time, and we shall proceed from that point. Standing erect with hands finger-linked across upper abdomen, the Affirmation of Individual Existence as an Entity is made. This is the simple statement of "I . . . AM." Just THAT. It signifies our All from Nil. Our expressed entirety. The most effective way of expressing this is by first uttering it silently as if from our far-down depths, then gradually sounding it louder and louder in our minds until it becomes an actual faint whisper passing our physical lips, slowly increasing volume with each repetition so that its resonant hum eventually vibrates through the whole of our bodies. The accent has to be on the "M" sonic all the while, and a good way of managing this is to make the "I" with an inbreathing, throwing the force of exhalation into the "M" with a steady and sustained effort.

Though obviously and deceptively elementary, this single act is of extreme importance. Not only does it link our central cosmic being with a sonic symbol coming into the control of our generalized consciousness, but it sets the standard frequency on which our various levels of consciousness will link together. In a sense, we are establishing the call-sign of our Cosmos which distinguishes it from all others in existence, and enables us to commence our channels of Inner communication with them along metaphysical lines of contact. By resonating our Selves in this manner, we automatically send out calls which will undoubtedly be received and recognized by those listening for such signals. Somewhere among appropriate Inner authorities, it will be registered and recognized that another Self has at least reached the stage of being consciously concerned with its own Cosmation while in physical incarnation, and a response will normally be made in some way. Whether we are capable of translating responses into understandable terms will depend on our own recognitive abilities, and these may take some time and effort to develop. So there is no need to assume our calls have been unheard if we do not instantly receive a stamped addressed reply in return.

The principles of our call-sign are very simple indeed. Everything (and everyone) has what is known as a natural frequency which it will resonate if energy is correctly applied. Strike a note on a piano and it resonates its tuned frequency. Rub the same wire feebly with damp cotton wool for hours, and no noticeable reaction is aroused. We all have our particular natural frequencies which resonate clearly enough when "struck" in the right way, and here we are attempting to resonate our fundamental frequency from our cosmic centers so that in effect we are saying "Here I am" to the rest of existence. By our original winding of the Cosmic Circles around our Self-Nuclei, we have constructed a tuned circuit of resonant energy similar to those used in radios, except that our magical resonator operates by proclaiming our Names, or radiating the Selves we really are through Cosmos, somewhat as a radio transmission is diffused through other dimensions.

This fundamental frequency amounts to the true Name of any Self which has to be so carefully guarded and preserved as a sacred secret. It is obvious that if a really hostile agency deliberately forced disintegrative energies along any particular Self-frequency, that Self would inevitably suffer degrees of damage which might have very serious results. Fortunately for most Selves, this is no easy procedure, and as Selves individuate, their fundamental frequencies become more and more attuned to higher ranges of the spiritual spectrum from whence the risk of intentional injury grows increasingly remote. Nevertheless, the principle of safeguarding a magical Name is a very sound and valid one to be taken quite seriously in symbolic procedures. The sonic symbol of "M," used to signify our central Cosmic Selves, or I AMness, is of great interest. It is centrally placed in most alphabets, and is the central Mother

Letter of A-M-Sh combination. It is the center of AMATh, or Truth. It is even the initial letter of "Middle" in English, and its very shape indicates two pillars conjoined from top to bottom with a meeting junction uniting centrally. Again, in English it is the leading sonic in the word "Me." However one deals with the letter M, it always seems to relate with centrality and living identity. In homely language, we begin our Earthly beings as microscopic pieces of protoplasm in MUM, and "Mum" is usually our first intelligible word in this world. What may not be realized to any great extent is that I . . . AM, and the ritual sonics of AMEN, AUM, and similar mantras, have an identical meaning. This knowledge should put a lot more meaning into our use of these Words of Power.

While we are resonating AMEN, AUM, or such sonics, we are in fact asserting our Self-Identity with one single concentration of consciousness. Every time we make use of them therefore, we ought to realize: "This is ME. I AM willing this. I AM this," and such Self-assertions. For that matter, no conscientious Magician should ever utter AMEN to anything unless entirely in Self-agreement with it. The AMEN is a Divine Name of Self-significance amounting to a fiat of Force and Faith by entire accord of Intention. It should never be uttered lightly or carelessly. If, by any chance, some sincere magical practitioner should be engaged in ritual work with others, during which phraseology might be used with which he could not accord, then he most definitely ought not to utter an AMEN to that particular piece no matter how many others did so. To utter a false AMEN is to betray one's beliefs in one's Self and in the Divinity from whence we are derived. AMEN should be treated as carefully as that.

We are really fortunate from a magical angle that I AM in English resonates so nearly to AMEN and AUM. Literally, AUM means "Mother," and takes for granted that whosoever utters the Word regards himself as a Child of Cosmos. In a childlike way, we say this in English when we instinctively link Mum and Me to make "Mummy." The mantra AUM is thus an attempt to relate the Self to its Primal Principle in the most intimate and lovable way imaginable. A Cosmic Child calling for Mother from the depths of its being—and who ever heard of a Mother refusing to hear the cry of a beloved babe? All this may be borne in mind while resonating the I AM call during our exercises.

A pleasant symbolic refinement may be introduced if a central Staff is used. The magical Staff, of course, is emblematic of its owner and his beliefs or spiritual structures of awareness. There are so many ways of indicating any individual by means of his Staff that they cannot all be described in detail. Let it be assumed that a working Staff is the same height as its possessor, and is colored, decorated, carved, or otherwise art-worked so that it proclaims to whom it belongs and what he stands for. Traditionally, its lower end should be iron-shod in spear-fashion, or formed so that it may be stuck into the ground and remain upright. For Temple use, a weighted socket or even a large flowerpot full of earth may hold the Staff erect by itself. In this present exercise, however, the Staff is held in front of the body by the hands being clasped together around it at about midpoint, the Earth-end between the feet. Such a stance gives a feeling of poise and stability from a central point of leverage, and this is what we should be trying to translate into metaphysical terms.

Once a nice sense of balance is felt, the silent stage of I AM resonation should be commenced. This synchronizes with nostril breathing—"I" while inhaling, and "AM" while exhaling. If the magical Name of the Individual is already in use, it may be superimposed Inwardly upon the resonance, but naturally must not be enunciated aloud. The I . . . AM formula is actually adequate as it stands, because everyone's fundamental frequency can only announce his specific Self-Identity when it resonates, and a magical Name is just a convenience of consciousness for covering this identification signal on spiritual levels. Therefore we continue the I . . . AM breathing, putting a little more power into each cycle until virtually the whole body tingles from head to foot with the effort. In the most controlled manner possible, the silent nose-breathing is changed into barely audible nose and mouth enunciation, the "I" always being with inhalation and the "AM" with exhalation. Volume must gradually be increased so that the "AM" can be maintained at a comfortable middle pitch of sufficient strength to make the body vibrate in response. The attitude of awareness to adopt during this practice is a sense of I-AMness, or Identity by itself being radiated from the Central Self equally around and about our entire Cosmos. Only that at first, and no more until practice enables the operator to sustain the pressure at a reasonably constant rate for several minutes of Earth time. If the Staff is being used, this may be considered to represent a species of antenna with one end grounded and the other pointing Heavenward, so that its holder broadcasts a Self call-sign to the remainder of Creation. This is what happens anyway, whether the Staff is there or not, but its supporting symbolism can be very helpful, especially during first attempts at the exercise. It is far better and quicker in the long run to persist with this Self-signal until it becomes assimilated into normal living, rather than rush ahead into the remaining practices without a sufficiency of the Self-stability which this particular practice is intended to produce.

Our I AM exercise is not meant only as a Temple procedure, but for extension through all angles of living. Once the trick of associating it with breathing becomes a regular habit of consciousness, we can do it anywhere on all convenient occasions—while walking, sitting down, travelling in vehicles (though not advisable if driving, unless very greatly practiced at multi-consciousness). It is important that the I AM remains unqualified during initial exercises. There should be no insistence at first that I AM anyone or anything in particular except just plain ME, whatever I AM. All else comes later during the next few practices. No matter how advanced we may suppose we are, or how superior to others we might consider our Selves, it is always a most valuable exercise to pick our Selves up again at Primal Point, and go back to being no more than a simple I AM, with no other complications of consciousness. In this way, we may seek a relatively fresh start with each breath of life we draw anew. When we achieve some degree of ability at being I AM as and when we Will, the follow-up procedures may be commenced.

These consist mainly of extending our Selves elementally along our cosmic axes, so that our living Energy aligns itself into distinct creative categories which, by combination with each other, will ultimately produce all we ever shall be in our Selves. We shall extend our Selves energetically along lines symbolized by the potencies of Divinity, Humanity, the Four Elements, and Truth, tying everything together. These we shall personalize into Archangel-concepts, and control with visual, tactile, and sonically recognizable Key-symbols at each point. Even though those ought to be familiar to every student of these subjects, we shall recapitulate them here for the sake of reference.

Point	Element	Symbol	Sonic	Archangel
Above	Divinity	Crown	Breath	Metatron
Below	Humanity	Cube	Z	Sandalaphon
E	Air	Sword	E	Raphael
S	Fire	Rod	I	Michael
W	Water	Cup	O	Jivrael
N	Earth	Shield	A	Auriel
Around	Truth	Cord	U	Savaviel

It may seem a formidable program to relate our Selves to all these distinct divisions of Cosmos, but it is really not so difficult if everything is taken step by step in its proper order and put together as we go along. A good plan is to devote one day's work for each associated set of concepts, then fit them together one by one until they can be combined together as a whole. On each occasion, of course, we must begin with the standard procedure of symbolically emerging into Entity from Nil and centering our Selves in the Circles of Cosmos. This is normally done by the Circle-Cross formula. Again at the risk of repetition let us recollect its ritual arrangement. Despite its external simplicity, when properly used and understood it operates from the fundamental depths of existence, linking the basis of our being with our points of life in the Here-Now. It is a symbolic recapitulation of all we have realized since our beginnings, and a plan for projecting our Selves properly right up to the completion of our Cosmos into Ultimation.

First, the indicating gesture of the right hand comes to heart level, and the phrase IN THE NAME OF is uttered. This should concentrate attention on the Nil-nucleus out of which the entity of the invocant emerges. From thence all else proceeds.

Second, the pointing fingers travel to just above the head and then down to below heart level, sketching around the Event-Circle of the Cosmos being formed. The phrase uttered is THE WISDOM (head) AND OF THE LOVE (below heart). This outlines the divine qualities we hope to encounter and build into our Selves through all we shall experience in existence.

Third, the fingers are carried over to the right shoulder and then the left in a rapid indication of the Time-Circle. The phrases AND OF THE JUSTICE (right) AND THE INFINITE MERCY (left) show that we expect to balance out every event of an Evolution. Here is the fulfillment of Fate, or the completion of Karma by means of these divine principles applied through Cosmos.

Fourth, the fingers travel around the Space-Circle while the phrase OF THE ONE ETERNAL SPIRIT is uttered. This tells us of the Containing Consciousness of the Supreme Spirit which is, "around all, in all, through all, comprehending and containing all." As the *Baghavad Gita* says, "All things in Me, Not I in them."

Fifth, the fingers return to the original point and the AMEN or I . . . AM resonated. This proclaims both the Name of Divinity and the Name of the utterant together. A life-link between these extremities of existence has been at last announced as an Identity. Cosmos is conceived.

Who might have suspected that so much metaphysical meaning lies behind so little material movement? Yet this is an example of how Magic works, and why all these exercises should be preceded by the Circle-Cross formula. In a matter of moments it puts a practitioner in a position of poise with Cosmos, and ready to realize whatever is Willed therein. From a state of I-AMness, therefore, we begin elementalizing our upright axis first. Consciously extending our Selves away from the I AM center, an attitude of awareness must be directed toward Divinity. Naturally everyone will have his own ideal conceptions of the Supreme Self, but whatever these are, they must be brought together into a single focal point and aimed above the physical head of his body. If an Inner sensation of uplift, which used to be called "rising through the planes," can be managed, so much the better, providing we can easily bring attention back to center again. The action should be as if we were selecting everything in us, indicating a Divinity-Concept and sending the whole energy thereof like a stream of Light beamed toward this highest objective of our lives. From our central source of Power, we are emitting an attuned frequency of force which responds only to consciousness concerned with Divinity for whatever this may mean to us as Individuals. We may expect to receive replies along the same channels once they are correctly and sufficiently connected.

This "in-and-outing" is an important factor with these exercises, and must never be neglected. What we send out of our Selves must come back again by one cosmic route or another, however long this may take, or whatever strange alterations might have occurred on the way. Here, we are directing definite amounts of Inner energy toward whatever category of cosmic consciousness we regard as divine in the sense of a Supreme Entity. There has to be a reply somehow or other, whether we recognize this or not. Now we must try and catch even the faintest echo of a response. The only way of doing this is by "listening out" along the same frequency we have been projecting, as if we had switched from "transmit" to "receive." Once again the breathing sequence makes a helpful linkage with the switchover operation. By pushing out power during the exhalation of breath, then changing this to a reception of returned energy through the next inhalation, a complete cycle of consciousness can be conceived.

Perhaps for the next few occasions of this exercise, therefore, it may be necessary to practice the push-pull of power between our Selves and our concepts of Divinity before we shall be ready to use the same technique in the other directions. There is a very strange, yet incredibly rewarding, conviction that Someone is definitely on the "other end," as this reciprocal radiation grows stronger and stronger. When we come to realize that we are not merely talking *to* our Selves, but *through* our Selves to a far greater Self than ours, we shall be ready for the remainder of the exercises. Then they will have a depth and quality of meaning we could not have reached without all these preliminary conditionings of consciousness. A very great deal could be written about this "In-Out" practice alone, for it is an essential part of the process which makes everything come alive into motivated manifestation. It should always be considered cyclic in nature, for really, as soon as we begin to project power in any direction we must of necessity be pulling its other end in at the same time, so to speak. This may easily be illustrated by an endless cord or hoop fed from hand to hand in one direction. All the while we keep apparently pushing it upwards, for instance, its far edge is constantly coming down toward us, like the rope of a service-lift. Eventually, we shall discover that what we send out of our Selves by one way automatically comes back by another, processed by whatever it has passed through elsewhere—Karma in operation.

The next practice takes us to the other end of our upright axis. This time our attitude of awareness must be tuned to the nature of our Humanity linked with all other life-types, usually thought of as lesser than ours in the scale of Evolution, but at the same time being one with us in the sense that they, like us, are living creatures forming their particular categories of the Single Living Self. No matter what they may be—animals, reptiles, birds, plants, or even microorganisms—they share with us the fundamental principle of life, and this is how we should be relating our Selves to them all now. Again, we must emit energy from our central Self-Source which is directed toward our cosmic companions of degrees lower than our own, as we would hope for contact with those of higher degrees in cosmic development than ours. Now we should realize the other end of the endless Light-loop we were pushing upward in our last practice returns to us. As above, so below; "what is done to the least of the little ones is done to Me," etc.

As this exercise develops, the circulation of energy around the entire axis along its Internal Power-path should be experienced. We may recognize our Selves as the natural mediators of life between Divinity and other living creatures. There is a constantly flowing current of force connecting us all together into a complete circuit of Cosmos. By directing our Selves toward Divinity, we are opening up pathways for the progression of lesser living beings. By invoking Divinity through them, we are opening up a path for our Selves. It is all one and the same chain. We may now relate our breathing sequence along this entire axis by an out-breath, which pushes our energy upward to Divinity, followed by an inbreath, which pulls in reciprocal divine force from all that is beneath us. Then we may reverse the cycle by sending our Self-energy down toward those below us, which causes an inflow of force back from Divinity above us. One way or the other, we must realize our relationship with the entire life-circuit, and recognize the pivotal extremities of our existence upon which the whole of Truth must turn for us. The cosmic circulation of an Initiate of Light is toward Divinity, because this automatically returns through infra-Creation back to Humanity, and allows all who will to follow the same upward trend of evolution.

When our all-important upright axis seems consciously clear, and can be called into experiential existence readily enough, we may proceed with the other Elements of Life at the Quarters. For the present we shall evoke them purely as typified force-concepts, for those are what we shall build the remainder of their attributions from. Taking the Quarter directly ahead of us as magical East, let the concept of Air be brought to life at the focal point of our concentrated consciousness. All we believe about Air, and associate with it symbolically, should come into our single cover-concept of the total force thereof, and be projected from the Self-center forward and ahead of us. As this energy encounters forces of its own frequency beyond our immediate Cosmos, they will return it to us again along its proper cyclic path. Depending on contacts made, our initially emitted energy may be altered, amplified, diminished, or otherwise modified by whatever it meets with on its road of return. Any such changes are bound to affect the conditions of consciousness within our Cosmos, and this is exactly the reason why we should set up our selective system of force-fields so carefully.

For this part of the exercise, the Elements should be considered only as distinctive life energies derived from their sole central source—pure powers alone. They are each characteristic of a peak-point upon our perimeters of power or equators of energy which divides our total cosmic potential into four different categories. Strictly speaking, there is only one fundamental Life-Energy, but the cosmic circulation of this around the humano-divine axis as it turns on Truth results in four recognizable points, much as the revolving Earth has Dawn, Noon, Dusk, and Night, or the Four Seasons. The Elements of life connect together in relative ways. Though differing from each other in manifestation and effect, they are really four methods of experiencing Living Energy. In correct combinations, they make up any life conditions of living creation capable of Cosmation. We are only dealing with them separately here for the sake of controlling their specific effects in and out of four cosmic Self-areas.

Adopting an Air angle of awareness, therefore, a force-flow of consciousness should be directed ahead of the Self-source, and received in return. Although the actual energy used is only symbolized by physical air, it may help if we imagine our projected power as blowing out of us like a wind and being felt returning to us with a corresponding force. Once more, regulation of the In-Out rhythm by means of breathing will prove valuable. Furthermore, we can determine the degree of power by this. With an out-breath, for instance, we might only emit a small amount of energy symbolized by a very gentle breeze, and with an inbreath admit only a responsive current of wind. Then again, with an exhalation an absolute blast may be released, and a hurricane received in return by inhalation. It is generally best, however, to keep such variations of force within degrees of tolerance for cosmic comfort. Yet it might be remembered that a wind strong enough to be most unpleasant when met with in the face may be positively helpful from behind. Providing our returned Air energy completes its cycle and comes in behind us to push us along as we are Willing to go, we shall be helped and not hindered. So we must arrange our Cosmos with this effect in view.

When we have gained some experience in Elemental Air-concept control, we must turn around and complete this axis by its balancing Water principle. The reason for not proceeding immediately to Fire at its logical sequence of South at this stage of our proceedings is that at first we need to build up balanced axes of equation between the Elements. Physically Air and Water are both gases in differing states of density. Air can be liquefied, and Water made gaseous. Air and Water exchange natural energies with each other by atmospheric cycles of rainfall. Here we are attempting a relative process by metaphysical means.

Facing West, a concentration of Water-consciousness must be released from the Central Self-source in a forward forceflow. Once more we may vary the degrees of this Elemental energy anywhere from a mere seepage to a full flood, regulated by our breathing. We must just "live Water" with our Selves through its spectrum of strength in order to make this exercise mean what it should. Once we have Water fairly well under conscious control, it has to be combined with Air to complete this Elemental axis. A happy way of relating the two Elements is by conceiving our Selves at midpoint between them, which is to say on top of the Water ocean, and at the bottom of the Air ocean. Facing West, the Air will blow us as we Will upon the Water, and facing East, the Water will supply us with its vital moisture in the Air we inhale. Between the two in balance, we live and move as we should. Only when we are able to handle both Air and Water concepts, either independently or in working harness with each other, ought we to tackle the remaining axis of our Cosmos.

Again it must be emphasized that with each separate occasion of these exercises, all of what has gone before must be recapitulated by the most rapid sweep of consciousness possible. The Circle-Cross symbol commencing every exercise should by now be showing its upright axis as a humano-divine exchange of Elemental life energy, and its horizontal axis as an Air-Water interchange of energies. These form part of the permanent Circle-Cross pattern, and as we fill in other details, so must they stay with us always. Whenever we make the Circle-Cross sign, it has to be considered as complete as our consciousness has made it up to that moment, and capable of containing all else we shall ever intend our consciousness to comprehend and include in our identity.

Dealing with the next Element of Fire calls for care. Though we cannot live without it, we may only live with it in very limited and controlled degrees. Therefore we must be careful to conceive it only within ratios of reason. With outbreaths we might allow our Selves to radiate no more than maximum heat for enjoying existence, and with inhalation receive back something like the best sunbathing sensations. At the same time, there should be a realization that only our present structure prevents us from coping with vastly greater amounts of the Fire Element, and as we evolve into more spiritualized states of being we shall come closer to Fire than we may while only mortal. There is an esoteric legend to the effect that those fires which are supposed to torture the souls of the damned so greatly are pleasant and stimulating to the souls of the blessed. The same Elements meaning Heavenly heat for advanced souls amount to Hellish horror for corrupt ones. We must become very, very pure indeed before we dare risk coming too close to Fire in our relationships with it. It is advisable during this particular part of our magical exercises to treat the Fire Element with all the respect and circumspection it deserves.

It should be remembered that Fire is not essentially a manifestation of flaming devastation or burning at destructive degrees of temperature. Fire, as a Life Element, is more nearly a metabolic process, changing the constitution of otherwise inert matter into much subtler types of energy so that these can circulate around Cosmos more freely. It releases potential into kinetic force, and on spiritual levels helps to liberate us steadily toward Light if we treat it rightly. Without the Fire Element, only frozen stasis would remain. Water would be solid, Earth barren, and lifeless Air unreleased. It is Fire, properly proportioned, which allows the other Elements to be free-flowing and mobile through our cosmic circulation. That is how we should consider Fire when isolating its Concept in our consciousness. Strictly within degrees of friendship—not otherwise.

One point must be especially borne in mind when considering the Fire Element. It is not to be confused with the Light-principle of life, from which, like the other Elements, Fire is derived. Our primal principle of Light in the Holy Mysteries thereof derives directly from the Nil of Zooic Zero, and therefore consumes nothing as it comes into Cosmos. Fire, as an Elemental differentiation of original Light-energy, is a consumer of the other Elements which it changes back into conditions of Light from whence they are reissued into the cosmic Elements again, and so the Cycles of Cosmos continue. In dealing with the Fire Element, we are concerning our Selves with that part of Primal Power which

works the operation of "radiant return" so that other parts
of the same Power may perform their purpose, complete
their cycles, and being regenerated through Fire into a condition of First Force again, return by pure Radiance into
Elemental energies ready for another round of activity. Fire
is well called the purifying Element, and we should so consider all magical practices.

After we have conceived Fire satisfactorily at the South
station of our Cosmos, it has to be balanced by Earth at the
North. As a Life Element, Earth is that adaptable and
amendable component of Cosmos which may be made into
virtually anything at all through the activity of the other
Elements. Even Humankind was reputed to have been made
out of mud, and has certainly seemed to stick in it ever since
in many ways.

Elementally, Earth supplied the bulk-basis of energy
out of which the bodily forms of all subcategories of Cosmos are created. These, of course, are impermanent and
subject to the cosmic cyclic changes controlling their natures.
Only their archetypes in the Eternal Awareness are permanent to the extent of Cosmos itself. What comes from Earth
reverts to Earth again, but the Idea invoking its expression
is immortal. That is why we are seeking to identify our
Selves with the Idea behind our beings as Earth entities.
Our Elemental Earth may be thought of as "formable
Force," out of which our consciousness may construct whatever we Will within the limits of our cosmic confines,
though naturally we shall need the other Elements with
which to modity this medium. Even to make a model man
out of clay calls for water to mix it with, and a draught of
warm dry air to set it solidly in shape. In concentrating upon
Earth we should consider it as the power-point from which
we may form up whatever we intend to bring into more
definable dimensions of being. Earth is the energy through
which the Abstract commences its condensation into con-

crete forms of energy-expression.

Though its physical symbol may seem solid and inert enough, Earth as an Elemental Energy has its tides and rhythms which may be represented by breathing while performing these exercises. Magically, we might think of Earth as a kind of motile and convertible matter, capable of pouring from the central Self-source in a stream composing all its constituents, or being steadied, stabilized, and changed at will into whatever we decide its temporary appearance should be. As we exhale, let a steady flow of this conceived Force be projected, and with each inhalation some formed-up type of natural matter (no kind of artifact) will be realized. Degrees and amounts of this may be experimentally varied.

Balancing Earth and Fire along this axis comes next. Here we must bear in mind that Earth provides all the fuels for Fire and also the Fire-resistant properties which make it possible for Fire to consume fuel in a controlled way and not just explode Earth entirely. Proportionate poise between these two Elements has to be exact in order to produce a properly compensated Cosmos. Fire needs fuel fed to it from Earth's readily combustible constituents in order to keep it going. It also needs accommodation by the less burnable integers of the Earth Element, so that its burning rate can be maintained within reasonable limits of cosmic circulation. Otherwise energy will be expended to a greater degree than it is being generated, and a collapse of Cosmos must follow unless compensatory energies can be introduced into the circuitry otherwise.

So, when working our Fire-Earth axis, we shall have to conceive the two Elements in complementation of one another the whole while. A crude analogy might be a hypothetical Fire fed and controlled by a dualized stream of small-coal and sand. If Fire should burn the fuel up too quickly, the stream of sand will reduce the blaze, and conversely, if the Fire is in danger of being extinguished by sand, an increase of coal will bring it up brightly again. If the action is fully balanced, correct burning will follow, and this is what we must accomplish by our Selves along this axis of our Cosmos. In the proper course of nature, Earth-fuel vaporized by Fire would ascend into Air, precipitate into Water, then come back via Earth again in chemical shape over the centuries, and so Cosmos would continue its cycles. That is also how we have to keep each minor Cosmos going for our Selves, and is as near to the idea of perpetual motion as we shall ever get.

Thus Earth and Fire act as controls upon each other through the mediation of whatever "Me" is able to equate them together. Should Earth amass too much, Fire burns up its surplus, and should Fire consume more than it ought to, Earth brings the blaze down to normal again. There is an ideal average at which all the Elements ought to interact with each other, and this is what we should aim for in our magical Cosmo-creation. At least we may be assured of reaching a far more practical life-rate with our Inner arrangements than the masses of Humankind are doing around us in external Cosmos on Earth. Humanity is burning up natural Elemental resources at a far greater rate than normal replacements allow for. We are destroying our world by Fire far more than is realized. Perhaps if enough stabilization can be accomplished along Inner lines of Cosmos, the effects of this may be passed through into our Outer world, and the risks faced by future humanity be considerably reduced, or even altered to more bearable possibilities altogether.

At this point in our exercises, we should have produced a complete tri-axial Elemental Cosmos, which now needs to be "tied together" by a Truth-concept telling us that everything in existence comes to mean something in common as a Whole, and we can trace this meaning out if we follow along all the connecting links. Maybe we are reminded of the children's puzzles in which a lot of numbers jumbled about on paper have to be joined in sequence, so that in the end an entire picture is drawn which conveys a complete conscious idea to the viewer, producing an intelligent outcome of what was a magical mess. We are faced with much the same type of problem presented to us by our cosmic components. If we knew how to draw the Line of Truth from point to point all through the incidents of our lives on every level and incarnation, this would outline the sort of real Selves we are as spiritual actualities. This means we should be Identified, and Know Our Selves as a total Truth. That is what we should be conceiving the Truth-tie for in the course of these practices: to realize around our Selves until our consciousness has covered whatever we ARE, and we may "announce" or "Name" whoever we believe our Selves to BE.

Incidentally, if an actual Staff is being used as an aid for directing attention during these Elemental concentrations, here is one simple and practical way to employ it. First, align the Heaven-Earth or Divine-Human axis. Next, rotate it clockwise by its middle through an angle of 90° so that it indicates the lateral axis; then lastly, move it horizontally in the same plane to point backward and forward along the axis being worked. This gives the sensation of balanced axis-building, and provides a symbolic basis for the construction of conscious Inner counterparts. There are other movements to be made which should suggest themselves naturally to intelligent workers. Some Staffs are equally divided into black and white halves, the white to signify radiant projection of power, and the black standing for reception of returning energy. Quite a good deal may be done with practical symbology like this.

To "tie our Selves up with Truth" at this stage, we need to connect all the Elemental points together in order, one to another, so that we can hold a concept of them as a Whole. This means we should "go around the clock" of our Cosmos in sequence in order to obtain an outline. A logical circuit is to begin at center, conceive the point of Divinity above, then Air in front, Humanity below, and Water behind. Then turn left and link around the Earth, Air, Fire, and back to Water points again. From there, rise to Divinity and continue clockwise via Fire, Humanity, Earth, and reaching Divinity for the last time, carry our Truth-tie to center where both ends are united and the whole Cosmos closed. The idea is to follow the lines of Cosmos from center to circumference and back again, taking in all salients on the way.

This completion of the entire picture with the Tie of Truth is of incalculable importance. However necessary it may be to focus attention on each item of our cosmic Identity step by step, understand how they all fit together, and get every component of our consciousness into good relationship with each other, it is obviously of overall concern that we should be able to handle everything successfully as a whole for any particular purpose. Otherwise we shall be like expert mechanics getting a vehicle into perfect running order which will be of no use to us because we cannot drive the contraption. It is the Truth-tie which pulls all our cosmic points together into correct relative tension, and provides us with the means of controlling our Cosmos as a whole with one operation. We might think of it in a sense as being like the reins of a chariot, or perhaps like a lead which controls a motor when the ends are connected by a switch. To hold Truth in our hands properly calls for careful cosmic driving! Yet until we can encompass our Selves with Truth and tie things together, we can scarcely take our Selves anywhere worth going in Cosmos. That is the value of this symbolic exercise.

When we can be conscious of the entire Elemental

Cosmos of Energy coming from, and continuing around, our central Self-source, we shall be ready to extend our exercises into more focused fields of definition. Next will come the sonic symbols of association which have already been mentioned. These are a "First and Last" to cover the Divine-Human axis, the vowel sonics linking up the other points, and of course the "M" in the middle of everything.

Having rapidly recapitulated everything up to Elemental status, we should concentrate on Divinity above while enunciating a sonic difficult to describe verbally. It is simply the sound of breathing through slightly open lips. An indeterminate sonic, vaguely vowel-like, but otherwise unidentifiable. It might be the beginning of any sound we are capable of uttering, and is little more than audible. We might describe this as "pre-alphabetical," or a sort of preliminary sonification of consciousness, prior to speaking at length. An almost unspoken invitation to Divinity to be behind all we say. This is its import here. If we began everything we said from the point in our Selves nearest to Divinity, how very different our lives would be. Now we should be trying to link the fractional period of our pre-speech with that point of our consciousness closest in contact with our sense of Divinity. If we can do this with any degree of success it could change our outlook on life very considerably, and undoubtedly alter what life is likely to do with us in return. It sounds like a simple concept to produce such a great result, but in the long run it can have an incredible effect.

So this is what we must aim for with our "suprasonic" symbol. What we are doing in effect is pushing our consciousness up to the highest point of our Self-development, and telling our Selves: "Don't start speaking until contact has been made with the very finest type of intelligence our Identity is capable of making contact with." It might be difficult to imagine a Humanity which only spoke from that life-level, and there is little likelihood that we shall do it our Selves on every occasion, but at least our exercises will take us to a much more advanced speaking-start than we would have had without it.

In addition to uttering the sonic symbol our Selves, we must also receive it in return to complete the cycle, and once more this may be regulated in conjunction with the breath. So we exhale our "suprasonic," which has sometimes been likened to a "puff" or a "fffff," though there is no definite "f" audible, and during the return inhalation "listen out" silently for an echo of the "still small Voice" which wordlessly tells us what we ought to say or, more probably, leave unsaid. This action is actually an unspoken petition for what is sometimes called Higher guidance over whatever we might think or say. It develops a propensity in our Selves to refer our consciousness automatically to this all-important point prior to making any statements, or even coming to conscious conclusions about anything. Such a trait in any character can only lead to the very best formation of its forces.

Next, we turn our attention to the other end of this axis and, plunging to the lowest and final "infrasonic" in our range, utter "Z." This is given as a deep buzzing, as low as possible, so that even our feet on the floor are tingling. With this, we try and put our Selves in touch through our own humanity with every kind of lesser living entity. Maybe it is a very pleasing poetic connection, but the deep buzzing of bees links with the fabled bowstring of the Indian God of Love, which was magically made from these creatures of pain (the sting) and pleasure (the honey). It is also the reflected echo of the "still small Voice" completing its cycle commenced in the Heights. Difficult as it may be for us to catch this sound of Divinity reaching us via the depths, we should try our best to receive it. Even stones will "speak the Name" to those listening closely enough with intent, and it is this secret we should be seeking here.

What we must realize while we develop our "Z" sonic as a symbolic contact with the remainder of lesser life is that it links us back with every stage through which we have already evolved, and so is helping them fractionally in their advance along the life-line of Light. The Z will put us in touch with these lesser levels, and not only pass back what Divinity tells them through us, but, maybe more importantly to us, what they have to tell us about the Divinity toward which we are still evolving, in cosmic company with all these lesser lives. When we are able to hear spiritual speech in the cries of every creature, or the whispers of the smallest insect wings, we may achieve at least an inkling of what Cosmos is all about. All that lives proclaims aloud its cosmic connection, and we should be prepared to listen for this story not only in the animal, but in the vegetable and mineral kingdoms as well. This must be borne in mind while "buzzing" our sense of contact with life on levels we might suppose to be lower than ours. Therefore, as we exhale our Z's, let us try and pass on some impression of our Selves mediating Divinity toward other lives, and during the inhalation receive whatever they have to pass on through us toward the same Ultimate we are seeking with them in our Selves.

Be it noted as a matter of interest that these combined sonics of "puff" and "ZZZ" amount to a snore, or the natural noise of a sleeping human. This is good symbolism, for it signifies that while we are asleep, and our consciousness comes in contact with much deeper levels of life than the trivialities of human civilization, we automatically make sounds linked with the opposite ends of existence which we are uniting in our Selves.

Once we have established sonic links with our upright cosmic axis, the other points may be dealt with "around the clock" from the E station. Here, the concept of Air is evoked as usual, and the vowel sonic "E" uttered at length. It must be heard as the Elemental voice of Air, or the fundamental frequency of that force. As yet, no more should be attached to it, and it is given forth and received in the sense of being an audio-communication between our Selves and all In or Out of us concerned with Air as an Elemental Energy. We may imagine it as rising or falling in pitch, increasing or decreasing in volume, by constantly maintaining its sonic nature as E. It should be easily associated with wind or air movements of any kind.

With these sonics, we conceive the Elements in action or kinesis. As they work, they sing, and this is their true tone. We know which Element is operating by its "signature tune," and by these associative exercises we are learning how to call them into our consciousness and also receive their replies via the same channels. With a single sonic, we shall be able to call up clearly concepts that have taken hours of painstaking efforts to build. We can even combine them with each other to make a species of Inner speech which will translate down to terms appreciable even on ordinary living levels. Vowels are the first fundamentals of sonic speech, and that is why they are connected here with the first Forces or Elements of the energies we are proposing to combine and proliferate into our constructions of Cosmos. The consonants will come later when we get the complex of our Tree into shape. Nothing makes any sound spiritual sense, however, unless these fundamental Forces are firmly brought into being at the base of all we are building, so we shall continue with our sonic symbolism.

At S, we call up our Fire-concept and utter the "I" with our usual in and out breathing. It may be associated with many Fire noises, and although there are other links possible, we ought to try and keep our concepts and sonics as uncomplicated as we can during these Element exercises. Long and involved chains of consciousness will all develop later along this one line if only its closest connections with our Selves stay clear enough. What we should be concerned with here is gaining an ability to keep our consciousness attuned to a Fire-concept synchronized with and convertible to the sonic of "I" being resonated by the audio range of our projective and perceptive awareness. When we have successfully joined the concept of Fire and the sonic symbol of "I" in our Selves, so that they come together in our consciousness and we thenceforth connect them automatically, we shall be ready to move on to the next Quarter.

This is the West, with Water to be united to the "O" sonic, which should not be at all difficult, with its suggestions of sea and pouring streams. Even the shape of the mouth while uttering "O" suggests drinking from a vessel. During inhalation, it is easy to suppose Water being taken in through the O of the lips. Tempting as it might be to think of this as some favorite drink instead, only the purest possible ideas of Elemental Water should be used here, all refinements and extensions being saved for subsequent stages. Not one of those beverages would ever have been possible without the Elemental Energy of Water, anyway, and that is the concept we are working on at present. Therefore, the purest power of Water and the clearest sonic of "O" must be linked and locked together here until we cannot think of one without hearing the other, or in some definite way considering the two topics under a single symbolic heading.

After the "O" sonic comes the Earthy "A," sounded more as "Ah" at the North Quarter. Linking "Ah" with Earth should be easy. It is generally associated with "down to earth" country dialects in any case, and suggests the sort of noise made by a fall of earth, or something striking the ground flatly. Also it makes a kind of satisfied sound, instinctively uttered by most people when whatever they have wanted materializes or appears in solid form. "AH" is the natural exclamation of anyone stepping safely to Earth after a sea or sky journey of uncertain security. There are many reasons indeed for Earth-linking here, and a satisfactory symbolic junction between the Earth Element and the "Ah" sonic ought not to take very long in practice.

In order to make the exercises a little more interesting, we might add a visual association with these vowel sonics around the Quarters. Taking the shapes of the letters representing them, E, for Air, could be outlined as a swallow or swift darting through the sky, I seen as a lively column of flame rising straight up, O like the outline of a pool, and A as a pair of legs walking along the ground. Whatever the choice, the subjects should definitely be natural and in no way artificial. Artifacts will be brought in from our subsequent stages onward, but for the present we need to be as near as possible to pure Nature in its first formed state.

The last vowel is "U," or "OOO." This is taken on a two-tone note nearly as: "oooo-oooo, oooo-oooo, oooo-oooo," and the sonic is rolled around the entire cosmic circumference with the Truth-tie. It ululates as it goes, and we can almost trace the Truth-track it leaves while it travels. In a way, it is somewhat like a sonar beam, echoing back everything it encounters so that the submerged Self in its cosmic depths is able to know acoustically all that comes within its environment. This is the principle we must have in mind while sending out and receiving the "U" sonic. The intention should be that by means of this symbol we are emitting signals concerning our cosmic state at any given point thereof, and receiving in exchange information and intelligence respecting other cosmic states relating to us. As a "natural noise," the "U" mainly resembles an environmental echo which, though it may originate with our Selves, nevertheless answers us with the voice of whatever returns it to us. On our interpretation of this depends our understanding of our cosmic circumstances.

So, in conjunction with our Truth-concept, we send the "U" sonic spinning around our cosmic Time-Space-Event Circles, bringing back to our Selves at our center the vital data we need to keep our Cosmos on its correct course. It is this particular sonic which symbolizes the correct correlative assessment necessary to every controller of any vehicle or contrivance of consciousness in existence. To maintain our consciousness, or anything whatever, in constant equilibrium and correct condition, we must be continually in accurate touch with all the force factors determining such a desirable state. Our "U" sonic signifies our overall awareness directed in all directions to gather this essential information and sum it up as a steady stream of good guidance. Whether we act on this or not depends on our own Will, of course, but the more accurate and reliable our sonic survey of cosmic circumstances becomes, the better for those Selves skilled in its usage. Sufis in particular rely very much on their reiterated "U" for prolonged periods in order to stay *au courant* with their Inner spiritual status and increase their experience of life on finer force-levels.

When all these sonics are successfully linked with their correct cosmic stations, they should be gone over and over again until their "wholeness" is realized as a major force-factor of Inner life. Together they form a mantra which amounts to what we might as well consider the "call of Cosmos." This must be repeated and repeated audibly and inaudibly until it gets to be so much a part of personal procedure for recognizing realities that it becomes a normal means of controlling consciousness. Whenever this cosmic call is uttered either aloud or clearly in the mind, an immediate awareness of Inner Identity and its relationship to the finer fundamental forces of Life should arouse our spiritual sense of Self reality and responsibility toward the remainder of our cosmic kindred.

The completed method of this cosmic call should be

practiced very carefully and conscientiously. It consists of the sonics uttered in symbolic sequence as follows:

		Note
Center	MMMMMMMMMMMMMMMM	F
Above	(Puff) as high as possible a note	—
Below	ZZZZZZZZZZZZZZZZ as low as possible	—
East	EEEEEEEEEEEEEEEE	B
South	IIIIIIIIIIIIIIII	G
West	OOOOOOOOOOOOOOOO	E
North	AAAAAAAAAAAAAAAA	C
Around	UUU UUU UUU UUU UUU	A-D
Center	MMMMMMMMMMMMMMMM	F

It should now be seen that, in fact, this entire utterance is the fabled AUM sonic code of Cosmos which sums up in itself the whole of all anyone actually is, or Will be. The point at issue here is this. Anyone merely muttering AUM (or anything else) with no notion of its significance, or without any previous practice in bringing it to this condition of conscious clarity, does no more than make senseless sounds. Those who by devoted effort and exercise of consciousness have conditioned the AUM sonic to invoke their own Identities from the cosmic depths of their own beings are expressing themSelves with all the force it focuses for them. In other words, AUM is a convenient sonic Key for releasing energy already stored up in the Self because of prior practices. It will not make available anything not already prepared for use. Hence the necessity for all the basic work being mastered first. Neither AUM nor any other magic word will produce from one stockpile of our Self-possessions something we have not arranged there ourSelves or made contact with in other states of Cosmos. That is the secret of magical Words of Power. Once they become Keys which unlock the treasure house of an individual Cosmos, they will give access to what lies within that Kingdom of Heaven, which in turn depends on what has been stored there. An initiated Magician utters words to open himSelf. If, within himSelf, there are contacts leading to other states of Cosmos, then the Words will make convenient conscious connections with these; otherwise, no connection will be made. Much indeed may be done with Willwords, providing power has been piled up behind them properly. That is the reason for all the wordless work which has to be done during preliminary practices. It is said that the Supreme Self caused Creation by uttering its Identity. However, without the prior "brooding on the faces of the waters," we would still be waiting for that Word of Life.

By now, therefore, we should have reached the stage of ability to call our Cosmos into consciousness about our Selves in a complete Elementary condition by a single utterance of AUM, OM, OON, or whichever sonic symbolizes an abbreviation of the cosmic call. It is actually composed of the sonic symbol for the circumference "U," and center "M" of our whole cosmic Self-condition, or Total Truth. In that way, it sums up Self into a single sonic comprising every possible combination, and that is the meaning of this most magical of mantras. It makes I AM become What is Willed as a state of Self-Cosmos.

Once this sonic significance of the AUM is realized, and by its repeated use a state of conscious Cosmos can be summoned out of and around our Selves in a matter of seconds or less, a considerable amount of "pay-off" in return for all previously expended effort should ensue. This will generally come in the form of a right-feeling with life which cannot adequately be described, a positive sense of belonging to a Cosmos infinitely greater than any to be made in this Earth-world, and an ever-increasing awareness of one's own Inner Identity and life-linkage with the Supreme Self. There will come a consciousness of being alive in very different dimensions from those which limit us to our mundane mortality, and by our altered attitude to life, we shall not only experience the sense of our arising Self-authority but become completely convinced of the necessity for continuing this magical creation of Cosmos. In addition, there are likely to be side effects of improved physical and mental health, increased abilities of concentration, clearer thinking, and a number of other outcomes compatible with a better balance of being and more harmonious relationships between Self and all that affects the state thereof.

It would be wrong to expect any spectacular results in the form of material gains, or attribute any apparent good fortune experienced during this period entirely to the Magic we are practicing. Such is not its prime purpose, though it is not uncommon to encounter all sorts of surprising alterations in circumstances due to changes made on deep Self-levels which are found to affect the affairs of our ordinary lives to some degree. These ephemera ought not to be our aim or objective in continuing with our Cosmation. There should always be one single objective motivating our Magic, and that is to become the Self originally Intended at our Origin, and attain the Identity which is truly our own in Living Light. Whatever assists this process of perfection we must welcome, and whatever inhibits it we must avoid if possible. Magical life is as simple as that.

As yet we have only put our Selves into a state of consciousness consisting of Elemental Energies controllable by sonic symbols. In order to go further than that, we have now to project these forces still further so that they focus and form up into personifications of appropriate Archangels. With all the experience we should have gained in our previous practices, this will not be as difficult as might be supposed. It is mainly a question of sending forth our forces as usual, and building them up before us at our cosmic perimeters so that they "bounce back" from their externalized encounters with their own force-frequencies and form into Archangelic Telesmic Images. These will become our own representations of the living realities on every life-level which we shall mediate with them, and they will cover the whole of our Cosmos with a type of intelligent consciousness which we can appreciate even on these low levels of our mortal manifestation.

The visualization of the Archangels is the easiest part of the problem. Anyone with even the slightest ability at making mental pictures can do as much with a modicum of practice. As such, our Archangels would only be empty shells and pretty pictures painted on the blank walls of our cosmic surroundings—only decorations. They have to be given more than an appearance in order to serve their best spiritual purpose. They must actually come alive and function quite freely within their appointed categories before they can possibly fulfill the specific duties for which we are calling them into our Cosmos.

How are these Archangelic Images to be given a semblance of life? In the same way our Selves were given life—from their creator—which in this instance is the Self invoking them. When and if we are capable of animating these creations of our own consciousness, their archetypes will continue our work and consolidate what we have done on higher levels of cosmic life. Then our Archangelic Images will pick up energies along their particular frequencies from far greater sources of living consciousness than we could supply from our limited Selves, and become our closest cosmic companions of Light, keeping us in constant touch with whatever may be most needed for the development of our Self-structure toward an ultimate state of union in Divinity. They also act as insulators protecting us from inimical influences as much as possible. As we gain their confidence, they will tell us all we need to know about them. The immediate necessity is to bring them into being in their places at our cosmic perimeters.

The best way of conceiving Archangels is not by imagining their idealized externals first, but by building them from their insides out, using pure categorized consciousness, and then after this becomes effective, covering the whole construction with whatever Archangelic appearance we choose giving them. Spirit first and skin last. This is the sensible and cosmic way of working. We being their creators, they have to be made up in our own image and likeness, which should automatically link back to the Original Image in which we were initially made. Moreover, they have to be evolved from a nucleus of energy, just as we were, except that their nuclei are those of the special Life-Elements they are being made to mediate. That is to say the Archangelic Concept of Raphael is derived from Air-energy, and Michael from Fire-energy, and so forth.

The general manner of their making is this:

First, it is necessary to isolate whichever Life-Element is being used and attune the Self-consciousness to that particular force-frequency. This must be projected along its path or axis normally, but instead of letting it flow forth freely and return from whatever deflects it back to us from outer Cosmos, it should be held at the distal point we have decided to pitch our perimeters, and allowed to accumulate into a concentration of power pulsating in accordance with the frequency at which we are fixing it. From a sort of globular and growing mass, this energy must be mentally manipulated into a roughly anthropomorphous force-form which has to be set in shape by conditioning it with those qualities called for in the Archangel under construction. These are sent into it from our Selves along the connecting axial line joining us to our Concept, literally an umbilical cord between the conceiver and the conceived. In order to do this, we have to call up all these qualities from our central Selves, and then project them into our Archangels. This is what brings them to life and makes them come true for us.

They must be made as real as our own qualities, and then "extra reality" will come to them from elsewhere, which we shall be able to share with other dwellers in spiritual dimensions.

Supposing we try a run-through of elementary Archangel conceptions around our Cosmos, commencing as usual with our upright axis. Here we shall make up Archangel Metatron, whom we never expect to see very clearly anyway, but whose presence and "person" have to be readily recognized. We begin by isolating in our Selves whatever instincts and motivations lead us to look for Divinity as a spiritual Self-state filling the whole of existence with its Entity, and controlling the whole of cosmic Creation. It is necessary to attune our Selves into this attitude of awareness as a force-focus, while others are held in abeyance. Once this is done, let the power of all we are conceiving be projected upward along its axis, and brought into a concentration just above our heads. Since this is really part of our Selves, and we are personified people, let us regard it as that much of a person in its own right and name it Metatron. Along the connective axis we continue to pour into our Metatron whatever we conceive in our Selves which impels us to deal with Divinity in any way. No matter what it is, we must send it out and incorporate it in the Metatron we are making. During this exercise the actual name Metatron should be enunciated with rhythmic repetition almost inaudibly at the highest possible pitch, only the vowels being audible at all, and the consonants filled in mentally. This results in the Name being uttered almost as if with a speech impediment, four distinct syllables being barely heard. It sounds like "-e-a-er-augh," to an external listener, but of course the entire name must be clearly heard Inside.

Metatron is conceived as an "uplifting" Archangel, yet one who must stoop to our level in order to reach us. For the sake of relating his force with our forms, we may conceive him above our shoulders (Wisdom and Understanding) while reaching to the Highest on our behalf, and placing his hands on our heads (the Summit of Self) while contacting us at the command of a higher cosmic authority than our own. We feel and hear him far more than we see him, but the visual impression we get is of one so bright that we dare not look at him directly, though we know his face would look like our own, transfigured into an appearance so remote from our Earthly features as to be quite beyond terms of comparison.

When it seems quite clear that we are properly connected to our Metatron-concept by the axis along which we shall always continue to exchange energies with Divinity through this Archangel, we may fix the summative symbol which acts as a sort of heading under which all the consciousness we direct with a divine end-effect can be classified. By the use of this symbol we can select the category of Cosmos it represents with the greatest facility, and keep our attention concerned therewith while we hold the symbol in mind. In this case it is the simplest form of Crown imaginable, amounting to no more than a circlet quartered by two half-hoops surmounted by a single jewel of Light at the top. Symbolically it is the upper half of our Three Circles of Cosmos. Those meaning to make a practical form of it for ritual reasons have only to cross an ordinary skullcap with gilt braid and hem it with the same, completing the work with a clear glass or crystal button in the top center. It signifies the intention of completing Cosmos under the guidance of Divine Light. To place it on the head either literally or metaphorically sends out a summons to that order of Inner Intelligence we have named and contacted as Metatron.

After Metatron, we deal with his other half, Sandalaphon, underneath us. Here it is useful to work a little trick of pronouncing the Archangels' names so that these correspond with the sonic symbols with which they are associated Elementally. So if we if we enunciate this Arch-angel's name as Zandalaphon, we shall bring in the Z sonic and nominate the Archangel at the same time. Zandalaphon is another Archangel we seldom see very clearly because he is actually holding us up on his broad shoulders, and we should try to feel the steadying support of his capable hands guiding our legs in the way they ought to go. To conceive Zandalaphon, we must project power down along his axis and attune our Selves with all lesser life forms than our own, and also with whatever we were throughout the long line of evolution which brought us up to our present point. It is Zandalaphon in us that has pushed us so far, even though he is the same as Metatron pulling from the other end.

The name Zandalaphon is audibly "buzzed" in four syllables, *Zan-dal-a-phon*, on the lowest frequency we can reach. All the while we should find our Selves teaching down with fellow-feeling (like Metatron) toward every living being we can possibly help evolve in their way because of our efforts. Through Zandalaphon, we must send out our recognition of these lives which have not yet reached our level, but must yet do so if we are all to reach Ultimate Union in Peace Profound. Through Zandalaphon also, we shall receive an impetus from that direction which will help us along ahead of those others, so long as we are willing to lead them forward toward the same Light we seek our Selves.

If we could see the face of Zandalaphon, it would be our own again before we became human, looking forward with every possible hope that eventually we should find the Identity we sought through each incarnation, rising steadily toward this aim of Attainment as our spiritual development and experience increases from life to life. It is the face that higher beings than us see as our cosmic countenance during our Here-Now life-state. Zandalaphon appears to us as we appear to our spiritual superiors. If we notice any robes at all around Zandalaphon, they will be so multicolored and variegated that it would be a waste of time to decide what they are. As long as we are closely enough connected with the "power-Plasma" we have projected as a life-core for our Zandalaphon-concept, and are continuing to link our Selves with lesser levels of life by this means, the rest will follow in good time.

The summative and summoning symbol of Zandalaphon is the Cube composed of a pyramid in a pyramid, which is the Crown squared. There is no need for enthusiastic ritualists to make this in solid form unless they really insist on taking such trouble. One square of hard board, marked diagonally and painted so as to represent the basic beliefs of whoever stands on it, will serve as a symbol. It signifies the interchanges of energy going on between any single living being and all the multiple other lives which help to hold that being in Cosmos. We might think of it as one human and all the millions of separate cells composing that person's body, or for that matter, all the animals and plants they have eaten to support physical living. Zandalaphon is well named Co-Brother.

When we come to personifying the Four Archangels of the Quarters around us on our own life-level, it will be found that these "come through" in very considerable detail. They are, after all, the most familiar major attitudes of awareness with which we generally face life as we find it in our immediate states of Self. The other Archangels link us up with living into recondite ranges of Cosmos, but these Faithful Four, as they are sometimes called, enable us to deal directly with the problems of living confronting us in contemporary condition. Moreover, they provide the balancing factors of our being which allow us to turn truly on all our axes and become the sort of Selves we should be in relation to the remainder of existence. So the chances are that we are likely to feel more at home with the Faithful Four than with the others, though those must never be neglected or omitted from our cosmic calculations.

While all Four Archangels are of equal importance, it is normal to commence their conception with Raphael in the East and continue clockwise around the Circle. To link Raphael with the Air Element, we shall enunciate the name as *Raph-EEEE-a-el*, the "E" being drawn out at length. Again we need to call up every "Raphaelic" quality we have in our Selves, and project these along the axis connecting us with our Concept so that they build up into the Archangelic force-form we are constructing. The characteristics of Raphael should be known too well to need another description of them here. While they are being evoked from within our Selves, they should be attuned to the "E" sonic symbol, and Elementalized as the Air of our own nature.

The *Raph-EEEE-a-el* we are producing is a projection of our Selves as young, eager, and entirely alert beings, aware of all likely dangers and competent to avoid them. Of keenly flexible intelligence and penetrating perception, willing and able to learn anything life has to teach, resiliently recuperative, unquenchably optimistic, able to rectify any mistake rapidly, looking for the best of life everywhere, and prepared to defend all principles of belief with every possible effort. An idealization of our finest forces personified into the spirit of Eternal Youth, and an essential part of our Immortal Identity.

It may be helpful when attempting to harden all this consciousness into recognizable objectivity to ritualize a little formulary which utilizes the Staff again. This time, the Staff is held with both hands at center and at arm's length away from the body. The Archangel is then conceived as being built up in the area of proximity defined by the Staff, almost as a sculptor creates a clay model around a crude wire armature. We are, in fact, doing much the same thing, except that we are using consciousness instead of clay. It is quite permissible to elaborate this practice, and make actual modelling movements with the hands around the Staff standing upright by itself in the ground or some form of base. In this way, it is possible to formulate the actual feel of the Concept we are creating before us. Texture of hair, robes, and responsive moves may all be built in as we go along.

The face of *Raph-EEEE-a-el* will be a version of our own as we would wish to look like if we were free to choose a countenance suitable for the sort of Self-style we are creating. The light brown hair coloring usually associated with *Raph-EEEE-a-el* is for identification purposes, and we can arrange it to suit our tastes. Robes will conform with our ideas of awakening awareness, and are conventionally suggestive of dawn, but it is more important to bring the Inner qualities of an Archangel into terms of living consciousness than worry unduly about details of dress and appearance. Once we get the Inner Force of an Archangel (or any other Concept) flowing correctly, the Outer Form will make its own appearance.

Though the summoning symbol of *Raph-EEEE-a-el* is a Sword, or Arrow (which equates with an Airborne Sword) we should not suppose this sign to be purely, or even intentionally, aggressive. An arrow, for example, may be used as a message-bearing missile, and it symbolizes a shaft of intelligence sent ahead as a probe to gather information. It may be an indicator of direction, or a pointer to whatever we are seeking. The Sword is not only a weapon, but a tool with an edge and a point. It might be a surgeon's scalpel saving our lives, or a craftsman's instrument cutting out whatever work we are engaged in. We have only to hear a sword or arrow whistling through the air, and it will remind us of the "E" sonic associated with *Raph-EEEE-a-el*. The more we meditate on this symbol the more it will link us with our

Archangel in the Eastern Quarter of our Cosmos.

Since we are using these Archangels as mediators of the Elemental energies between our Selves and other cosmic states of existence, they should be conceived as facing in toward us when they are conveying consciousness to us from other Self-states, and facing outward when acting as agents on our behalf toward those same others. Above all, they are animated and articulated according to their characters, though they will only move and speak within the limits of their category. This, however, extends until its margins encounter those of its neighbors on either side. Thus, the province of *Raph-EEEE-a-el*'s communications is centered mainly in the sphere of his specialties, but can diverge each side to roughly a 45° angle where contacts are made with the Archangels of Earth and Fire.

To emphasize and define the duties of these Archangels, they may be addressed ritually by an injunction or "Charge" which covers their fundamental purpose in the following formula:

> *I Am*—(Chosen Name). *Thou art*—(Archangel's Name). *Permit no power to pass along this living line of Light connecting us in Cosmos, saving what is needed by my spirit of thy nature for the sake of Self-identity immortalizing into Perfect Peace Profound. Amen.*

It is also good ritual procedure to make a very slight bow or indication of recognition toward our Concept when we direct our attention to it, and when we turn our attention elsewhere. Any courteous gesture which acknowledges our commencement and completion of a conscious energy-exchange with the Concept will suffice.

After *Raph-EEEE-a-el* has come to life in the East to some degree, we may turn South and address our Selves to Michael, whose name we shall vocalize as *Mik-IIII-e-el* with all the accent on the central "I." Here we have to turn our Fire-force into Archangelic form as *Mik-IIII-e-el*, the Prince of Light.

To do this successfully, we must evoke from our Selves all our associations with uprightness, leadership, fair dealing, honesty, dedication to duty, sense of Self-discipline, and every possible Michaelian quality we can isolate and recognize as belonging especially to this Archangel. These have to be brought together and focused through the force of Fire into the form of *Mik-IIII-e-el* by our usual process. Once more we resonate the sonic symbol "I," and build up our *Mik-IIII-e-el* bravely into the fine form he always assumes.

Mik-IIII-e-el has the kind of face that might be ours if we had his position of powerful leadership and command over a whole host devoted to divine duties. A face that should inspire instant and complete confidence in anyone called upon to follow the cause its owner upholds. If the traditional coloring of hair is gold, and the eyes blue, we might remember our ability to appear as we Will within our own Cosmos, and assume *Mik-IIII-e-el*'s character and appearance with a glad sense of privilege.

It might also be well to remember that our Archangels can smile and laugh in their particular ways if occasion calls for good humor, though they should never be verbose or in the least pretentious. Nor are they given in the slightest to preaching or moralizing. Any apparent tendency to sermonizing or exhorting should be strongly suspect as a malfunction due to our own faulty programming and should be "edited out" during subsequent sessions. We do not actually receive any messages via the Archangels in verbal form but as impulses of energy we have to translate into word-terms from our subconscious supply. It is the accuracy— or inaccuracy—of this process on which we depend to make coherent sense of what we obtain through the agency of our Archangels. Hence the need at first for keeping to the simplest and least misunderstandable forms of symbolic communicative contact throughout our Cosmos.

With his symbol of the Rod, or Lance of Light, *Mik-IIII-e-el* holds up the Standard of our cosmic code of conduct which we ought to follow for our Selves if we expect to evolve as we should. There is no denying or doubting what we fundamentally know in our Selves is right for us, even if we may be apt to avoid such a realization on less exalted life-levels. Our *Mik-IIII-e-el* will not function as he should for us, unless we place in his hands the symbolic Standard or Emblem of ethics which we realize quite well within us signifies the straight Rule of Life we must accept for the sake of our Self-salvation. For those able to take the traditional Ten Commandments as a complete code, the Rod of *Mik-IIII-e-el* may be considered as a decimal Rule displaying a commandment in each division. Others will have to make whatever arrangements satisfy their consciences.

It is *Mik-IIII-e-el* who mediates most of the influences tending to heal diseases of body, mind, and soul. These may not reach us in any particularly miraculous manner, but through quite ordinary methods and medical treatments. What *Mik-IIII-e-el* does is to so assist our favorable reactions with such items and events that recovery ensues in the most expeditious way. Neither *Mik-IIII-e-el* nor any other Arch-angelic agency will attempt to keep a human body alive which has passed the point of practical preservation and needs renewing through the reintegrative processes of death and rebirth. Now and then it may be necessary to extend the Earth-life of some initiated individual for a par-ticular purpose, and this is made possible during a limited permissible period. The cosmic laws of nature are never entirely suspended for anyone, but as we become aware of them from higher viewpoints we may take advantages of them which are imperceptible on lower levels. The Rule of life indicated on *Mik-IIII-e-el*'s Rod is translatable into terms of conduct to be followed for obtaining harmonious health. No sensible soul dare break these deliberately without risking disease. The Rod of *Mik-IIII-e-el* has a great deal to tell us for our good once we learn how to read it rightly, and only *Mik-IIII-e-el* can teach us the methods.

From *Mik-IIII-e-el*, we turn Westwards to Gabriel, who with the soft "G" is sounded *Jivrael*, and whom we will have to call *Jivr-OH-e-el* to link with the "O" Water-sonic. Contact with the *Jivr-OH-e-el* Archangelic concept can be a very wonderful experience indeed, because it is connected with life and love in the most intimate and trustful terms. This is one reason why the Western position is normally taken as being behind us in our Circles of Cosmos. It represents something so confidential in our Cosmos, and sacredly secret to our Selves, that we would ordinarily place our Selves in front of it in a protective position, so highly do we value it. Placing the Grail traditionally in the West is an accurate attribution. While actively conceiving or dealing with it directly, however, we face along its axis as we associate our Selves with Archangel *Jivr-OH-e-el*.

To call up this Archangel from our Selves, we shall have to isolate and project all in us that is compassionate and loving, friendly and fertile, tender and trusting, merciful and beautifully benign. Every quality we would so gladly exercise around us if our cosmic circumstances permitted. The sort of being we would be in this world among all other Selves, except that sad experience and inborn caution warn us to preserve this Quarter of our Cosmos as a private Self-sector into which only our most intimate and trustworthy associates are allowed. Here we must be as we should with our very closest and most beloved family connections. Here we meet the Waters of Life, which personified as *Jivr-OH-e-el* as Archangel of the resurrection, can conduct us all the way through the hidden side of life we consider as death, and launch us again around our Cosmic Circle.

Through *Jivr-OH-e-el*, we pour out all the love and friendly feelings we dare toward other Selves, and receive back whatever returns are forthcoming. Though this naturally includes even the least degree of love motivating sexual contacts and fecundity of body, mind, or soul, *Jivr-OH-e-el's* function is to exclude from his Quarter of Cosmos all sexual proclivities motivated by malice or unlovingly committed. The Archangel is no arbiter of morals, but of attitudes and awareness. Sad, lonely and hurt souls seeking only some kind of comfort or consolation from peculiar but harmless sex practices, because no alternatives are available, may certainly have confidence in the compassion of *Jivr-OH-e-el*. On the other hand, anyone treating sex—or any other aspect of love—with contempt, abuse, cruelty, and an antipathetic attitude can never expect to make real contact with this Archangel.

Reaching *Jivr-OH-e-el* may be almost as difficult as trying to handle Water literally. If we make a clutch at this Element it slips through our fingers, leaving us only with moist skin. If we hold our hands together closely in hollow form and dip them carefully, we shall gain the Water we need. That is how *Jivr-OH-e-el* needs to be handled—with loving care and a caressing manner.

The Archangel's face is our own, expressing the side of our Selves we would want whoever we love most to see— that special expression which only those who love each other in the deepest and truest way ever recognize in their countenances. Maybe it is the sort of expression we might only see once in a lifetime with another human, but it is one we should expect to find constantly meeting us from *Jivr-OH-e-el*. He will try to show us reflections of it in other Selves, if he can find them, and if he cannot, we shall never see it.

Being at the sunset position of the Circle, we can make

Jivr-OH-e-el's robes really colorful and glamorous. It makes a nice little gesture to try to sense the feeling of our Concept's robes between our physical fingers, or to try to feel them if we lay a hand on them. All materials have their unique feel, and it helps in bringing our Concepts to life if we add such a detail to their data in our consciousness.

The summative symbol of a Cup is of the deepest significance. Traditionally, the Cup of the Mysteries is a hemispherical bowl poised on a square pyramidal base, but it may be a Chalice of any type, or even a drinking horn. Its symbology should not need reconsideration here. What really matters is that this symbol should *only* be associated with the best and most beautiful essentials we would draw from our lives and build into our real Identities—whatever we would willingly have as permanent parts of our Selves to live with forever. The contents of the Cup are usually considered as "God-Blood," but may be interpreted as our own spiritual blood-group which confirms our Inner kinship with Divinity, and communicates to us a sense of this royal relationship.

Perhaps a little reluctantly, but necessarily moving away from *Jivr-OH-e-el*'s Quarter, we come to that commanded by Auriel, whose name we shall resonate *Aur-AH-e-el*. At last we are down to Earth and invoking the Archangel of that Element. To do this effectively, we shall have to bring out of our Selves all our "solid" qualities such as resourcefulness, dependability, patience, perseverance, quiet good nature, tolerance, and even long suffering. Adaptability is a special quality of this Element, and it produces whatever we call for to live on its surface. Most of us realize pretty well what Earthy qualities are, so there should be little difficulty in isolating them.

Aur-AH-e-el personifies our Selves as experienced and mature entities, though he should not be thought of as "old" in the slightest sense of senescence. It is as if we simply continued living indefinitely, getting wiser and more experienced all the while, yet remained immune from bodily deterioration or any sign of aging past a point of maximum maturity recognizable as representing a most senior authority. *Aur-AH-e-el*'s manner rather than appearance conveys this distinction, for he always has something of an *in loco parentis* way about him. He is calm, deliberate, considerate, and positively protective in his attempts to screen us from the worst effects of our wrongdoings. Again and again he directs us back to the lessons we ought to have learned long ago, and patiently waits for us to catch up with whatever cosmic condition we should have reached. He is the "old " side of our Selves guiding and providing for our newly emerging energies which we are trying to control in our Cosmos—the influence of what we have done upon what we propose to do.

The *Aur-AH-e-el* figure building up on top of these Inner qualities takes the form of a dark-haired Elder with perhaps a suspicion of grey here and there. He is not, however, a bearded being, and the face might be that of either sex, though of course it is our own as we should be if we actually occupied this place of power in the North. Not that *Aur-AH-e-el* should ever be associated with coldness, ice, or any uncomfortable linkage with that Quarter. Rather, he should be connected with cool and calm consideration, quiet and orderly behavior, sober good taste, and wise generosity. Though his robes may seem dark, they actually shine as starlight, and may be as beautiful as a brilliant moon on a clear night. Earth-light is reflective, and *Aur-AH-e-el* tells us over and over again to reflect carefully on all we propose before committing our Selves to any course of action. He is far from being any kind of a wet blanket, but he does counsel us that before we rush past his position into activity with *Raph-EE-a-el*, we should listen to what he has to say first. This is very sound advice indeed.

Since Earth is the Element of materialization, it is through *Aur-AH-e-el* that we may expect to gain the various commodities and possessions we shall acquire during our incarnations. Not that *Aur-AH-e-el* produces these by himself without the energies of the other Elements, or will provide them for us unless we exert our efforts. What he does offer without being bidden is opportunity. Even then we have to recognize the potentials and possibilities of this from what we learn by looking in *Aur-AH-e-el*'s magic mirror which is fixed in his Shield.

This Shield-symbol has very many facets of meaning which ought to be familiar to students of magical lore. As a filter-screen, it interposes between our Selves and others a mutual protection from possibly injurious effects on one another, not necessarily intentional. It reflects us to those others in our possible light if we know how to use it for this reason. Held out as a kind of platter, it may offer any particular thing we may ask for in life, providing we know how to select this for service. On the surface of this Shield we may read the secrets of nature, once we learn the language which only *Aur-AH-e-el* will teach us in his own time. There also may see outlined our plan for Perfection and temple of Truth. It is the background against which the characters of our illuminated consciousness become visible, so that we may distinguish and understand them. There are so many unsuspected uses for the Shield in various guises that we are only likely to hear about them from *Aur-AH-e-el* himself when we come into close enough contact with him.

After *Aur-AH-e-el* has definitely become impressed into our consciousness, we must complete the Archangelic arrangement of our Cosmos with Savaviel, whom we shall have to call *SU-vU-ve-el*, the accent being on the *U*'s. Possibly this is the most difficult Concept of all to follow, since the Archangel has no fixed station, and may be anywhere or everywhere at once. At whichever point of our Cosmos we direct our attention, there is *SU-vU-ve-el* passing by. He travels at the speed of thought—perhaps even faster. The Circles of Time-Space and Events are all the same to him as he relates them together to tell one tale of living. He is our Cosmic coordinator and continuity expert.

It is virtually impossible to visualize *SU-vU-ve-el* with any very distinct degree of definition. For one thing, he signifies Truth, and who recognizes Truth when he sees it? Our perception of Truth changes so much from point to point of Cosmos that only its movement keeps us in touch with what is happening both in and around us. Truth as a principle is unchangeable, of course, but only our alterations of angle toward it will ever encompass it as a whole for us. In a way, this is comparable to a tape recording which has all we want to know on it but means nothing until movement at the right speed in the right mechanism translates it into comprehensible sound. That is like *SU-vU-ve-el*'s function as he circulates around our Cosmos making it mean something as a complete Creation. His job is to relate its spiritual story so that we can see for ourSelves what everything adds up to and go on spinning the tale for our Selves AS WE WILL. We might almost think of *SU-vU-ve-el* in the sense of a recording stylus or Light-sound head, which we can switch to "record" and "play" as we intend. On "record," he will output our own constructions of consciousness into our Cosmos so that it modifies accordingly, and on "play," he feeds back whatever is impressed on the cosmic "grooves" into our awareness. Ideally, our Truth-transcript should consist of the very finest selections from all that we, or other Selves, have printed into our cosmic circuits.

In such a way should *SU-vU-ve-el* help us to build up the best sort of Self we shall ever become. Suppose we might be able to take only the most perfect pieces of our Selves from incarnation to incarnation and fit these together into our greatest Self-Truth of Identity. Suppose again, on a far lesser scale, we were able to filter out our worst bits day by day and combine the better ones together as we went along, in order to come closer and closer to the Cosmic Truth we intend to represent. *SU-vU-ve-el* acts as the selective point which picks up the various items needed for this assembly of awareness. He operates our ability of linking chains of consciousness leading anywhere we Will through our Cosmic Circles for the sake of Truth-finding to even the slightest degree. Hence the symbol of *SU-vU-ve-el* is aptly a Cord. The Cord is a symbol common to all systems one way or another, and it has a wealth of meaning almost beyond belief by those who have never considered a Cord worth any deep thought. It is our Line of Life, cluing us through all the mazes and labyrinths we have to follow everywhere in existence in search of our Identity. It is every train of connected thought we make throughout all our lives. It is the Cord of Birth joining us with our Mothers' wombs, and the Cord of Death severing our contacts with Earth-life. *Yama (Yaum)*, the Indian God of Death, took lives with a noose, symbolically. His secret side, never shown, converted the Death-noose into a Birth-cord, and merrily on went the Wheel of Life. As a modern analogy, we might think of the Cord as being like an electric cable carrying power wherever wanted, or bearing pulses of energy to be translated into terms of intelligence however we Will. It is through *SU-vU-ve-el* that we may contact other Selves with mutual advantage, maintaining ties with them for perhaps many lives, which are helpful to all concerned. Through this type of linkage we are able to keep contacts with each other even during disincarnation. By means of the Cord we bind our Selves to the Truth as we believe it, for it acts as a safety belt during violent cosmic disturbances. Those who are tied firmly enough by the Magic Cord to their Seats of Reason and secured to their Thrones of Truth will, in the same manner, survive any shaking they are likely to meet with in the course of their cosmic life-travels toward Truth. Only *SU-vU-ve-el* can show us the secrets of the Cord and its Knots which afford us those degrees of spiritual safety.

When this last Archangel of our magical Cosmos has been dealt with sufficiently to obtain a sense of his Inner actuality and action, we shall have completed the entire covering system, bringing us into a state of correlated consciousness and personification at every salient point of our spiritual Self-hood. Once this is accomplished even to a relatively minor degree, everything else becomes a follow-through leading us steadily along our cosmic course toward our Self-Identity at the edge of Infinity. What we have done in effect with all the work accomplished so far is to construct a species of spiritual auto-compass which is life-linked with a "homing-beam" guiding us inevitably into our Ultimate Identity, uniting with Perfect Peace Profound. Providing we maintain this Cosmo-Compass in working order, it simply *has* to direct us properly along our Paths of Light. Surely this is the most valuable magical Instrument we could possibly possess for our Selfsearch, and even if it took years to construct, every moment would be well spent. It need not take nearly so long, however, and once made it stays made indefinitely, unless sheer neglect and indifference interferes with it, or deliberate and intentional misuse results in serious damage to its delicate circuitry. With normal use and maybe even minimum attention, our Cosmo-Compass will continue directing us faithfully as we Will toward the Identity we originally Intended to become. It can also lead us through many interesting and valuable experiences on the way. Let us take a comprehensive look at where we have arrived so far, and assess our achievements for what they amount to in the sense of spiritual acquisitions. They are worth rather more than might be supposed.

Chapter Seven

In Whose Name

In order to construct our Cosmos-Compass up to this point a considerable expenditure of energy in terms of event-efforts has been called for. Now what exactly have we got for it, was it worthwhile, and what can we do with the thing now that it exists in our experience? Perhaps more important, how do we proceed from this point, and why? Although all answers to these vital queries are really individual ones, there is certainly a general outline which may be considered here.

First and foremost, with regard to the world we live in, and the conditions of consciousness with which we are expected to cope during our ordinary Earth lives, we have constructed for our Selves a spiritual area of relative Self-security which will provide us with a chance of becoming what and whom we ought to be in our own Individual right alone. The medieval magician with his chalked symbolic Circle believed (or more likely hoped) he could exclude demonic and other ill influences from his immediate environments. The chalked circle did nothing of the kind, of course, but it provided a framework for the magician to make up an effective equivalent out of his own consciousness—if he knew how—which one suspects few medieval magicians ever did. The modern magician has rather different demons to deal with than his predecessor, and needs a much wider range of knowledge and experience to control the forces influencing his cosmic career as an Individual. Otherwise, a rough parallel may be drawn between the two cases.

The medieval magician was surrounded by immediate pressures from cultural, social, religious, political, and economic sources which exerted effects upon him just as these do upon us today. Imposed on these, as again with us, were the slightly more remote energies directed from and by other than human intelligent entities for their specific purposes. The older type of magician personified these powers as demons if they were inimical to him and as angels if they seemed favorably disposed. This may have been a somewhat rough and ready classification by our present notions, but the basic idea was fundamentally sound. Our current fetish of depersonalizing, demythologizing, and generally reducing our conceptual capabilities to a very low common denominator has opened no new Inner portals for us, and, indeed, has cut us off from very considerable areas of consciousness leading to life on what can only be described as spiritual levels. It is not that we ought to go back to medieval outlooks, but should progress these forward into our modern ideas of personal relationships with entitized Inner energies, and realize that such relationships must grow ever closer and closer through our future improvements of them, until the common ground of a mutual consciousness is reached. Thus, we shall see our demons and angels in a very different light from that of the oldtime magician, but they are there just the same, waiting and working to affect us for good or ill, according to how we react to them and deal with their force-fields.

For example, we now see a great deal of our angelic and "diabolic" influences operating directly through purely human agencies, but this knowledge does not by itself alter the effects of such energies. It is the use we make of such knowledge that counts, and the Cosmo-Compass is about the most practical construction we can make with our consciousness along modern magical lines. Properly built, it provides us with the immediate spiritual security we need for developing our true Selves while still living among world-conditions which are becoming increasingly inimical to this vital Individualistic process. At the same time, it affords us an ideal means of maintaining contact with all that this world can offer through the built-in agencies of our Archangels which process everything going out of or coming into our Self-area in the most beneficial way possible for all concerned. If we set up our Cosmos properly, it ensures that the best of our Selves goes out toward others, and only what will be best for us is admitted Inwardly from them. That is what we hope to gain in return for what we have put into our previous exercises. A perfectable Energy-exchanger, or consciousness-converter, between our actual Selves and All else.

Not only does this offer increasing immunity from the various pressures and persuasions directed against those who dare to claim their cosmic rights as Individual Entities, but it also enables us to neutralize these, if need be, with counter-energies on our own accounts, or on behalf of others asking for aid. Our Self-areas in this world become less passive parts of a mass mind susceptible to manipulation by other mentalities for their own reasons and, far more positively, part of an Original Identity capable of creating currents of consciousness at Will. We will tend to do our own thinking, rather than take ready-made thoughts as they become available. No matter what external or other insidious influences are aimed at us, or which we encounter in the usual course of living, we shall be able to deal with them as they deserve in whatever way our Wills determine. Now that we have the Telesmic tools, we can complete our original contract with Cosmos.

The magician of old believed with the then theologians that invisible and actual evil entities summed up in a sort of Group Overlord endangered the spiritual evolution of Humanity but, if directed into divinely appointed channels, might be made to serve entirely opposite ends. Using other phraseology, a modern magician takes much the same standpoint. It does not need very much imagination or credulity to realize that we are living in a world where intangible but very real energies are being brought to bear on all of us more and more insistently for no particular noble or sound spiritual reasons. These are generated, applied, and utilized by intelligent human entities for motives which would scarcely be called altruistic in the very slightest degree. So far so bad, but what unhuman entities are back of these people again, encouraging and assisting their human associates in a common anti-cosmic cause? If we call them demons and be done with it, this seems as good a general description as any. To that extent, there really *are* such beings as devils, or of-evil entities, whether or not they have human bodies attached to them.

Such ill-intentioned energies are the devils which our genuine Magic Circle of Cosmos resolutely excludes from entry into our Self-areas. If, in fact, nothing except what we create consciously with our own Wills and intentions exists inside our Self-Circles, then no evil of any kind can possibly penetrate there unless we invite it in or make it our Selves. That is a very important asset of our Cosmic Compass. Whether we prefer to call it a magical or a psychological phenomenon is beside the point. Its practical value is beyond dispute either way. No Self can hope to survive in any conditions of conscious existence without some kind of Self-system adaptive to the types of awareness necessary on those life-levels. Our material bodies are full of systems involving fluids, electrical processes, and a whole host of other physical principles. Without those we could not inhabit these flesh-forms. Without other kinds of systems working equally well and maybe better in metaphysical terms, we cannot operate properly as people in spiritual states of Self. Building up and developing just such a Self-system through which the consciousness of our own Cosmos can freely and effectively circulate is exactly what we have been doing during these magical workings. Could all the time and energy expended possibly have been put to better or more profitable use?

The question arises as to how we are to summate symbolically the whole of our Self-system so that it may be dealt with as a complete unit of universal consciousness in its own individual right. Conventionally, this is accomplished by means of a magical Name, or Identification which amounts to our own assessment of our Selves as an entity independently of our incarnate personifications. As with Divinity, we must announce our own ideas of what we are in order to establish who we are. Since we are but human, this is bound to be an imperfect realization, but at least we should follow the life-rules of our Self-system and make a nomination which will be a satisfactory substitute on present levels for the reality we are confident of reaching later in our evolution. It is correct magical procedure to create an identifying concept carrying the inherent proviso that as our consciousness with it progresses, so can we alter and adapt our symbolic specifications to suit the enhanced conditions of our awareness. This is very true in the case of our magical Names. Though we shall always be the same Identity, our conceptual consciousness of this Self-source varies not only from one incarnation to another, but is liable to alter during any Earth-life as initiatory status improves in degree. That is quite a normal thing, and simply has to be dealt with as the problem appears. Here, we are faced with the issue of how to obtain a magical Name in the first place.

Perhaps the best starting point is to realize that our True Identity already has its Name which we shall never discover until we ultimate into it. The most we can do is to adopt "Names for the Name" according to our capabilities of conceiving it. Once this issue is grasped clearly, we may go ahead with a clear conscience and an inventive intelligence. Achieving a Name is a major magical operation of primal importance. This is because by the utterance of our magical Names alone, we call the entire force-form of our Inner Self-state into a cosmic condition of consciousness in the swiftest and surest way possible. We are literally invoking our deepest conception of our own Entity with a single Key-symbol of consciousness. The implications here are very significant, and should be considered most carefully.

In normal Earth-living, we have personal names to cover our incarnatory presentations. These may even be classified into formal, friendly, and intimate categories. Our associates call us one thing, our friends another, and our intimates give us special pet names. We react quite differently to each appellation, since appropriate varied responses are needed to answer all types of summons. Though we are still the same person, we have to alter our attitudes relatively to at least these three calls for contact with another course of consciousness. This procedure is so commonplace we scarcely give it a thought, and yet how very necessary it is for the sake of human convenience. Someone calls us and we reply with that part of our person they have invoked. Eventually the response becomes automatic and builds itself into the lines along which we live. If we extend these factors toward the state of spiritual Self-Identity we are seeking, we should see why an adequate magical Name is so very important as well as the principles behind its adoption.

In this ordinary world, our name is what other human beings call us, and what we call our personalities in relation to them. In spiritual dimensions beyond Earth-living, our magical and secret names are the Self-symbols by which we are known to others living in that state of being, up to and including the Life-Entity Itself. We gave our Selves our most secret Name of all when we emerged from that Entity into individual existence, and we shall never know this Name again until we equalize with it at the end of our separated Selfhood. That is the Lost Word which we have to learn by completing our cosmic circles of life. In the meantime, we have to progress from one substitute to another in stages which come successively closer to the reality we are trying to reach. So our magical Names are actually a succession of Self-summative symbols enabling us to extend auto-awareness through all the lines of life connecting consciousness from one end to the other of our entire entity.

The value of magical Names to us while we live in this human world is that they enable us to invoke and call into the force-focus of our consciousness those potent and amazing latent life-energies which normally operate along much deeper and more remote levels of our living. In effect, they link our True Selves with the personal presentations of those Selves as humans and with all energy to be transferred from one level to the other. Sometimes, this energy may almost seem miraculous to an uncomprehending human observer. What looked like another ordinary human of rather average qualities has suddenly and unexpectedly appeared in some almost Godlike guise to meet an emergency demand for so-called superhuman characterization. We all have such capabilities in us to possibly unsuspected degrees, but it usually takes drastic or painful pressures to make us call deeply enough in our Selves for their release to surface levels of life, and then perhaps not for very long or with sufficient strength to accomplish much. By means of our magical Names, providing they are properly chosen and preserved, we can call these needed qualities from within our Selves in a controlled and cosmic manner so as to develop them naturally and normally into a pattern of our Self-projection at any life-level we choose. Put in very simple terms, if we want to find any sort of Deity or Divine Being, then we must call that Entity out of our Selves by the Name It will answer.

The immediate problem confronting those who have built up a Self-system of Cosmos in a magical manner is the choice of a nominal Self-symbol to act as a Key-call for the whole life-edifice. Not an easy problem at all. Somehow, the Name chosen has to contain a complete Self-realization of one's own Identity in relation to life throughout one's entire Cosmos. It has to describe evocatively one's existent Self-state toward all angles of awareness, and also indicate clearly one's intentions for further evolution toward ultimate Identity. Above all, we cannot obtain our magical Names from any other source than our Selves. It has to be the Inner epitome of not only what we really think we are, but what we believe we are becoming—the essence of our Selves concentrated into a single symbol containing the whole of our Self-consciousness. To find such a Sign with any good degree of satisfaction is a truly magical operation.

Legends are full of fanciful tales telling how various individuals achieved this Name-knowledge—some recognizably, and the majority disguised euphemistically. The most familiar pattern is probably that of the cauldron which had to be boiled for a year and a day until its contents were reduced to a single drop, which must then be consumed in order to transform someone into a magical, immortal, or otherwise quite out-of-the-ordinary sort of being. In other words, all the contents of a consciousness had to be simmered down to a single summation which signified "This is ME" in the most absolute idea of our Selves we can reach after a prolonged period of processing all our thinking toward that end. Not just a glorified opinion or wild guess at what we suppose we should be if we were given all we demanded gratis by an over-generous God. Nothing like this at all. What we need is a solid estimate of our own entity arrived at after life-experience in and as this Individuality. Our end-product is the Golden Drop, and all the rest is but smoke and steam arising from the efforts at producing it.

Although it may take a whole lifetime to achieve the magical Name for that incarnation which acts as a spiritual Self-seed for our next appearance in this area of awareness, most of us need something rather more ready at hand for practical use during that period. Therefore the sensible thing to do is invent a symbol-Name to stand for the Self we are seeking, and employ it much as the symbol X substitutes for the unknown quantity in mathematical problems. Even this operation calls for the greatest care and precision, involving the same principles which will lead us to the reality it represents. Yet, as with all magical operations along the Inner paths of Initiation, there are only three ways we can set about it.

These three Ways, aligning with the Three Pillars of the Life-Tree, should be familiar to all serious students of occult matters. They are, of course, the Hermetic Way and Orphic Way of the outside Pillars, and the Mystic Way of the Middle Pillar. It is equivocal if references are made to right- or left-hand Pillars, because these are reversible depending on how one faces. Only the central Pillar, or Way, is constant, yet it is the least promising, because it involves direct inspirational relationship with Divinity along the highest Light-Life lines. This is not only the most difficult, but also the most dangerous path for humans in attempting progression. So we are left with parallel Ways of intellectual Hermeticism, or emotional Orphism, unless we are clever and experienced enough to combine the two like the serpents on the Caduceus, and weave them into a Way of our own around the mystical Middle.

To attempt this with an expectation of success, we have to arrive at summative verbal symbols representing our finest feelings for life and clearest intelligent concepts of the cosmic Life-Spirit, then combine these into a synthesis expressive of what we are Inwardly convinced is our Entity. Thus, one Pillar provides us with what we *feel* our Selves to be. The other Pillar tells us what we *think* we are, and the Middle Pillar informs us what we *believe* our Selves are becoming. So do we derive our magical Name by the Tree of Life pattern, and this way of working will give us very good results if properly planned and carried out.

Since Names are words which comprise syllables and letters, these should in some way link up with our cosmic Self-system so that they call up its pattern into our consciousness as we invoke or utter them. This is usually done by relating them to the salient points of our symbolic system in such a way that they will indicate this Self-state by associative linkage. For instance, the vowels might be attributed to the appropriate quarters of our Cosmic Circles, and remaining consonants to top, bottom and middle points, with extras or repeats located in the quadrants. Only someone knowing the method of attributions around the Circles could possibly pronounce the Name. An old way of working this was to arrange the letters of the alphabet in a circular or spiral design in some special sequence, then draw connecting lines from one letter to another spelling out the Name in proper order. The resultant glyph obtained would then become the personal signature of its arranger, and be used as a magical Seal for that individual. There are all sorts of practical systems for relating letters to magical cosmic patterns that spell Names as required. Competent magical operators are expected to be capable of making their own designations.

In the case of the Tree of Life, its Paths have definite

letter-associations which can be translated into virtually any tongue. Both Hebrew and English alphabets should be familiar to most Qabalistic workers. Once the spiritual sense of a Name is known, there should be little difficulty in verbalizing it and linking it up with the Life-Tree. The major problem is finding adequately expressive phraseology capable of compression into a satisfactory summative symbol. How can we express our whole Self estimation in a few letters?

As an example, we have the Divine Tetragrammatic Names, such as IHVH, and AHIH, or AMEN to encourage us. In four letters only they express entire cosmic concepts recognizable to initiated intelligences. Given a few more letters, we should easily be able to surround our Selves with symbolic sense in terms of nominal identification. The shorter, simpler, and more concise the Name chosen, the better. In old times, Initiates took very brief magical Names descriptive of their immediate intentions, and then changed these fairly frequently as their Self-status in the Mysteries increased. The tendency now is to find a Name associated with a longterm life-purpose, adopt that on deep levels of living, and then use a disposable cover-Name to conceal the underlying realization. This certainly seems to be a practical step in the right direction. It ensures the necessary factor of secrecy as to the actual magical Name linked with the Identity, and also allows allusions to this which may be invalidated or altered to suit requirements almost at any period. This makes magical living much easier for the Initiate concerned.

Even knowing all these minor details about magical Names may not help in achieving one, though they are decidedly useful for arranging a Name after it is arrived at. The act of Name-knowing is essentially one of Self-realization accomplished by means of meditative and mediative Magic applied in Inner areas of awareness. One might almost call this process a controllable method of cosmic comprehension, or perhaps intelligent inspiration. It means we must reach and recognize the deepest Inner drives linking our Selves with life, then embody these into a satisfactory Name-symbol. Let us try to follow the action of this through the strivings of some imaginary Initiate in search of a magical nomination.

We shall suppose such a Self looking for its Identity label and asking the vital question, What makes me especially different from all other entities? coupled with the query behind our Eternal Quest, How am I to Ultimate? This is our inquiry into the enigma of our existence and the perpetual pursuit of our purpose. Needless to say, no instructed Initiate would expect to find more than relative replies to these issues. Be it noted also that this line of investigation is not concerned with whatever makes the Initiate just like everyone else, but with what distinguishes his spiritual identity from all others, or sets him apart in a sacred sense. This makes him unique in the Universe, or special as a Self.

Whatever this factor or factors may be, it should not be sought in the realms of matter or even mind, but in as close to states of spiritual consciousness as possible. It is not the physical or mental peculiarities of a personality or a Pseudo-Self which are being looked for, although these may provide clues leading in the right direction. The Initiate is seeking fundamental characteristics of the deepest Self-levels he can reach—his "Me-motives," or his spiritual genetic patterns which, by subtle differences from all others, determine our purely human inheritance of nature.

Using the Three Pillar scheme of inquiry, the Initiate asks himself what he considers as his dominant intellectual life-relative characteristic. After careful and sufficient meditative work, he comes to the conclusion that he is predominantly analytical. No matter what he encounters, he must always be trying to sort out constituents and discover why they work together as they do. He never seems to accept anything just as it comes, but is constantly analyzing and separating out the integers of everything and everyone he meets. This is an overall factor which conditions his intellectual life-relationships, so he duly notes it down for naming. Next, he considers his emotional feelings for life. He has a great dislike of disorder or dirt, and is happiest of all when things are calm, clean and comfortable. His feelings are for quiet and unadventurous living, preferably in beautiful surroundings. Emotionally, he would describe himself chiefly as an appreciator of quality, and so he enters his Self-estimate. Lastly, he develops his central theme of mystical aspiration. What he believes he ought to become as an immortal Identity. This may take a good deal of determining, but after a rather long session with himself, our imaginary Initiate decides that his greatest spiritual need is an ability of life-love, or delighted discovery of Divinity in all his experiences of existence. It dawns on him that this yet unattained aspect of his individuality is what makes him keep taking things to pieces all the time, seeking what he has not found or will ever discover by mere dissection. It also accounts for his continual preoccupations with feelings of peaceful orderliness, since he automatically associates Divinity with Cosmos and Perfect Peace. So he sets this Self-factor aside for naming, and now has a three-point estimate of his spiritual entity to fix into suitable phraseology.

This is generally done by what might be called inspired mechanics. The three known factors have to be codified into nomenclature associable with the cosmic pattern of the Self-system being followed, which in this case is the Circled Cross and Life-Tree. There are many ways to do this. The factors of Self may be simply designated by initial letters, hybridized into Greek or Latin compressive terms, abbreviated from plain English words, or indicated in any way, leaving no doubt of their meaning and distribution to the Initiate concerned. After all, he is the only human being who should ever know what and where these nominal symbols are in his scheme of Self-Cosmos. So far, our Initiate has classified himself into three categories which he heads under the generalized descriptions of Analyzer, Pacifier, and the composite term of Amadeist (God-lover). These verbal symbols cover his Self-Cosmos to his temporary satisfaction, so they will serve as roots for his comprehensive magical Name.

At this stage, the Initiate could actually term himself Frater A.P.A. and have done with it, but this would be sadly lacking in enterprise and imagination, both very muchneeded qualities in his field of living. Besides, the letters will not distribute nicely around his cosmic design. This particular Initiate has decided he needs a ten-letter Name, one for each Sephirah of the Tree, and enough to outline his Circle Cross also. By simple arithmetic this means that three ideas have to be associated in ten letters, or three letters per idea with one to spare. If all five vowels are to be used, then there can only be consonants to combine with them. Is this possible? With the aid of a little elementary Latin for the sake of convenience, and a certain amount of word-bending, quite an original and connective magical Name can be made as follows.

First, the central theme of "God-loving" is taken as "Deo Amator," and abbreviated to DE.AM. Next the description of "analyzer" is equated with "explication and examino"—to explain and examine. Pacifier, of course, links with "Pax" and "placidus." Out of all these words, a ten-letter selection must be made which suggests their meanings and nominates the Initiate joining himself with the principle they indicate. Apart from informed inspiration, a reasonably reliable method is to write the letters separately on small pieces of paper or on cards, then play around with them as if trying to solve an anagram. The five vowels can be retained and the remaining consonants juggled around until something sensible begins to make a clear pattern. Eventually, an arrangement will be found which somehow seems right, for reasons obvious to the Initiate if to no one else, and the magical Name will more or less declare itself. The action of this is symbolically related to Cosmos coming out of Chaos as the Original Name of All was uttered. In this particular hypothetical instance, the magical Name emerged as DEXAMOPIUS, which interprets in this manner:

The "God-loving" theme is indicated by the DE-AM combinations, and the central syllable of AMO (I love) sets the tone-meaning of the whole Name. EXAM, of course, signifies the inherent propensity for examining everything in order to explain (analyze) its nature. The termination of PIUS shows a dutiful, kindly and religious person of a necessarily peaceful disposition. If we "far fetch" a shade, a conclusion of I (the Initiate) in the middle of OPUS (the Work) can be reached. Other relevant interpretations should be found by most intelligent individuals. For example, the Name could spell out the precept or injunction, "For the love of God consider all carefully with dutiful devotion." All sorts of magical mottos may be made up from its letters with even a minimum of ingenuity. OP.MAX.DEUS.I can be translated into "The Greatest Work of God is Individuation" or, PAX.DEO.M.SUI.—"The Peace of God in His Great Mystery" (Magnum Mysterium). Altogether the magical Name DEXAMOPIUS would be an entirely valid one for an Initiate obtaining it for himself by the methods outlined. These are by no means the only methods, of course, and there is no obligation to use Latin or any other particular language for the purpose. The major factor is that the name-finder shall feel entirely confident that the Name of his choice indicates his own Identity at the highest life level he can reach with his consciousness. It is possible to do this by the way we have been considering, but should that not be acceptable, then other approaches must be used by those who prefer them.

Having found a magical Name at last, what then? What should DEXAMOPIUS do? In the first place, resolve to keep it entirely secret from everyone else, even his nearest and dearest human associates. No one must ever know it except himself and his highest types of Inner contact. This is of paramount importance, and the reason is an entirely genuine necessity, having nothing to do with mystery-mongering or any such rubbish. The fundamental purpose of the Name is to create a clearway of consciousness between the Initiate and his True Identity. A sort of direct line to Divinity, or straight "I-Thou" relationship between an individualizing soul and its Self-source. To keep this contact effective, there must be nothing whatever "on the line" except the energies transmitted from one end of its conscious connection to the other through the Cosmic Circle so formed. Thus, a magical Name should not be used for any other reason whatsoever except intentional contact between our Self-consciousness on human and divine life-levels. It serves the purpose of focusing the forces of our awareness and Will along this most vital Light-Life-line, and once it is working to any degree, no Initiate dares risk damage or "defilement"—as it used to be called—to his magical Name, since what injures it also automatically interferes with or injures his sense of Identity. This instinct to "keep one's name clean" is more or less inherent in most human beings, but in the case of instructed Initiates has this very special and particular purpose associated with our most profound basics of being.

So even the symbolic magical Name by which DEX-AMOPIUS identifies himself as an Inner entity extending from one end of his existence to the other should be treated as a sacred affair entirely. For him alone, it should be his God-Name, or the term through which he reaches Divinity in himself and receives divine responses at the incarnatory end of his Self-extent. Nowadays, we might say it amounted to a "hotline" leading between him and God. It should certainly be treated as such, and utilized with no less degree of dedication and discretion. From time immemorial, the various Mysteries have devised all sorts of safeguards against desecration or misuse of this life-link. This was the origin of much concern over blasphemy, or ill-treatment of Holy Names. It was the principle behind this practice which mattered. To defile a Name meant that contamination would cut people off from the Self-source the Name identified, and in the case of Group-Gods, this was and still is a most terrible deprivation. Either collectively or individually, intentional mis-association of Names or ill-employment of them is of very serious consequence in the Mysteries for these reasons. This is why neophytes are still trained in habits of "Name-security" with unimportant or relatively meaningless Names. When they develop the technique of dealing with these correctly, they can be brought into closer communication with sources of Inner intelligence that do not intend their classified information to reach beyond circles of consciousness capable of containing it in a cosmic manner.

Having adopted his Identity-Name, DEXAMOPIUS will then put the essential rules of sacred security into practice. He will never write the Name down, although some schools consider it permissible to have separately lettered discs or squares with a couple of extra dummy letters added, out of which he may arrange his Name for ritual purposes, then dismantle them afterward. This may be a nice symbolic gesture, but it is not really a fundamentally sound one in dealing with a magical Name. If the procedure is used for the cover-Name, which is normally invented to conceal the magical Name, then it is quite in order and will enhance any rite where it is employed. A magical Name should only be written on one place, around the individual it identifies Inwardly. So this is what DEXAMOPIUS does.

Calling his Cosmos around him, he attaches the letters of his name to the cross-points, center, and other significant places. In this case, he has a fairly easy distribution to make. The vowels of his Name will link with their stations to start with, the *U* having a roving runaround about the perimeter. Above, the *D* will stand for Divinity, and below, the *P* may signify Power, People, or whatever term is wanted. In the center, the *M* aligns with the AUM. The remaining *S* and *X* can be combined as a monogram occupying the Circle from top to bottom, the *X* being the Cosmic Cross, and the *S* the Serpent Path on the Tree of Life. All this makes a very practical and magical arrangement of the Name, indeed. The next operation is to fix the Name in place so firmly by repeated exercises that a single Inner utterance of it will automatically call the whole Cosmos correctly around the Initiate whom it identifies. Thus, DEXAMOPIUS need only invoke his magical Name properly in order to Cosmate himself forthwith. His Name becomes his Self-Key to Individuation. No wonder he needs to guard it so carefully.

Traditionally, a magical Name should never be uttered aloud except in very special circumstances, and then only below the breath or as a breathed whisper. The reason for this is to establish the balance of an Inner Identity at threshold point, or at the focus where our ordinary consciousness merges into our greater magical awareness in other life-dimensions than these material ones. If the magical Name were brought out entirely into our mundane conditions it would then belong with our mortal lives. If, on the other hand, it were pushed too far back into the depths of our subconscious we should lose effective touch with it here. So the compromise of the "threshold" is worked out, and both our Inner and Outer areas of awareness are given a sense of common identity by means of the magical Name used correctly. This means it must be brought up to the focal point of an intense identification just behind the act of utterance, yet never allowed to break into physical sonation, save through permissible safeguards.

The conditions of uttering a magical Name are those applying to the High Priest's annual utterance of the God-Name in the Temple sanctuary—solitude, silence, softly, and seldom combined as an act of sacred secrecy. In a spiritual sense, this amounts to a sort of sex-act on a sublime scale. The initiated individual "breathes his Self-spirit" into the symbolic stone chamber representing the Great Womb of All, and "impregnates with intention" thereby, so that in due course an outcome will issue forth accordingly. The High Priest, of course, was doing this on behalf of the entire people he stood for, while single Initiates will work on their own accounts, but the principles are the same. Different individuals have their particular ideas of putting them into practice. Some seek natural environments such as a hilltop at dawn or sunset. Others prefer a dedicated Temple. All sorts of ritual devices like caves, stone tabernacles, secret chambers, and other receptacles of Name-confidences have been, and still are, in use. The cup employed in sacramental rites is often put to this purpose. Nevertheless, the idea of "breathing Self" into the Infinite Identity and receiving back its cosmic counterpart is common to all variations of the custom.

Although the magical Name is not normally uttered, it is possible to express it openly and Outwardly by using a cover-Name or euphemistic version of it. This is sometimes termed a Lodge, or Temple, Name because it is generally confined to initiated circles when referring to each other's Identities in their common Mysteries. Even then, Mystery-

Names are used but sparingly, and often abbreviated to mere initials. Our friend DEXAMOPIUS is likely to adopt the extracted Mystery Name of DEOPUS from his full nomenclature, since this signifies "God work," a sound description of anyone's highest aims, and he would therefore be known simply as "Frater D." among his fellow Initiates.

By these and similar methods do magical Names come to life for initiated Identities in the magical Mysteries. Because of the need to feel a sense of identification with these Names on the deepest possible life-levels, some form of shock, stress, or whatever is likely to make the greatest impression on our Self-awareness is sometimes used to drive in the Name as fully and forcibly as is practicable. Devices for this are numerous and varied. Long ago, the candidate was occasionally isolated in silence and darkness for three days as if buried alive. Then came the dramatic "Calling to Light" in the new Name by which he was to be known in the Mysteries. Inwardly he identified himself with the magical Name he had adopted. Today's methods are not generally so severe, but may be relatively arduous, depending on the Initiate's capacity and endurance. It is also determined very much by what type of stimulus is most calculated to reach the required depths in any particular Initiate's individual make-up. Each sort of soul has its special kind of spiritual susceptibility. What works with one may have no good effect upon another. Here, the responsibility lies fairly and squarely upon the Initiate to know exactly what touches him most deeply, and to cooperate with Mystery colleagues who are willing to help him achieve a Name for himself.

There is no absolute need for any soul to depend on others for a Naming ceremony, however welcome this might be. Essentially, we must Name our Selves, and whether others assist with the mechanics of this or not, the validity of magical Names depends on the degree to which we are able to adopt them with our own efforts, for the sake of deep and definite associative links with a Name Identity; however, it is advisable to employ whatever form of dramatic ritualism seems likely to produce such a result. Something impressive and unforgettable, which need not be expensive, elaborate, or impossibly difficult. Ingenuity and imagination should suggest many ideas. For instance, water might be taken from some special spring or well, and a journey made to a solitary place considered sacred, such as a stone circle, or maybe just a secret altar set up with a few stones from the locality. At a selected time, the Name seeker might attend this spot and proceed more or less as follows. First, dig a symbolic grave or "womb-hole" in the earth, a handful or so being enough. The participants prostrating themselves on the ground, the new Name is barely breathed into this hole, while appropriate intentions are made. The hole is then filled in as if a seed had been planted, which is symbolically the case. Next, while kneeling, water is steadily poured over the top back of the head in such a way that it runs down the face and pours onto the earth. Again the Name is breathed during this process. Then, standing up, a wood or charcoal fire is kindled on the stone altar, incense added and the Name breathed into the flames and smoke. Lastly, perfumed oil may be rubbed on the face, hands and body, and a dance deosil around the altar performed as the Name is breathed in and out during the gyrations.

This rather beautiful and simple ritual has a profound significance of Elemental connections. First the Name-seed is symbolically sown in Mother Earth's womb. Then the Sky-Father sends down fertilizing Water in the form of rain. Next the warmth and heat of Solar Fire germinates the arising Name entity whose soul takes shape like smoke savored with its particular scent of Self. Last of all, the newly arisen Individuals move freely around in their fresh Cosmic Circles, sending their personal perfume into the atmosphere of Air so that all other Selves may become aware of them. They have proclaimed themselves in accordance with magical tradition reaching back to our most remote Elemental origins.

Whether this or any other method of impression is used to commence an Inner sense of Individual Cosmic Identity, the important thing should be to achieve such an end per se. Once this eventuates, the path to Inner potency as a True Self becomes really opened, and a Way of auto-awareness, or Knowing One's Self, lies before the awakened Initiate leading toward Infinite Truth. Certainly these eternal opportunities were there all the time, but now it will be realized how to take them properly. Every road has its right rules, and the road to Self-realization is no exception, but an example for the rest. When we know how to travel rightly thereon, all we have to do is follow these Inner constructions faithfully as they come into our field of consciousness. The first vital distinction to draw with the initial breaths of a new Inner sense of being is the difference between our initiated Identity and the everyday personality associated with our mundane manifestation in this world, subject to all the laws pertaining thereto. In other words, this is the difference between DEOPUS and his Earth-entity Bill Brown.

There are very many important divergences between these two characters belonging to the same Self which will be noticed immediately. Bill Brown is a mortal of limited intelligence born to human parents and destined to die at the end of his Earth-life experience. DEOPUS is an immortal entity born of himself in the manner of Melchizadek, having an indefinite capacity of consciousness, and destined to Ultimation in Divinity if he so Wills. Bill only lasts a human lifetime in very limited conditions of awareness, but DEOPUS goes on from one incarnation to another, learning with each some new and interesting lesson which improves the true qualities of his immortal Individuality. At least he should do so, and providing such is his sincere Self-intention, he certainly will. Poor old Bill may not have very much to offer DEOPUS while they associate with each other, but what he makes available is always of value to an Inner Identity able to assimilate and reduce it to terms of cosmic consciousness where it will add spiritual stature to the Self whose experience it enlarges. Bill lives in a bewildering world where other mortals affect him from all angles one way or another, and pressure persuasions push him around as those applying them intend. Bill may do his best, but this is seldom enough for his satisfaction, or even his safety. Sometimes he gains or grabs a nice large lump of advantage, and other times loses far more than he can afford. Since his whole outlook on life is limited to a single lifetime, his sense of values is necessarily confined to corresponding dimensions and he misses the point of anything extending beyond those material marks. He might mean well enough up to such points, but he cannot go further because he will never exist to those extents. Bill Brown has but one incarnation on Earth to live and no more. He knows this instinctively, so why should he pretend otherwise?

DEOPUS, on the other hand, has a much wider and fuller field of consciousness to cover. Although Bill Brown is his present focal point, he knows that he continues where Bill ceases, and that he began long before Bill was ever born. What happens to Bill is only a fraction of what DEOPUS can contain. The whole of Bill Brown is only an incident in the life of DEOPUS, while it takes Bill maybe most of his life to suspect that DEOPUS exists. It is a question of viewpoint. Bill looks rather small to DEOPUS, while DEOPUS seems enormously extensive to Bill. DEOPUS is not a person to be pushed around according to the convenience of Pseudo-Self grabbing what it can get from life until forced to release it in favor of greater grabbers. That sort of thing may, and usually does, happen to Bill Brown, but DEOPUS need not accept such treatment except as part of Bill's experience. He does not mean to affect his Individuality adversely, or even bother to remember unless as a guide to further life-ful-fillment. Whatever happens to Bill, DEOPUS can take or leave as he Will. The area of awareness governed by the Will of DEOPUS is much greater than Bill's equivalent extent ever will be. What is perhaps difficult for them both to grasp is that they are not really two individuals at all, but separated parts of the same Self. They should be comple-mentary to each other, and never antagonists, which is not infrequently the case for perhaps several incarnations.

In a way, Bill Brown has some degree of immortality insofar as he becomes an incident in the existence of the Individuality behind DEOPUS. Our higher Identities absorb the lesser parts of our projections all the while in this man-ner. What really matters is that we awake Inwardly to the realization of this process as a Self-intentioned act of con-sciousness, and that our Earth entities recognize what is taking place enough to assist the initiated action of their absorption into the Spiritual Self-stage whose magical Name they now know as a Self-symbol. The Initiate knowing him-self as DEOPUS centers himself in his Circle of Cosmos, and from there relates his auto-awareness through whatever his focus as Bill Brown brings in from the material world, in addition to the impression he is obtaining from his expand-ing consciousness as an independent entity of spiritual Self-hood. As their relationship continues through the course of cosmic development in the Mysteries, DEOPUS will take over the conduct of living more and more from Bill, whose ultimate death becomes no more than absorption into the existent entity of DEOPUS behind him, who continues in the same Cosmos they now share in common as a single state of being.

Failing this absorption into DEOPUS, Bill Brown still

dies when his body does, but he may also survive as an awkward and even embarrassing section of DEOPUS' otherwise advancing awareness, which will eventually have to be evened out by a process of Inner evolution. This is rather like the survival of child-personality in a mature person which can be the cause of certain character deficiencies and lack of life-ability. Just as a part of our ordinary incarnation-entity lagging far behind our normal point of progress is a nuisance during Earth-living, so can the equivalent state of unbalance due to previous personality persistence spoil the spiritual status of an Inner Identity attempting to advance normally along higher than human Light-lines of life. Hence the injunctions in the Mysteries against trying to "bring back the dead" as they were known on Earth during incarnation, and also prohibitions pronounced against insistence on remembering past incarnations or dragging back memories of past personalities which are not yet equated properly into the Inner Identity.

This is mostly why the Mystery systems as a whole are averse to spiritualism under its popularly understood meaning and practices. In seeking psychic contact with dead personalities under the names and having the appearances by which they were recognized during Earth-life, we would only be attempting to recall a relatively lesser part of the real being those attributes represented. Moreover, we should be interfering with a perfectly natural process which is essential to the evolution of the entity concerned. Far from doing any good to anyone, this actually causes inconvenience or, in some instances, actual damage to the structure of the Self in question if the past personality has not been sufficiently assimilated to pass beyond reach of injurious interference. Besides, nothing very helpful is likely to emerge from these encounters, since such low-level contacts are chiefly confined to already disintegrating personalities which cannot operate coherent chains of consciousness any longer, because they are now only bits of being and pieces of personality belonging properly to the spiritual Self-spheres which focused them together into incarnation.This is one reason why so many spiritualistic communications seem trivial, disjointed, inconsequential, and pointless. They arrive from Inner areas as odd items dredged up from the breakup of conscious collections once assembled by incarnate entities, which are in the course of return to the Self-stores recovering these energies for other purposes. They make no more meaning than a handful of snippets from a mixed lot of books would make if scattered on a table top and read at random.

After the physical death of Bill Brown, therefore, his fellow Initiates in the Mysteries should make no attempt whatever to communicate with that dispersing area of his consciousness. They should, in fact, do all they can to help its absorption into DEOPUS, their colleague and brother who once used Bill as a material focal point. They must certainly try to forget Bill Brown entirely and remember DEOPUS always. The sooner Bill becomes just an item in the experience of DEOPUS as an entity the better. It is therefore on the DEOPUS level of magical Identity that other members of the same Mystery expect to keep in contact with their co-Initiate when he no longer uses a human body for focal reasons. Now, however, the Name procedure will change, and the magical Name cover of DEOPUS which was kept so subdued and secretive when he was embodied among them will be sounded firmly and clearly if there is any need to establish conscious contact with him. This is only likely to reach DEOPUS as a very faint impingement on his awareness, but it arrives in a form he is familiar with, and so he answers willingly enough, though naturally in terms of his current consciousness. Only those understanding the same Inner speech will be able to translate such communications into any kind of Earth-tongue. That is the main difficulty in interpreting intelligence conveyed between these different levels of life.

By this time, the Self-situation built up by an Individuant by means of a magical Circle of Cosmos and Identity-Name should be clear enough to purpose and possibilities. After all the effort and exertion it has cost in achievement, we ought at last to have created a safe Inner area in which we can become our real Selves AS WE WILL, and not just anything someone thinks we should be for any convenient purpose suiting their special interests. Inside our Self-Circles we can truly *live* and develop all our finer faculties to a state of perfection during our cosmic continuity. The state of Self-Cosmos we are making is not for one incarnation only, but for as long as we live in Light-life as Individuals. Once our Inner Cosmos is operating correctly, all we have to do is keep it going through cycles of perpetual improvement. The initial arrangements are the hardest, and that is why we are called Initiates. Everything depends upon just how truly and deeply we are motivated by the life-need to BE OURSELVES. That is the determining factor.

Two other points have to be emphasized very strongly here in order to eliminate the slightest possibility of misunderstanding. One is that the axiom AS WE (or YOU) WILL is *not* synonymous with purely Pseudo-Selfish inclinations toward irresponsible or antisocial behavior involving the spiritual detriment of the True Self or any other beings. AS YOU WILL in the Mysteries specifically indicated the pure intentions of the True Self as regards the perfecting of all its projected parts in order to enter the highest Self-state of Perfect Peace Profound, thereby becoming one with Eternal Entity. The second point is that the creation of a magical Cosmos and a Named Inner identity does *not* in the slightest imply some artificial withdrawal from the world into some condition of fantasy unrelated to human happenings on the material scene of living. On the contrary, it affords greater ability to contact and comprehend the affairs of Earth-life from a much wider angle of awareness and considerably deeper penetration of perception than average mortals. It *does* mean that a soul in this state of Self relates its energies expended between external and internal living with initiated intelligence controlling the selection and processing of all that passes in and out of its perimeter. Relations between a Self and human society become far richer because of a magical Cosmos, but they also become much more finely balanced and delicately discriminative. Quality rather than quantity becomes preferable to those with well-poised Self-Circles constituted in a magically cosmic manner. The insulation of Selves in their magical Circles does *not* mean their unrealistic isolation from all other Selves. An insulated electric wire is intended for connection between correct points only, and in the same way a properly insulated Self is available for contact with other Selves only at appropriate points. That is all insulation is for—a safeguard and for the sake of providing a valuable service. So likewise with magical Self-Circles.

Thus far then, we have arrived at a Self-state systematized into cosmic circulation of Elemental energies controlled by an Inner entity identified by a magical Name. What now? That depends upon our intentions. There is considerable difference between a simple life-cell and a highly organized human body, though the latter is built out of and develops from the former. We have as yet only constructed the vital "cell" of Inner Life out of and with which we can build our Selves further into whatever being we Will. This has positively been the most difficult and demanding part of our Self-process. The rest of the work consists of organized growth and development from the elementary Cell we have created around our Selves. We shall need some kind of a pattern, plan, or system for this task if we are to build our being into a living force-form really worth cosmic consideration. What better basic pattern than the Tree of Life, which provides about the most practical plan of perfecting our Inner Identities that we are likely to encounter anywhere in our present condition of existence. Once a pattern is known, we have only to apply our Selves to life according to its principles, as we have seen with the Circle-Cross system. Although the Tree of Life may seem far more complicated than that, it becomes progressively easier all the while we grow it in and around us like the Circle. We do not have to make any spectacularly fresh starts as we produce our Tree out of our Circle, but just continue what we have begun so well along more sophisticated lines—no more or no less than that.

If our bodies started with a simple cell and continued living out of this Cosmos into increasingly more complex arrangements and accumulations of materialized life-energy from relatively few genetic fundamental elements, then we can surely do as much for our Selves at equivalent levels of spiritual existence. All we have to do is just go on growing according to the master-pattern within us, and if we determine for our Selves that this is the Tree of Life, then so it will indeed be for us. In the case of our human parentage, we had to accept the nearest genetic keys we could find suitable to our Self-requirements, but spiritually we are free to make our own, like Melchizadek. From the Inner genetic keys supplied by the Tree of Life, we may select our Self-makings AS WE WILL. Furthermore, this source of supply only offers the best materials. So we may as well help our Selves to the finest fruit it holds out for the picking.

Chapter Eight

The Tree Is "Me"

The next part of the "Me-making" program is constructing the Tree of Life power-pattern in association with our Selves as we did the Circle-Cross of Cosmos, until we are able to call it up completely with a single summative symbol like the magical Name that summons our Secret Selves into a force-focus at Will.

If we consider the principles of this process, they should illustrate very neatly how real Magic is applicable to the whole of our living. We expend energy and effort, construct all sorts of schemes and projects, produce this, that and the other outcome of whatever we do. Anyone may do much and more, but who is able to take hold of his complete cosmic command and direct its entire energies and capabilities toward specific issues of intent so that these are accomplished as acts of Self-determination? How many individuals work with the whole of themSelves, or as much of this as they can concentrate, while they are engaged with existence at particular points of any life-level? Far fewer than might be supposed. The majority of people generally use only very minor and often quite inadequate parts of themSelves in order to "get by" with the frequently boring or unsatisfactory affairs of external awareness and their confused Inner states of consciousness. It usually takes considerable pressure from environmental events such as imminent danger, or some exceptional Inner Self-stimulation causing a marked emotional response, before most people will really make the effort of bringing as much of themSelves as they can to bear upon any point of living. How is it that we seem so relatively unable to exist effectively, and what would happen if we learned how to live wholly instead of only partially?

To live wholly does not mean we have to exist in a frenzied state of total exertion, flinging our Selves around in all directions with full force until overcome by sheer exhaustion or stopped effectively by other Selves out of exasperated annoyance because of our activities. Whole-living is a definition of quality, not quantity. It is a carefully controlled application of Self to all "Otherness," and has nothing to do with aggressive Self-aggrandizement whatever. In whole-living, a Self is asserted quite naturally as an integrated individuality without any unpleasant inflictions or impressions upon others. This simply means we act and react to life on all levels as entire entities, and not just from locally concerned centers of subconscious automatism. Which is to say we become totally involved with individuation throughout its complete Self-scale of Cosmos.

This does not necessarily indicate that every aspect and level of our Selves is equally involved with every single incident experienced in the whole of its existence. Such a Self-state would be an obvious impossiblity for entities of our cosmic classification. We relate with everything by degrees, and different points of our Selves connect with other parts of us from very widely differing angles. At any given Self-location, something of us is maximally affected, and the remainder reduces to minimum concern. What really matters is that our entire being should relate appropriately with all we are engaged in at every life-level. We have to learn living in such a way that a correct proportion of our whole Selves goes into whatever our Cosmos is concerned with in its conscious continuum. Something of everything we are should be brought to bear on everything we do in life, so that even the least little item is put to the purpose of making us into what we ought to become.

This used to be thought of as being "whole hearted," and is indicated by the injunction to "Do it with all thy power." That is to say, with power derived from every part of a Self, rather than from one point only. Our life-need is to grow like a tree, as an entirety. Roots, stems, branches, leaves, flowers and fruits, the whole organism is one living unit, even if its items have their own proper periods and degrees of development. So should we. If we would really become our true and single Selves within the Greatest Self of all, then we must discover how to live with the Whole of a Self, instead of with bits and pieces of it here and there as we stimulate them. Since the Tree of Life is a Self-symbol covering Cosmos completely, it makes a perfect plan for this purpose.

To appreciate the importance of whole living, let us briefly consider what happens while we are in an unsatisfactory state of part-living. In this very average condition of Humanity, we tend to issue and receive energies from lower Self-levels without adequate reference to, or sufficient control by, our higher sources of Inner Self-authority. Though this may well be due to lack of evolutionary experience, or to other reasons imputing no special blame to the Self concerned, it still causes a great deal of trouble and inconvenience to those living with such deficiencies of cosmic character. Suppose, for example, some provocative stimulus is encountered, as it frequently may be in the course of our mortal manifestations. The Self-point at the receiving end of this takes it in, and instead of putting it through an initiated process of involvement with higher

Self-centers closer to divine discernment and direction, slams it straight across by a short circuit into an automatic action-arc of a repercussive nature without any particular consideration as to consequences. It is easy to imagine all sorts of damage and casualty sustained by such irresponsibility. Now let us go a stage better, and suppose the issue referred to a more exalted and cosmically competent Self-level, but still below the spiritual standards needed to ensure a sound and satisfactory course of cosmic conduct. In that case, things might work out well enough in some ways, yet fall far short of achieving anything worthwhile along more important lines. To live correctly, we have to arrange our Self-sectors so that each distinctive area is keyed by the one immediately above it in line with our Highest Light. In this way every part of our Selves depends on direction from as near Divinity as we can reach, and we begin living as a whole, rather than a lot of parts disagreeing with one another and making trouble through the Self-circuits they disturb and unbalance. Because the Tree of Life shows this ideal relationship among all areas of Self from lowest to highest, it is most likely to teach us how to achieve such a valuable state of Self, and therefore we shall set about growing it in the most practical way possible.

The first essential is obviously to become familiar in terms of ordinary consciousness with the design and details of the Tree, together with a general outline of its Paths, significance of its Spheres, and associated immediate issues. All this elementary ground is not going to be re-covered here. It has already been done repeatedly in other works which are readily available from libraries and booksellers, and these give adequate basics for the task in hand. Therefore, we shall take for granted that those studying this Self-systemization scheme have already acquired some idea of what the Tree means and more or less how it goes together. Should this not be the case, it is hoped that enough interest and enthusiasm will be aroused to send inquirers in search of the missing material. Knowing what the Tree stands for may mean required reading, but knowing what to do with it subsequently calls for persevering practice, and this means actually living in accordance with its principles and life layout, which is exactly what we have to consider here.

In very simple language, the Tree is a decimal Self-scale between Humanity and Divinity, indicating the working relationship between the two extremities of existence, and showing the principle force-flows throughout the arrangement of its major points. The Tree does not purport to portray all the issues of living as we find them in this world, but as they *should* be if they were put together properly in order to bring us maximum benefits. Thus the Tree of Life is essentially a plan of perfection, and we shall treat it mostly from this angle as we attempt to follow its implied instructions here.

Sublime as its concepts are, many people have been either bewildered or discouraged by the somewhat bleak and unattractive appearance of the Tree-symbol as it stands with branches bare and its spherical fruit cases apparently empty. It certainly has no appeal externally for anyone seeking only surface and superficial contacts with life, and this should make the symbol all the more important for those in search of the soundest spiritual basics to their beings. In this way, the Tree acts in an opposite manner to many showy and intriguing designs which seem to have such rich promises, yet the deeper we delve into them the less they offer and the more inconsequential they become. In the contrary case of the Tree of Life symbol, it looks as if it had so little that was worth the attention of investigators, but the further we go into it, the more solid spiritual ground we find, and the greater are the discoveries we make. From the unreal-looking exterior, the Tree leads us steadily In-wardly toward increasingly substantial states of spiritual living, and so fulfills its symbolic function.

Admirable as the Tree-pattern may be, one of the first difficulties to overcome in connection with it is thinking about it merely as lines and dots on paper. These must all be translated in our Selves into terms of living actualities related to each other as the Tree indicates. Unless this process is accomplished factually by Self-experience, the Tree will stay as we first saw it, no more than a printed piece of paper. So we must make it come true for our Selves by means of all the magical methods at our command. This means more meditation, more mediation, more experimental exercises with energies of consciousness, and more of the Great Work.

At least we already have the base and apex points of our Tree at the top and bottom of our Self-circle, so that all we have to do at first is connect these together by our main and Middle Pillar or Tree-trunk. If we watch how an ordinary tree grows out of its seed, we shall see that it first sends up a straight "Earth-Heaven" stem, then opens out into one pair of leaves at a time from its top. Its bottom leaves come out first, then subsequently all its higher dualities. We can scarcely do better than grow our own Life-Tree in the same way according to those laws of natural living.

Since all trees come from seeds of some kind which derive from other trees, we shall assume that we get our own Tree-seeds in a comparable manner. What this "seed" amounts to in a human being is an inherited instinct of individual immortality holding hopes of achieving direct relationship with Divinity. The Inner conviction comes to us from a very high Self-source to which we are linked with incredibly wonderful origins of Light-Life, so that we are actually upon our cosmic course of spiritual growth toward an ultimate status of Self. We might say that a Tree-seed is our most basic belief in our Selves as a humano-divine whole. Provided this faith-focus is implanted in favorable

ground, germinated by well-balanced elements, and cultivated carefully according to the best of our knowledge, we
can grow it and also grow with it as we Will. So far, we have
made the finest possible Inner conditions of Cosmos ready
for planting the Tree-seed. All Life-Elements are balanced,
controlled, and brought together harmoniously at the base
and apex of our beings. If we plant our faith-seed in the
solid Inner ground we metaphorically stand on, and then
allow our Elemental energies to germinate it as if it were an
ordinary seed set in garden soil, our Tree of Life will come
up in its due spiritual season and grow as it should toward
the highest summit of Truth it can reach while we rise with
it. By this action we shall be symbolically copying some of
the Genesis myth which showed Paradise as a Circle-Cross
enclosure, with the Tree of Life and Knowledge planted
therein. Here we are planting in our cosmic gardens the
seed from the Tree of Life which not only ensures our
immortality, but also brings us knowledge (DAATh) as and
when we are truly ready to receive it.

Now although such a seed is unquestionably likely to
have grown into some sort of shape already in the case of
anyone interested in the system we are studying here, the
helpful effects of a ritualized recapitulation should be easily
recognized by those intending to form whatever growth
they have made into a Tree of Life pattern. It is a question of
forming existent forces into required forms, and ritual is a
most reliable means of accomplishing this in Magic. There
is no need here for very elaborate or exotic rites, in fact the
simpler the better. Physical requirements will be few, and
metaphysical ones many.

A good way to begin is by using an actual pot or plot of
earth to represent Inner grounds for Tree-growth, and a
tree-seed of some suitable nature, such as an acorn, to symbolize the Life-Tree seed to be ceremonially planted. Then a
significant ritual must be devised for connecting the two

factors in our consciousness. An acorn is suggested only because it is easy to handle, hardy in growth, and needs virtually no attention. Also since it is likely to live far longer than the physical life of its planter, it does symbolize immortality to this purely relative degree. If an acorn should be chosen, however, there is a "trick of the trade" to bear in mind. To raise acorns successfully, they need to have ripened on their trees, and to have been kept moist the whole winter until ready for planting in springtime wherever they are required to grow. Should they dry out entirely they will lose their viability. A good way to keep them alive during the winter is just to bury them in a loose mixture of earth, oak-leaf mold and moss, then leave this pot open to the winter rains in a frost-free spot where it can drain easily. A few handfuls of humus and soil from underneath the parent tree will do very nicely. It is a good idea, too, if an acorn for such a purpose is selected from a special oak tree having personal significance of some sort for the planter. Another good touch is to use a little soil taken from somewhere sentimentally close to the planter's heart, although of course this must be suitable for tree-growing purposes. What really matters is that both acorn and soil should symbolize their attached Inner meanings adequately for the individual concerned, and how this is to be achieved is mainly decided by the intention and ingenuity involved.

Having obtained our soil and seed, it is necessary to meditate upon each until its Inner significance comes clearly into our consciousness. The soil, of course, is dealt with first. It is placed in its pot in a convenient position for attracting attention, and then seated or stationed comfortably before it, we call ourselves into a state of Cosmos by uttering our magical Names silently and signing our Selves into a Circle-Cross of Elemental energy. This done, we turn the focus of our consciousness toward the soil-symbol. A good position for this is on the floor some three feet away and if it can be spotlighted in contradistinction to subdued surroundings, this may be quite helpful. What we have to do now is attach meaning to our Earthly emblem by efforts of imagination and intention.

We might start by asking our Selves just what sort of soil we are expecting our Life-Tree to grow from. This is a sound question, because it begins where everything should, with basic fundamentals. Well, just what have we grown out of so far? What *is* soil anyway? Earthly soil is composed of constituents derived by breakdown from all available organic and inorganic sources of substance on this planet and possibly some percentage from other planets also. It is a reduction of past-living into a state suitable for the support of present and future living. In a sense, it is the excreted essence of old life for the nourishment of new life-forms. The final disintegration of once organized bodies before being rebuilt into other conditions of being. The powerpoint of reintegration and return through the Cycle of Life we continue incarnating with in this world. All these and similar considerations should pass through the consciousness in connection with the subject of soil, then be translated into comparable terms relative to the problem in hand.

The Inner equivalent of raising our Tree of Life is the aggregate to which we have reduced all our experiences of living, and the common ground we have made out of everything passing through our consciousness not only during our present incarnations but also from every previous personal heritage accruing by physical and spiritual genetics. Ordinary Earth-soil contains organic matter from the latest fall of leaves, and chemical elements derived from minerals deposited millions of years ago. In like manner, our Inner soil combines deposits from recent life-events, and traces remaining from our earliest conditions of conscious existence. If we could analyze it similarly to Earth-soil, we should find an odd mixture covering the whole of our cosmic history. It is composed of basic bits of belonging to all that has ever happened to Humanity, both collectively and individually. All of us are entitled as living entities to our share from its stores. We build our beings out of it, and break back again into it what we excrete from our Self-systems. Just as Earth-soil theoretically holds infra-microscopic fragments of every single human being who has ever lived on this planet, so does its Inner equivalent comprise fragments from the life-consciousness of all creatures combining in a common share of Cosmos. Each separate Self-Cosmos collects a deposit of its own soil-contribution immediately beneath it, and this will sooner or later absorb into the shared substratum. We enrich, or perhaps impoverish, our common Inner soil because of what we do with that portion of it we are passing through our Self-Cosmos. Inner soil can be poisoned or improved as in the case of Outer.

This Inner soil in which we intend to plant our Life-Tree seed is given the generic name of Malkuth—the Kingdom or "Territory" over which we must eventually become Monarchs, or "Self-rulers," rising above it with the help of our higher faculties directed from holier life-levels at the spiritual summit or Crown of Kether. From Malkuth we become as Kings, and from Kether we become as Priests in the Mysteries of Melchizadek, or the process of perfection developing Humankind toward divine living. The symbol of a King is a Crown, and that of a Priest is an Altar. If we imagine the King arising from Malkuth reaching up for the Crown of Kether, and the Priest from Kether reaching down toward the Altar of Malkuth, this will give us a wonderful symbolic sense of what energy exchanges are taking place between the two extremities of the Tree.

All this type of thought and motivated meditation should be directed at the practical pot of soil we are putting into ritual usage. It might help a little if the pot is cubically shaped, its sides being colored in the traditional black, light green, dark green, and russet sequence to suggest Tree-life through the four seasons. Appropriate symbols might also be painted around the pot if desired. In fact, a cubical cover could easily be made for an ordinary flowerpot and decorated in any way you wish. Any device is permissible which assists the action of consciousness employed in creative magical courses.

The essential end-effect to reach here is a realization of what Inner soil means for us, and how it compares in terms of consciousness with the specimen of ordinary World matter we are employing as a ritual example. Somehow, we have to see this "Insoil" as our most solid grounds for believing in our own divine destiny. It has to become literally our life-standpoint from which we hope to reach Ultimate Light. If we need to be modern, we might look at it as the launching pad for our take-off toward Total Truth. However we manage to arrive at these or similar conclusions, we must finish this stage of our practice by firmly attaching as many of such meanings as we can to our Inner and Outer soil-specimens brought into ritualized relationship. Only when this is satisfactorily accomplished should we continue our work with the seed.

Here the objective symbol of an acorn or other convenient focus of fertility should be arranged somewhat above eye level and clearly illuminated. The idea is to gain an impression of a Ketheric spiritual situation, as if it were our seed of life descending from a superior source of being. To convince our consciousness that this seed will produce the Tree of Life for us, a tiny diagram of the Tree design may be drawn on the outside of the acorn with appropriate colors in poster paint if required. Mere dots for the Spheres will do, as long as they are plain. The mythos of the story behind this symbolism is that our Selves originated in

Light, then separated away from our life-source and subsequently "fell" into materialization. Because we bear within us what amounts to a sacred seed of our Initial Identity, this offers us a means of sure salvation if it becomes "raised to Light" effectively. To ensure this end, the seed-bearing part of us must implant it in suitable soil, energize it with our living elements, then devotedly tend the growing Tree of Life, rising toward Ultimate Light with it from one incarnation to another and beyond embodied being until our Trees become tall enough to lift us into the Light we truly belong with. Such are the ideas we should try and associate with our symbolic seed.

Somewhere in everyone is held a secret hope of becoming better and more evolved entities than they immediately are. This is in no way to be confused with material greeds and ambitions. It is the present position of a Self-seed grown in the past and seeking finer fruit in the future. However slow its germination may seem, it usually provides our main incentive for living purposefully. Material equivalents are easy to see and sow. We may implant a seed-sum of money to grow and make a fortune for us—if we have the know-how and opportunity. There are plenty of physical seeds which mature within months and bring us rewarding results. Here, we should be seeking the seed of something quite different, namely whatever factor in our Selves deriving from divine life-levels causes us to grow constantly and cosmically toward our ultimate state of Selfhood.

That something of such a nature does indeed exist in individualizing entities, there need be no doubt whatever. Divinity is Humankind's deepest instinct and highest inspiration, disguise or deny this fundamental of our Selves as we may for whatever reason suits our minds at the moment. We can only refuse to acknowledge Divinity and spiritual Self-hood with our mental faculties. Our souls are unable to reject what they feel, and our basic intuitions can scarcely disinherit their origins. Say what we please, we know well enough quite wordlessly that somewhere, somehow, right at the back of whatever we are now, something connects our real Selves with cosmic life on a far greater scale of living than anything this world can possibly offer. Perhaps we might paraphrase a familiar saying and put it that in every human there is a God trying to grow out. Who is foolish enough to suppose that merely mortal status on this perilous planet is the best Humankind may ever achieve for itself? Who seeks not more than mortality deserves to die in other than physical dimensions. Those unwilling to find a finer future for themSelves than afforded by Earth existence alone may only expect a very limited term of living as any kind of an entity. Every Self has the inherent right to decide its own destiny. Let whoever denies themSelves life beyond a body be so bound to their extinction as they have determined. Let those of us who intend achieving our own immortal Identity seek out the Seed afforded this sort of living. Having found it, let us go on growing it faithfully and carefully, so that it will turn into the Tree of Life supplying us with everything worth living for as Selves of One Eternal Spirit.

When associations of this kind have been satisfactorily attached to our symbolic seed, we shall be ready for the actual implantation. It may take several meditative sessions to achieve this degree of readiness. There is no hard and fast way to determine this point, but a good guide is to estimate our own reactions with the symbols as we contact them reflectively, either physically or conceptually. If when we meet them with an Inner attitude of open approach they immediately start suggesting all the thought-trains we have been putting in to them, and even adding extra ideas as a bonus, we and they are ready for further work together. If, on the other hand, they mean little more to us than an ordinary acorn and a heap of garden soil, then we shall have to continue concentrating on them until they become satisfactory symbols and Keys to the areas of consciousness within us that we intend opening by their means. This is not unlike making a recording on a tape. We talk, sing, or play our piece, then rewind the tape and switch to playback. If nothing happens, or only disjointed and discordant sounds are heard, we correctly assume a fault in the mechanism somewhere, and when this is put right we have to re-record the whole sequence. The same is true in the case of impressing collections of consciousness into symbols. If they do not play back properly, then our practical procedure was faulty, and we should make what corrections we can and try again, persevering with our efforts repeatedly until the symbols are working well enough for us. Unlike a tape recording, however, a replay of a symbolic set of associations is likely to include extra or improved impressions which have developed during subconscious storage. Assuming we have put our soil and seed symbols to this sort of test and been satisfied with results, we can now connect them together ceremonially.

The form of such a rite is simple enough. It calls for only an empty planting-pot shaped as desired which may have a small stone or so from some specially cherished location in the bottom for drainage. This pot occupies the central position on a low altar table or the floor. Around it at the four proper stations are arranged the little heap of soil as Earth, an empty pot-holder for Air, a lighted lamp for Fire, and a small vessel or cup of Water. Around all of these a circling Cord may be placed. At a high level above everything, preferably where it has to be slightly reached for, the seed symbol is located. Failing any facilities for this, it may be borne in the hands and elevated when required. The rite may commence by blessing the symbols of the Elements in turn in accordance with the operator's normal procedure, and any suitable method employed to achieve the right magical mood necessary for impressing the importance of the issues involved as deeply as possible into the state of Self-awareness invoked.

Fixing the focus of intensified Inner consciousness upon the central soil-pot, let the force of all attached associations therewith be directed at the symbol and firmly connected consciously to it by the words:

> *Be thou my symbol of that spiritual soil from which my life ascends toward the Supreme Light of Total Truth.*
>
> *Blessed by thy kingdom unto me, that I may rightly rule my own responsibilities therein.*

or whatever phraseology to this effect may be preferable to the operator. When it is felt that the intended contact has become effective, then let attention be turned to the seed, which is held above the head with both hands so that it can be clearly seen and the Tree-design on it be observed the right way up. Here a sincere petition-prayer may be made to the Supreme Self that the precious spiritual potency represented by the symbol may be rightly received and correctly cherished. The focused force directed to it is formulated by the phrase:

> *Be thou my symbol of that spiritual seed from which my living pattern of perfection grows until I am identified in ultimate and greatest Light.*
>
> *Blessed be to me thy crowning apex of awareness, granting me the grace to mediate thy majesty as thy Divinity deserves.*

Now comes the union of seed with soil, a truly sublime act which might be considered as a sex-symbol in the finest sense of cosmic fertility. It is an act to approach with loving reverence and firmest faith in its Inner reality. Since it is

intended to implant and germinate the special Tree of Life
properly belonging to the Initiate conducting this ceremony,
all appropriate realizations of this objective should be made
as the seed-symbol is lowered carefully and deliberately
down into the waiting pot where it is still held between the
thumb and forefinger of the left hand. The ritualist should
do this from the North position of Earth, and may end up
kneeling there. This part of the procedure may be phrased:

> *Soil of living*
> *Seed of Light.*
> *Be forthgiving*
> *Love! Unite!*
> *Create my Tree*
> *Of destiny*
> *As I proclaim*
> *My secret Name.*

Here, the magical Name is infrasonically uttered into
the symbol which now represents a seed (the acorn) having
entered a womb (the pot). A few moments of meditation on
this marvel are in order. Wonderful as the act may seem, it is
still insufficient to ensure good growth into maturity. For
such a fulfillment, nutriment is needed, and the natural
source of all essential supplies derives from Elemental
energies. So now these are provided from each quarter of
our Cosmos. Filling up the pot from the heap of soil so that
the acorn is bedded about an inch down, every energy
associated with ideas of Earth contained in our consciousness is intentionally made available to the Tree we mean to
raise for our Selves in order to live by its principles and
benefit by the blessings we hope to have from its fruits. This
intention is directed formally by the injunction:

> *Let my energies equating with the Element of . . .*
> *(Earth) . . . flow freely forth into the present purpose of*
> *my Will and word.*

May the holy Tree of Life arise in me that I may also grow with it toward my greatest good in highest Truth and Light.

Going around the circle in a cosmic manner, the other Elements are associated with the Tree by the same formula coupled with appropriate activity. At Eastern Air, the planted pot is placed into the vacant container of that Element, breathed upon, and linked with all Air-classified concepts of the directing consciousness. At Southern Fire, the seed-symbol is imaginatively welcomed with warmth and radiated by whatever in our Self-Cosmos we connect with the best temperature to foster our growing Tree through our faith in its nature. Then at Western Water, the pot of soil is literally saturated with water, poured upon it as we also pour out our intentions represented by this Element. This done, a good symbolic completion of the Elements is made by leaving the pot placed centrally, and picking up one end of the Cord like a serpent climbing a tree. If we remember that the Cord symbolizes the Element of Truth, we shall appreciate how the Tree should be sealed, and what should tie its branches together as a perfect pattern. The standard formula may also be used for this action.

As a finalizing act to this small ceremony of great consequence, the planted pot may be picked up in both hands and, while held heart-high, dedicated to the Life-Spirit which is the Supreme Self of all. Each entity should find its own words for this Will-working, but the summation might well be formulated:

May I be
One with thee
My living Tree
Grown into Me.

After which, the consecrated symbol may be placed on an altar or other focal position, and a brief period of contemplation will complete this ceremonial session.

From this point on, whenever we call our Selves into Cosmos by the Circle-Cross formula via our symbolic Names, we must automatically include the Tree to whatever state we have managed to grow it by means of magical methods. Subsequent to the previous rite, for instance, we should be aware of our Life-Tree in a condition of primal planting at the base of our Cosmos. There we must consider it as our principle of "perfectibility," implanted in us by our own intention acting in combination with the Will of our cosmic origin. As it grows, so shall we grow with it. Its life-force is supplied directly from the Elements of our living energies. These combine and concentrate at two points of our Cosmos only—beneath us and above us. Between both extremities of our Elemental existence, we are now growing the Tree of Life which links us with our immortal Identity.

The growth of our Tree within individual Circles of Cosmos should in no way confuse or contradict our Circle-Cross conceptions. The Tree is an adaptation of the forces generated by our cosmic energies into the formation of its principles and the pattern they present to us as a growth-guide toward perfection. We have to feed our Elemental energies into the Tree from the bottom through the symbolism of the fourfold Kerubim associated with Malkuth the Kingdom, and from the top through their highest equation as the *Chioth ha Quodesh*, or Holy Living Creatures. This may be visualized as the interchange of energies from Heaven to Earth as outlined by the Emerald Table of Hermes. They descend from Heaven to Earth, and again ascend from Earth to Heaven for the performance of the wonders of one thing—in this case the Tree of Life.

Periodically, therefore, we ought to send the Elemental energies of our Cosmos consciously into our germinating and growing Tree of Life. This may be done quickly with the standard formula already given, or by any other ceremonial direction of consciousness that satisfies the Self concerned. A summative sentence might be made into a mantric "jingle" such as:

> *Air, Fire, Water, Earth,*
> *Truly bring my Tree to birth.*

This makes an effective circle-chant, since it associates all the Elemental energies with the purpose for which they are being invoked. Of course each Element must be clearly and concisely concentrated into consciousness as called on, which needs an ability of swiftly alternating attitudes of awareness during practice. Still, if commenced slowly and then steadily increased in frequency, the force of any such utterance can be built up to a very satisfactory degree of application.

Providing all this procedure is carried out conscientiously and rhythmically at regular intervals, the Tree of Life should grow naturally by its own accord in our states of Self-Cosmos. This means it will call the attention of our consciousness to its progress by contacting our specific Self-areas associated with its particular Sphere-principles. We are, of course, really growing "a tree on top of a Tree" by this ritualized reproduction of its formation, but the object of it is to realize and relate our inherent Tree-qualities according to the pattern of life we are following. Sooner or later we shall be aware that our Inner Tree has "come up," and is strongly thrusting its rising stem into our consciousness. This awakens our sense of Foundation or life-basis amounting to ancestral and genetic instincts, tracing right back through our reproductive links to the beginning of our lives as biological beings. That is to say, it is the whole of our sex-history which has brought us to the present life-point, and the potential it offers for establishment along future lines of finer breeding-methods.

Between our gestation-birth point in Malkuth and

arrival at Yesod, however, we have the Inferior Abyss mentioned previously in connection with its cloacal properties. It has a very important place in the Tree-scheme apart from this function, being the immediate dividing line between our purely physical conditions of living and all the qualities represented by the higher Spheres. Through it, we should obtain whatever we dispose of down the Great Abyss reduced to "least common denominator" state suitably fit for fertilizing the fundamental life-forces at the basic roots of our beings. It is the bottom of our Inner break-down process as it were, resupplying our previous rejections in a condition which enables us to use them again for fresh living. In a sense, this minor Abyss is like a sleep-state during which toxins and fatigues of the previous day are neutralized as much as possible, so that we awake with the same bodies but find them somewhat regenerated. The sleep-gap in our consciousness, which is an Abyss of Awareness in a minor way, has made such an improvement practicable. What this Abyss will do for us during a human lifetime, the Great Abyss will accomplish between incarnations once we learn how to use its facilities correctly. That is their relationship with one another.

We cross the Inferior Abyss on the Tree of Life by our intentional projections of purpose toward the Inner principles on the "other side" via any or all of the three Paths provided. However we get across, whether by Hermetic, Mystic, or Orphic way, or even through them all together, it is a life-necessity that we should keep aiming across this Abyss toward a state of "awakening beyond sleep" until we realize something of the Self-state awaiting us in spiritual dimensions if we learn how to live accordingly. In theory, an effective initiation ceremony is supposed to assist candidates of the Holy Mysteries in bridging this minor Abyss between their bodily consciousness and immediate Inner intelligence, but it is still something we must all do for our

Selves whether or not we have ceremonial aid available. Most people manage quite well without it, but once the way over this minor Abyss has been opened up in any incarnation, this is usually easy to recapitulate and regain in subsequent Earth lives.

As we come to the ritual point of our Trees where we recognize this Lesser Leap in its growth, we may formulate the crossing of our consciousness from physical to metaphysical living by pressing a hand to the front of each thigh as if bracing muscles just before a take-off, and saying thoughtfully:

> *Beyond physicality,*
> *To Inner reality,*
> *Let me duly awaken.*
> *Guide me, my God, aright*
> *Into most blessed Light*
> *By this Path I have taken.*

After which we should feel free to find the entire remainder of the Tree awaiting our climbing consciousness.

It is interesting to observe that the growing Tree contacts our Self-spheres in the same order these usually activate during an ordinary lifetime. The implantation levels with our gestation, and Malkuth brings our birth to this life-kingdom. After we cross the recapitulative minor Abyss of childhood, along the first rising stem comes the sex-sense at puberty (Yesod) which branches left and right during early adulthood toward the dual life-drives of Splendor (Hod) and Achievement (Netzach), then comes a central sense of power and purpose amounting to Balance and Beauty at Tiphereth. This again divides into a double acquisition of Severity and Mercy (Geburah and Chesed), complementary qualities mostly gained in middle life. These join into a point of indefinite position on the Tree termed Knowledge (Daath), or more simply Experience of Life. This, being an individual and variable quality of very uncertain constancy, is purposely left vaguely at the X position of the Tree immediately over the Great Abyss. Whatever Daath may be, it has to bridge this major gap between our general areas of living and the special or supernal states of our existence enduring independently of incarnation. These balance up as our deepest qualities of Understanding and Wisdom equated by the entities we are as our Selves. We normally reach our best contacts with these particular Spheres somewhat late in life, and should go on living with them excarnately in states of pure consciousness later still. All combine finally in the Sphere of Crowning Awareness (Kether), wherein all life comes to a single spiritual Point of Perception. We are only likely to reach a very minor and relative awareness of this Self-state while incarnate if indeed at all. After that attainment comes the Nil of Infinite Identity.

In raising our ritually grown Tree, therefore, we should expect to experience its Yesodic development subsequent to its planting, and this is the next area of consciousness to open up in our Cosmos. It means a great deal more than simply sex as a purely physical phenomenon. It signifies the entire basis of our creative abilities on all life-levels by the fundamental process of polarizing anything into two complementary principles, then re-combining these so that they will produce a modified version of themselves as an improved or more evolved life-unit. Whether this is done physically by ordinary sex-union between two humans or other creatures so as to breed a somewhat better version of their species, or otherwise along Inner lines of living, makes no difference to the Foundation-principle (Yesod) involved. On mental levels, we might take any concept, polarize it, put it through the equivalent of a sex-process in its own dimensions, then obtain the issue of this as another concept of somewhat higher quality. This type of action may be followed spiritually as well. It arises from the same Sphere of Yesod on the Tree, where selective fertility of life should start, and is the important consideration here—to breed better and finer conditions of conscious being for the whole of our lives, so that our entities are constantly evolving cosmically. That is what Yesod the Foundation is really about. It is essentially the Inner base from which we start improving and selecting the Self-qualities out of which we hope to achieve our highest state of Individuality.

Yesod has certainly nothing to do with the wastage, illtreatment, and contemptuously careless mismanagement of sex in all its forms which we so commonly encounter in this world. To regard sex (or productive polarity) as only a physical function entirely confined to bodily ability and the lowest levels of psychic gratification is a very serious mistake which not even a minor Initiate of the Mysteries would make for a moment. Physical sex-activities are the primitive forms of the life-forces we have to use in order to evolve from human into much higher types of entity. This does not mean physical sex is unimportant to us. On the contrary, it is absolutely vital to our progress that we not only learn how to handle it correctly but also discover how to apply and make the most of it so that it will help us grow and develop as Selves in the true sense of the word. When we achieve physical sex-ability at puberty, this does not imply we are "grown-up" as more than mere mortals. It means we can start growing up as spiritual life-entities for the rest of that incarnation. The trouble is that so many mortals seem to deliberately stop growing at this point, or perhaps are easily persuaded against advancement.

Yesod the Foundation is thus the point on the Life-Tree where we are supposed to realize that we can and ought to do much more with sex than amuse the purely physical ends of our entities with its activities. This realization does not call for unrealistic condemnation and denouncements of sex from muddled moral motivations at all. It just means we have to place the subject of sex properly in proportion upon our Life-Tree. What we must acquire in the Yesod Sphere of life is the art of making even minor material experiences of a sexual nature produce really deep and important consequences to our Self-structure in terms of our cosmically evolving consciousness. In like manner we must find out how to polarize a thought so that its two ends mate and produce a finer outcome which in its turn may be put through the same process. Then we have to do as much spiritually. Far from becoming less sexual as we move our attention away from physical foci, we actually intensify this life-ability in our Selves as we apply it to successively higher levels of our living. Our ultimate sex-act unites us with our own original Identity in Divinity, and That is That.

All this and associative items of awareness should come out of our contemplations in connection with Yesod contacts upon the Tree of Life. For the sake of ritual symbolism, this Sphere is considered to locate with the generative area of the human body. Although the average inclination is to visualize a sort of disc at that point, like the conventional chakra or spinning circle, it is best if an idea of life-energy about to polarize like the first fork of a Tree can be symbolized satisfactorily. Since we are going to construct definite Sphere-concepts as we grow our Trees of Life, it is probably best to consider them analogous with globular states of luminescent energy having a rate of pulsation (or frequency) relative to the nature of its force-field. We can codify this for convenience by the numerical label of the Sphere in question, and color our concept likewise. Here, for instance, the Sphere of Yesod the Foundation might be conceived as a globular mass of pure life-energy occupying the genital area of the body. It would have a deep lunar type of radiance, and a ninefold pulsation with a triply triple beat. For good symbolism, such a Sphere ought not to be imagined as having a hard restraining outline like the circles we are accustomed to seeing in the Tree designs, but as a bright core graduating into an indefinite edge which loses its light quite gracefully into invisibility. Where the Paths joining Spheres emerge together from their perimeters, this luminescence defines into clear channels of connection, the colors meeting and mixing into their combined shades, somewhere about the middle of a Path. As yet, however, we should still be dealing with the single Sphere of Yesod.

Again several sessions of meditation may be needed to create this Concept of everything concerned with the power-principle of Foundative life-force and symbolize it summatively as a Sphere of radiant energy with a ninefold pulsation. A helpful associative gesture is to join the hands at fingertips over the genital area. Also if any particular music seems to go with this Sphere (such as the Moonlight Sonata, for instance) there is no reason why it should not provide a favorable background. When the Concept seems well enough developed, it may be ritually set into the system by calling it ceremonially into position with the formula:

> *Thy Name is Yesod. Be unto me a firm Foundation for my faith in life, and secret Source of Self-fertility in all conditions of my consciousness.*
>
> *May I learn to polarize thy power correctly, and produce perfection through my living Tree in Cosmos.*

By linking the special Hebraic Name of this Sphere with a command and a petition, we are building up that Name into a Key which will call up everything we have put into the Sphere with a single summons. Moreover, if we find out how to call on deeper and deeper levels, the same summoning sign will connect not only what we have charged the Concept with by our own consciousness, but also more and more of what other Selves have attached to it by their efforts. In this way, we are able to share in the almost unbelievable store of consciousness accumulated in what amounts to the computer banks of our common Cosmos. We might even add our own modest contributions.

We ought to bear in mind that any healthy tree develops and grows as it does along two main force-lines. One is the centrifugal and gravitational force of the planet which tends to push the tree-trunk up in a line relating with the Earth's center. The other is the radiant energy of Light received from the Sun, and translated through photosynthesis into an upsurgence of growth. The planet pushes and the Sun pulls trees out of the ground. So it is in the case of our Inner Life-Tree. The force of our preceding life-efforts provides the gravitational mass whch pushes up the Tree for us, and the Light shining from our spiritual state of future finalization pulls our Tree toward it by the top. At this point of Yesod, we should try and feel this interchange of force taking place in us and study what happens when the uprising Sphere of Foundative Life encounters sufficient pressure from the Light of higher spiritual states directly above it.

The effect of this superior Light energy upon Yesod acts something like a laser beam concentrated into a force-focus. The result is to split the emanations of Yesod equally so that they polarize into the twin Sphere principles of Glory (Hod) and Victory (Netzach). These correspond symbolically with the first fork in the Tree above ground level, and the two leaves initially produced by a tree-seedling. Although they are numerically identified as the eighth and seventh Spheres of the Tree respectively, we must always consider them together as complementaries of each other rather than isolated items of Tree-fixtures. Even though we shall have to think about each of these two Spheres separately, we should still realize they belong to opposite ends of the same level, as their mutual relationship on the Tree testifies. In order to try and get this sense of polarized interdependence, it is a good idea to deal with both Spheres during any single meditative session, alternating from one to the other a while at a time.

We might start by sensing and imagining the beginning of this mitosis from Yesod itself. First of all, two Paths emerge out of the Sphere like horns rising to right and left. Nearest to Yesod both these Paths are the same violet color, but as they extend so do they change through intermediary shades into green on the left and orange on the right. We know quite well that this order is reversible if we turn around and face the other direction, but for the purpose of our exercise, we shall see our Selves between the Pillars so that the Black Pillar is on the right, and the White one on the left. This gives an "Inner looks Outward" view of life. When the Paths (or branches) reach suitable situations to each side of our Middle Line about hip-top high, they will grow into proper Sphere-principles appearing in a similar style to Yesod but brilliantly green and orange in color, the orange Sphere (Hod) having an eightfold beat of two triplicities and a double, while the green Sphere (Netzach) has a septuple pulse of two triplicities and a single.

These Spheres of Splendor and Victory are the principles of life which our sexually-based impulses of being divide into upon the next higher level of living. They equate with intellect and emotion, mind and soul, thinking and feeling. Our dualized consciousness attempting to find out how widely we can extend our Selves away from the center-line of life. The metaphorical bottom branches of our Tree reaching away from the trunk in order to establish the proper proportion and degree of duality needed to produce a perfect Tree-design. If we are sensible, we shall keep our Self-proportions according to those of the Life-Tree. This means we must match our qualities of Glory and Victory as equally as we can, not allowing one to grow beyond the other, and use each to encourage or control the other's rate of growth.

These two Spheres are really extensions of our Foundative fundamentals into complementary living-incentives. We might think of them as impulses of inquiry and achievement. Humans want to know, and they want to accomplish, to pursue and to profit, to seek and to be satisfied, to follow and to find. Here, we are travelling in both directions at once on the Tree. We have to combine the activities of the mind and soul in proper proportions so as to live levelly and advantageously between them. This is a problem frequently encountered during the early years of living. Those torn between impulses from "heart" and "head" in different directions usually have a terrible time when facing such dreadful dilemmas. Those forced by economic pressures to apply their minds through channels entirely uncongenial and unwelcome to their emotional inclinations will appreciate the difficulty of this dichotomy. When our minds are driven one way, and our souls another, life becomes very bewildering and unhappy unless we are able to push on to a stage still above this and balance everything out beautifully. Short of this solution, we need to develop the knack of playing both ends of our mind-soul line against the middle so that each keeps the other countered and the two principles develop at approximately equal rates. That is the action we are ritualizing just now.

Despite the need for keeping parity between the principles of Glory and Victory, the former has actually a leading edge on the latter as we go up the Tree. Glory motivates Humankind to achieve Victory. One of our greatest tragedies is that we have applied this natural order of living so much to wars and so little to welfare. We need desperately to become more than mere sex-reproductive mortals with no greater life ability than our animal colleagues of Cosmos—if indeed as much as theirs. Our twin drives immediately raising us above that level are an ambition for Glory, Splendor, or intellectual gains coupled with a desire for Achievement and Victory bringing us the benefits of comfortable and enjoyable living. On the one hand, we want to be honored and respected by our fellow-beings, and on the other liked and loved by them. Sometimes these may go together in a well-balanced life, or otherwise during periods of unequal development. If we fail in both directions, then distrust and dislike most probably ensue. Our concern here is to avoid this unhappy outcome by training both these branches of our Life-Tree along the Paths they should follow together in company and not in competition with one another.

This means we ought not to try to increase our intellectual capacity unless we are capable of improving our emotive abilities. Nor should we attempt enlargement of our emotional aspects without correspondingly developing more intelligence to guide them along the right lines. We must not think without feeling, nor feel without thinking. That is the problem we have to cope with at this part of our Tree. So we ritualize the action by separating our hands from their low clasp and extending them sideways a little, approximately hip-high, as if we were balancing the two Spheres levelly in that position. Maybe we might think of a weightlifter's bar without a sensation of heaviness, but simply of balance. The magical image of Yesod symbolizes Strength, and we certainly need spiritual strength to hold Hod and Netzach apart in their proper places so that they stand in equipoise. Therefore we must concentrate upon the radiance and frequency-rates of Spheres Hod and Netzach distributed evenly between our right and left hands while remaining in correct relationship with Yesod. All three Spheres should be clearly conceived and felt as Inner actualities connected with each other along direct Paths. It may help a little if a very slight motion of a "balancing" type is imparted to the hands, as if they were actually supporting tangible though unsubstantial masses of energy. A visual symbolic device is to imagine that because of unbalance the colors of the two Spheres are running together and spoiling the look of either. Too much Netzach flowing into Hod will turn the bright orange into dirty brown, and adulteration of Netzach by Hod results in its pleasing green becoming muddy. If we can get the feeling of holding the Spheres level, so that they both stay clearly colored, this will symbolize the Inner attitude we must adopt to maintain our Middle Path poise on the Tree.

These Spheres are ritually set into the Self-system by formulae addressed to them separately and together, so:

HOD

Thy name is Hod. Be unto me the Glory I shall gain
by learning how to live through my intelligence.
   May I hold with honor whatsoever special secrets
of this Sphere my reason may reveal to me.

NETZACH

Thy name is Netzach. Be unto me as Victory won
with virtue and procured through peaceful practices.
   May I be guided into grace by every finer feeling
of my sentient soul.

BOTH

Glory forever be
Even as Victory
Joined in dependence.
Rising upon my Tree
Equally leading me
Into resplendence.

When it is felt that Hod and Netzach are properly set in their positions right and left of our center-line of Light, they have to be linked with this Light-wise at the Solar point of Harmonious Beauty (Tiphereth) which is possibly the most wonderful Sphere for any human to work with on the Tree.

The higher Spheres may be more ethically and meta-physically important, but they are also much more remote from our ordinary sort of living as incarnate mortals. Tiphereth represents the most advanced condition we may reach and still remain mortals subject to the laws of the birth-death-birth cycles of Cosmic being. Once we can withdraw our Self-living past that point of the Tree, we no longer have any need to return to ground level, unless we absolutely insist from purely altruistic motives. Marvelous as living beyond bodily limitations may be, however, this state of blessedness is somewhat beyond our present means as a permanent possibility. Nevertheless, we may fairly expect our due proportion of it in principle, as we symbol-ize it for our Selves on this lower level by reaching Inwardly toward the most beautifully balanced state of happy, wholesome, and healthy Harmony we can find within us.

Trying to describe the state or Sphere of Tiphereth is like attempting to run rings of words around a Power of Light which out-illuminates them into insignificance faster than they are formulated. Still, something may be said sym-bolically. Tiphereth amounts to our Point of Poise between all aspects of our cosmic awareness. It is a state of con-sciousness connecting all our parts together into a sense of wholeness among them, and a recognition of their status in our Selves as integral items of a complete Cosmic Identity. Here, the body, mind, soul, spirit and every unit of living energy associated with them find a common force-form fac-tor which contents them.

Maybe Tiphereth is best described or symbolized as a state or Sphere of Royal and Rightful Radiance. How often during our Earth-lives do we feel in this superlative condi-tion when everything seems exactly right, and we are entirely radiant and equal to any royalty this world might raise? Rarely? Only once? Perhaps never, no matter how much we might want to experience such an enviable Self-state because of what we believe it could be. If something of that sort ever happens to us for even a moment to be remembered for the remainder of an incarnation, it would be a touch of Tiphereth. If we can imagine what life would be like in such a state as an extended experience, it might give us an idea of what people in the past thought "Heaven" was. Though somewhat short of actual Perfection in Peace Profound, Tiphereth represents as high a Heaven as Humanity is likely to reach for a long while in Light-evolution, even if we surpass it symbolically as we raise our Tree beyond it by magical means.

It is the Light radiating down on Yesod from this Tipherethic life-level which divides the life-energy at that point into the duality of Hod and Netzach—the Sun shining on the Moon to signify fertility on Earth. Now we are combining these energies back into their more subtle and spiritual states, or putting them through a process amounting to purification as they ascend the Tree of Life. We symbolize this action ritually by raising our hands slowly and clasping them together at the epigastric Solar region. Not over the heart, which is higher up. As we do this, we may imagine the colors of Hod and Netzach trailing away from our fingers and filtering out their sections of a spectrum as they combine in the middle. The blue of Netzach's green stays behind, and so does the red of Hod's orange. From both emerges their common component of clear and beautiful golden-yellow, merging into the Middle Sphere of Tiphereth. The irregular pulsations settle into a steady six-beat rhythm of two triplicities. We have arrived at the Golden Mean of the Living Tree.

This is the principle-point from which we may look at life about equally in any dimensional direction. To an entity on a very low level of evolution the Sphere of Tiphereth would seem unbelievably advanced, while to an Individuate approaching imminent attainment of Identity and Ultimation into Peace Profound, Tiphereth might look like the beginning of such an achievement. It all depends on which side of incarnatory existence we live. At Tiphereth we are able to appreciate both viewpoints and adapt our Selves every way of Will-working. Just as the Sun shines equally upon all inequalities of life on Earth, so does a Tipherethically centered Self radiate its living energies equitably around it. True, these energies are changed and modified as they come into contact with other categories of Cosmos, but the area or Sphere of Tiphereth itself should be so equably constituted that nothing will disturb the regularity of its rhythm or interfere with the quality of its Golden Light.

Tiphereth means Beauty in the deepest sense of the word—far beyond any sort of mere external appearance. It is the actual state and being of Beauty, needing no beholder to confirm or deny its truth. Above all, it is a condition of cosmic Beauty, calling for complete order throughout its totality so that it may exist as the spiritual standard against which all other degrees of Beauty are determined. No Self with an activated and correctly constituted Sphere of Tiphereth, properly positioned in its system, can ever be ugly, whatever its external appearance. Beauty begins in our very middle, and it is there that we must begin growing Beautiful upon our Tree as we awake the golden-yellow radiance of this Sphere in the center of our spiritual Light spectrum. By symbolic ritualized means we should hold this precious power of being beneficently bright to all Being closely to us—with both hands. If we need to feel "outgiving" about this, the hands may be held a little apart from each other, the fingertips nearly touching, palms turned upwards and wrists against the body, almost as if we were holding something very valuable in our care for the benefit of others. We might even ritualize this further by holding a lighted lamp in this position as we stand in an otherwise darkened room. While stationed thus, it should be realized how responsible we are to ourselves and others for maintaining our central Self-Light level, steady and burning clearly with a bright yellow illumination. Only by living as this action symbolizes can we appreciate how much Tiphereth should mean to us and everyone in contact with our Self-sphere of influence.

Once this kind of thinking has been successfully attached to the symbolic Tiphereth-Sphere glowing and growing ever more beautifully in its proper place on our Inner Tree, it may be formally fixed there with the recognition-phrase:

Thy name is Tiphereth. Be unto me the Beauty of my living in a balanced state of spiritual life.
May I be held in healthy harmony and happiness throughout my whole experience of thine effulgence.

There comes a point in the life of all ordinary trees and persons when they and others concerned with them feel reasonably certain they are likely to live sanely, soundly and relatively successfully through the remainder of their life-span if they can continue along the lines they have developed. During early life-efforts and attempts at growth so much may go wrong so very easily. After the roots have taken good hold of the soil, the trunk has become thick and strong, branches and leaves have opened out firmly, and a further extension of the main stem is showing every sign of rising as it should toward Light, we have every right to believe that the remainder of our Tree ought to come alive correctly, providing it survives as a structure of Spirit. Likewise, we may well be confident about a Self in an equivalent state of growth which has reached an Inner-life point where the beautiful balance of its being becomes evident as an act of attainment. We might truly say such a one had come to terms of equality with the Tree-principle of Tiphereth. Though we may only be doing this in a lesser degree relatively by ritual, the attempt will certainly carry us much closer to the actuality it represents. Hence the need to be careful and conscientious while working the ceremonies.

An assurance of good growing is indeed very heartening, but it is not an absolute guarantee of ultimate attainment of original aim. Tiphereth is the end of spiritual adolescence, but only the beginning of spiritual adulthood. From there upward on the Tree, we shall need to develop qualities of life enabling us to expand our Self-state into far more evolved conditions of Cosmos than those experienced on lower levels. Once again we shall have to repeat our procedure adopted at Yesod, and reach upward and outward toward whatever Light is immediately above us, polarizing our energy sideways, as it were, so that it may re-combine as a finer type of force to another stage closer to the possibility of perfection. Here, we must extrude from Tiphereth the ends of its spectrum as twin streams of force running to right and left of us and forming into the Spheres of Severity (Geburah) and Mercy.

These two qualities must always be considered in combination with each other, controlling their activities together just like Hod and Netzach, but in a superior style of Self-development. Geburah has nothing to do with Severity in any sort of vengeful or spiteful way at all. It signifies strict Justice coming from a cosmic appreciation of necessity for disciplined order and sense of duty so that life may be continued in a controlled and rational manner for all categories of Creation. Chesed does not mean Mercy in a sloppy or sentimental fashion. It stands for Compassion stemming from a strength which is greater than any weakness with which it has to deal. Mercy is essentially a quality which can only be extended to a less potent being. Mercy is power modified because of compassion or fellow-feeling for weaker beings. So here on this level of the Tree we have to gain sufficient strength of Self to exert directive discipline over all we are capable of controlling in our Cosmos, and an equal amount of compassion to prevent misuse and promote our application of these amplified life-energies. Between Might and Mercy we must maintain our balance of being as perfectly as we can, never trying to develop one quality without developing the other. The exercise of Might alone would lead to attritional destruction of everything, and Mercy alone would result in accretional disasters everywhere. If the economy and ecology of existence is to be maintained in a condition of cosmic constancy, then the divine qualities we recognize on human levels as Might and Mercy must continually be applied universally.

Geburah and Chesed are principles of life we need if we are to advance to spiritual or material adulthood. It is rare for their qualities to be possessed by very young people to any marked degree. They generally come later in life, after we have gained enough experience to come to some terms with Tiphereth, which is why they are placed on the Tree in their particular positions. As a rule, they are associated with a senior Self-state which has evolved enough authority to govern everything below the level of its active being. This authority is not synonymous with any worldly rank or Self-situation whatsoever. It means the auto-authority each Self exercises in its own Cosmos over all its components. It is the degree to which we rule our Inner Kingdoms, regardless of social status in the Outer world. It is true that the better we are able to govern our own Inner affairs, the better fitted we become to manage those of others insofar as they accept our authority for such a purpose. It is also true that we shall never control our own constitutions correctly until we learn the art of balancing Might with Mercy, and gearing our sense of Severity with feelings of Compassion so that the two will act in unison consistently instead of irregularly and unreliably. To use them accurately, we have to arrange matters as we did lower down the Tree with Hod and Netzach, letting neither Geburah nor Chesed work apart from each other, but always as a polarized power applied together for a common cause.

It is very important that the habit of employing Geburah and Chesed in unison should be formed as deeply as possible within our Selves, so that we become conditioned sufficiently to carry this admirable sign of cosmic conduct from one incarnation to another. Thus we can ensure a fairly favorable start to almost any life, because we tend to take up a new incarnatory Self-expression in more or less the same spiritual condition (not social status) as we left off formerly. Moreover, the better we are able to control our Might and Mercy Self-Spheres, the more easily and effectively we shall cope with any life-situation we encounter in bodily or disembodied states of Selfhood.

So although we may study Geburah and Chesed separately as we might consider any two ends of a single issue, we should always see each end against the background of the other, so to speak. We should no more try to bring one to bear at any point without involving the other than expect to pick up one end of a Rod apart from its complementary opposite. The best way to hold any Rod (or climb any Tree) is by the middle, and this is how we should learn to handle the enormously potent life-energies of Might and Mercy.

This ability may be ritually symbolized by separating the hands from the Tiphereth position upward and outward so that they are held apart with fingers together, palms forward, and elbows in to the sides, taking up the characteristic attitude of priestly prayer. Indeed, that is why this position is adopted for such a purpose. It not only indicates, but also induces, a balanced state of spirituality and a mediative cosmic condition in those accustomed to reacting in such a way. It signifies Humankind in medial relationship with Divinity. As the hands take up their places for this part of the Tree ceremony, they should be seen as separating the colors from the middle yellow into distinct

Spheres of red and blue at the right and the left respectively. The red Sphere of Geburah has a three-two beat, and the blue Sphere of Chesed a three-one rhythm. We should try to feel them pulsing in our fingers while we try to balance the colors of the Spheres as we did with Hod-Netzach. When we are satisfied with the way we have got our symbolic Spheres into place, we may fix them there ceremonially with the formulae:

GEBURAH

Thy Name is Geburah. Be unto me a sense of spiritual discipline and duty arising from my recognition of the living law.

May I judge others as I would be dealt with by Divinity myself, in strictest justice for the sake of my salvation only.

CHESED

Thy name is Chesed. Be unto me the Mercy which I hope and pray with my whole heart will make myself and all Humankind more perfect.

May I direct my Inner kingdom as Divinity intends, and I affirm, with kindly and compassionate control of whatsoever comes within my Cosmos.

BOTH

Be every Severity
Tempered most mercifully
Into beneficence.
Justice and Charity
Brought into parity
With true magnificence.

Once we are able to hold these principles in polarized power together, we need to think a little more about their point of balance. At lower levels they equalize through Tiphereth, but we have not yet reached the top of the Tree.

How are we to relate our Selves by their means with higher qualities rightly belonging to a divine, or supernal, state of life? It is the absence of those qualities in us which divide us from Divinity by what is termed the Great Abyss. And with what is an abyss frequently compared? *Ignorance!* A lack of knowledge and an ability to apply it, reaching right down to our very roots and dividing us from what we should be as a spiritual Self. If ignorance is abysmal, then Knowledge must be the best bridge for crossing it. Here we are faced with a cosmic Chasm separating us from our rightful state of supernal Self-hood. Only the right kind of Knowledge built from the balancing point of Might and Mercy will bridge this Great Gap in our lives between our human and divine ends of entity with spiritual safety.

In Tree-terms, this is called Daath (Knowledge), pronounced almost as "Doth." It is not a Sephirah but a vacancy which we have to fill in by our own efforts. Everyone must make his Daath individually for himSelf, and as we all differ from one another distinctly, Daath cannot be shown upon the Tree with any certainty, hence all the mystery and vagueness about it. What Daath amounts to is the experience of life turning toward Truth. Knowledge as a living being not only of, but also *in*, a state of truly spiritual Self-hood which bridges our ignorance of what Individuality actually means as an awareness on the highest life-levels. Real Knowledge should signify that we have brought our Selves up from the basis of being to the point on our Tree where we recognize the Great Reality behind all living. In effect, we raise our Malkuth to this Daath position, and so "redeem" the primal pledge we made to our Selves as we plunged down into materialization. Here, at Daath, we have at least returned within spiritual sight of our ultimate objective.

Determining Daath is an exceptionally delicate occult operation. For that reason alone, it is usually symbolized as crossing a Sword-Bridge along the edge of an imaginary blade by a hair-breadth line of Light connecting us from one side of the cosmic Chasm to the other. Once safely across, we shall be on the firmest spiritual ground imaginable, but it is the actual crossing which is difficult. Many Selves miss it life after life, looking for it everywhere except in the right place, or falling while attempting to cross it without sufficient experience. Only those able to combine Geburah and Chesed in exactly the right proportions are likely to cross the Chasm confidently by Daath. This is somewhat like bringing two colored beams together with such accuracy that they produce a precise cross-line of light having a central frequency at their meeting point. Or it may be compared to beaming two sonics so that a true harmonic crosses between them. To equate this action here, we have to tune our qualities of Might and Mercy into an absolutely precise balance, and then direct our attention to right angles as it were, so that we cross the Abyss along this finest edge of energy, thereby connecting the two conditions of living.

It must also be remembered that the Abyss should be a major spiritual service in our lives. Its chief function is to dispose of all which is unfit or unsuitable for building our Self-systems as integers of our Identities. In another sense, it is like an omnivorous mouth which devours whatever we push into it, reducing everything into a condition where we are able to separate the best and the worst for us in our stomachs, and retain what we need for Self-sustenance, expelling the residue through our evacuations. Very few otherwise practical Qabalists seem to realize just what an important contribution the Abyss makes toward a sound state of spiritual health. There is a great need for study and research in connection with the Abyss-principle of the Life-Tree. When the true significance of its nature and possibilities are explored in depth and applied correctly to our consciousness, we are bound to become healthier and happier people as regards our spiritual potentials.

The Great Abyss is primarily the clearing place of all we do in any incarnation, which should not be brought into another if this can be avoided. On a grand scale it should send out of any life-scheme whatever is cosmically unfit to remain within it. In minor ways, it is capable of clearing our consciousness from day to day, if we connect our Selves to it properly. We must learn to treat the Abyss on the Tree of Life with the same respect and consideration as we devote to our ordinary bowels and bodily interior mechanisms. Then it will begin making real spiritual sense.

We may ritualize this symbolically by bringing the hands upward and forward again so that they meet and cross over the throat with the thumbs at each side. Since the balance-point between red and blue is violet, we should visualize only a Light-line of the finest ultraviolet nature, dividing and also uniting the blue-red ends of our Self-spectrum into a complete cycle of cosmic comprehension. The beat-frequency of Daath which controls the Abyss cannot be determined by any definite symbology because it is an individual problem. Relative to the Tree it may be a three and a half count, but usually it is best to regulate this as a steady reverberance of about medium-high pitch or thereabouts. Almost any ritualistic idea is acceptable if it conveys deeply into the consciousness some realization of a fine and firm balance between our existent Self-state and everything we believe we shall ultimately become as spiritual Identities in living Light.

The neck-clasp symbolizes this situation on the Tree very well. In a sense, the throat is a narrow life-passage between the trunk of our bodies and our heads which, like the supernal level of the Tree, contains the chief organs of our consciousness. With this hand-grip, the thumbs press lightly on the sides of the throat like Pillars. Undue pressure here would kill our bodies quickly, so we have metaphorically brought them to the life-death edge of an Abyss. It is the hollow emptiness of a trachea conducting air in and out of our lungs which is of value to the throat, and another traditional symbol of Daath is the "empty room" or vacant space we have to fill in our Selves. Via the throat-bridge between our heads and bodies, nourishment descends (or falls) into our alimentary systems, and rises again as metabolized energy through the nervous system of the spinal cord, back to the brain and once more through the throat. Similarly, in our Tree-system, we convert all our living experiences into a summative quality of Knowledge, which has to be passed back into the highest Spheres of consciousness by the connective bridge we build at Daath. There is naturally a return-flow of energy available in the opposite direction. We literally hold our lives in our hands as we symbolize the Daath-position on the Tree by a throat-clasp, just as we do figuratively while crossing our metaphorical Sword-Bridge. Altogether, an association of Daath with the throat makes for very satisfactory symbolism.

The setting of all this into the Self-system ceremonially may be done with the formula:

> *Let living experience*
> *Be my best evidence*
> *Of the direction*
> *I am led lightfully*
> *As I come rightfully*
> *Close to perfection.*

Now we should have crossed the Abyss safely, and come into a realm of pure Consciousness. Here, we are not aware *of* anything or anyone, but *as, in,* and *through* them. At this life-level we are coming closer and closer to the Identity we have been seeking all our lives. Once again we must polarize our energies and reach out in two ways at once for the last time on the Tree. What we are reaching for here is the basic breadth we need for fulfilling our life-purpose of comprehending our Selves as Cosmic Individuals. Putting this another way, we might say that the human ends of our entity have come to the point where they may meet and link up with their divine counterparts. Humankind gets to Know its Self, or we finally realize conclusively that there really is a Supreme Life-Spirit in Whom we all live, and each of us finds the God we have been seeking for so long.

Here, we should have divided our energies as equally as possible between the extemities of our conscious range, considered as Understanding (Binah) on the right and Wisdom (Chockmah) on the left. Once more we must treat these as opposite ends of the same stick and use them conjointly rather than separately. They are often thought of as feminine and masculine types of awareness, but they are really two ways of directing the same energy, or polarizations of a common power.

Understanding (Binah) is otherwise Intuition, or the ability to "take things in." Wisdom (Chockmah) is the ability to "make things out of" our consciousness. Together they amount to complete comprehension. Whether we are males or females, we need them both in our Selves before we shall be able to Individualize entirely. Only by the degree we balance these qualities in and by our Selves shall we approach our true Identities closely enough to establish our cosmic claim thereto. It calls for a very advanced Self to control these ends of conscious energy together so that they lead toward a single conclusion. We are usually too inclined to develop or depend on one or the other of these finalizing faculties. True, a man frequently uses the Wisdom end of his consciousness rather than relying on Understanding, and a woman tends to neglect the Wisdom factor while relying mainly on Intuition. Neither attitude of awareness is cosmically correct. Binah and Chockmah should form a proportionate partnership of power together in any Individual. No sensible Self would dream of developing only one of these qualities and then expect another Self to supply its complementary condition. It is true that partnerships between Selves in a position to compensate one another's deficiencies are advantageous to both, but only because each then has a better chance of correcting his or her own unbalanced state of Self-hood. Sooner or later every one of us must become a complete Cosmos and a fully grown Life-Tree for our Selves. That is what initiated living into Individuation is all about.

At this Tree-point, we are up against a very difficult operation: balancing out our Self-sexual components of consciousness so that they level up to our apex of awareness as a single-Self-state. Sex is a polarized state of being which may or may not be a perfectly proportioned balance in any entity, human or otherwise. In the world-living we are familiar with normally, the great majority of humans are very far from being sexually honest with life. They preponderate heavily toward one sex polarity or the other. The younger we are and the more active our physical gonads, the greater our unbalance is likely to be. It is generally only in later life that we become more able to stabilize our sexual balance between both poles, and this we can only do with the right combination of Understanding and Wisdom. Hence the placement of these principles at the top of the Tree where we are nearly full-grown Selves, at least in theory.

An ideal Individual is one in whom each sex has reached equality of spiritual status. Anyone of such a cosmic condition could only properly mate with another of the same development. That is why such stringent rulings were made in the Mystery Faiths, where these matters were understood, about marriage and breeding procedures, celibacy, and other customs relating to all sexualized distributions of life-energy or consciousness. What these amounted to was an agreement among them all that only those who had reached a spiritual state of Self-balance in regard to sexual polarities should be allowed to invite other Individual entities into incarnate expression. In other words, only the best beings were permitted to breed in those circles of Cosmos. The remainder worked out their adjustments until they achieved such spiritual status by various techniques taught during the process of initiation. Though this ideal is theoretically excellent, it cannot operate practically in this world unless a sufficiently adequate and capable section of society were unanimously in favor of its adoption among them, as well as being willing to abide by and carry out all the requisite measures for success within the scheme. In the world as we know it now, this possibility seems highly unlikely. The spiritual balance of sexually polarized life-energy must therefore remain an individual responsibility for each Initiate of the Mysteries in modern ages.

It is only possible to polarize and balance our sex energies properly and satisfactorily from a spiritual viewpoint at this supernal stage of the Tree where they exist as states of pure consciousness. If only we could get our sex-consciousness into correct proportions at this vital point, the remainder of its course through the rest of our beings will work out well enough. Heaven alone knows the extent of damage among Humanity traceable to sexual imbalance. It is more than probable that modern changes of consciousness regarding sexual matters, and most of the instability in those areas, are actually wild and often desperate attempts to achieve sexual balance on higher levels of life than was commonly believed possible. The Keys to this superlatively important Self-adjustment lie in these Spheres of Binah and Chockmah, between which both types of polarized consciousness must eventually be blended into a poising point as near to perfection as possible. We all have to do this for, in, and by our Selves, however much we may be able to help one another toward this achievement.

The ceremonially symbolic indication and placement

of these two Spheres in our Self-system is similar to former procedures except that we have gone beyond the range of color associations, having moved much higher up the Inner Light spectrum. Binah is represented by black, which absorbs all colors into itself, and consequently symbolizes Understanding very well. We do not think of colors here, but simply about the principles of absorption and radiation. Light is both radiated and absorbed in return through its cosmic cycles. If Understanding is the absorbent end of Light-energy, then Wisdom approximates its radiant complement. Wisdom here, however, is not symbolized as pure white, but as light grey. There are several reasons for this. First, if white were used, it would be impossible to represent the last Light-stage of Kether except by some kind of radioactivity, which would hardly be practical. Then it must be remembered that the quality of Wisdom, wonderful as it may be, is not the point of ultimate perfection but only one of a polarized pair. Therefore, the Sphere of Chockmah is not so much grey as imperfect white.

The pulse-beats of Binah and Chockmah are triple and double respectively. So to symbolize these Spheres setting into our Self-system, we should remove our hands from their throat position and bring them out sideways and upward again, until they are just above the shoulders, in the "hands-up" style. This is not an easy position to hold for prolonged periods and is even more difficult to keep the principles represented thereby upheld and balanced in that position, so the symbology is good. With this gesture, of course, goes the realization of what the Spheres stand for, and their imaginary energy-forms. In this case, the concept should be that of Chockmah radiating and Binah absorbing their respective qualities. Wisdom impregnating Understanding, which then conceives and brings forth another "child of consciousness." So must we learn to live creatively as we "create our Selves out of our Selves," according to the same pattern originally outlined by the Divine Designer with Whose image we are supposed to identify.

Another sound piece of symbolism here is the attitude suggestive of hanging from a tree-branch. If we are indeed hanging on to life by Understanding and Wisdom, we have three possibilities open: (1) We can release our hold on these finest faculties and fall down the Tree to the bottom; (2) we can swing our Selves along hand-over-hand from branch to branch; or (3) we can exert enough effort to haul our Selves up to the next level above us, which in this case is the last. It is our confident handling of Wisdom and Understanding which finally takes us right up to the top of the Tree. Here we are poised for the leap into Light.

The setting formulae of these Spheres are:

BINAH

Thy Name is Binah. Be unto me the universal Understanding of my life, and every law that leads me into Light.

May I come to comprehend whatever is designed by the divine Will working in me.

CHOCKMAH

Thy Name is Chockmah. Be unto me the Wisdom of whatever way will individuate me into true illumination.

May I determine what Divinity intends my Will to be in all I am aware as an Identity.

BOTH

Let my intelligence
Sensible sapience,
And wise intuition,
Being together brought,
Bear me the way they ought
To final fruition.

The next move on the Tree is the penultimate rise to its apex from the point of balance between Binah and Chockmah to our Self-summit at the Crown of Light at the first Sphere of Kether. Naturally this is a state of being no ordinary human could possibly exist in per se, so what we are trying to do here is to identify or isolate its "trace-presence" in us. Any Self which has developed enough to realize the existence of Life-Entity in Which or Whom they hope to Individualize obviously has some traceable degree of the Ketheric Sphere in its makeup. At this Self-stage, therefore, we should attempt to direct the attention of our awareness *as a whole* toward the single Sphere-principle of Kether.

This Sphere of the Crown (Kether) is taken in the sense of being a summit, an apex, a *ne plus ultra* point, zenith, or degree of life where Humankind and Maker meet into one ME. It is as high as we can reach and still remain a single Self. Beyond in the infinite Nil of Zooic Zero, or the spiritual state termed Perfect Peace Profound, we Ultimate into the Utmost Identity of all. That is the Mystic Union which every Faith acknowledges under different descriptions as the very most that Humankind, collectively or individually, may ever make of itSelf. It is the state of Superself—beyond any sort of being we might possibly conceive below that level. We cannot know or even guess what this is in actuality. We only realize it IS NOT anything, or even everything there IS. We may only know it by its Not-being, yet this state of Perfection in Peace Profound is our ultimate aim of life. Kether, the apex of our Life-Tree, represents the entire point of our whole purpose in and with life, the *raison d'etre* of our existence as living entities. Once we catch up with it finally, we shall be free forevermore from any need to exist except if and as we Will.

The function of Kether in any life is to keep its course pointed the right way to perfection. It is our inherent awareness of Kether in our Selves which directs us through all the dangers and difficulties of living toward successively higher Self-states until at last we Ultimate in Light Limitless. In a way, Kether is like a kind of built-in homing device which keeps correcting our cosmic course so long as we do not deliberately interfere with its action. The source of any such interference is usually traceable to the Pseudo-Self. We can see the relative effect of Kether in the lives of most individualizing entities intelligent enough to realize a spiritual need for some kind of divine direction in life. They generally start by "not-knowing" what they are looking for. Nothing seems right, nothing appears to satisfy their needs. Did they but know it, the Nothing, Nil, or Perfect Peace Profound actually is their ultimate life-aim, which they are trying to symbolize by rejection of all they encounter. The way we are made, however, only *something* can possibly lead us to that Nothing (Ain-Soph-Aur) which alone is ALL. This factor of "something" leading to Infinite Identity in Nothing varies with each individual in essence, but is universal in principle and that principle is Kether. Once we find this in our Selves, we have only to follow it along its line of Light.

The Ain-Soph-Aur is the Great Unknown that we live for and unto. Kether is the single solitary point of purpose in each of us which is able to reach up so high in life and take us with it. As soon as we learn how to direct our living *as a whole* toward the Ultimate Unmanifest with Kether in the lead, and the rest of our Selves related thereto in Line of Light style, we may really begin living in the true spiritual sense of the term. We might think of Kether as the datum-point of our Cosmo-compass upon which we have to align our whole Selves in order to follow the original intention initiating our Identity—the single spark of Light we must never lose complete sight of in spirit if we are to survive as truly living people. That is how important Kether should be for us, and it is reachable on the Tree of Life along the exact

Middle Line between our Spheres or qualities of Understanding and Wisdom. We have to balance these precisely, and push ourselves along Light-lines which join us directly with Kether, almost as if we were in a boat with one black oar and one white one, trying to steer an absolutely straight course toward a guiding star on the horizon.

Our Kether-concept coincides with the top of our Cosmic Circle axis, and so the Tree has finally grown up to occupy the Inner Space-Time-Event Cosmos we have previously constructed for our force framework. Again, the Elements meet and concentrate at the Ketheric level personified as the *Chioth ha Qodesh* or Holy Lives. The Elements of life sublimated into their highest spiritual essences, all "come to one" as a single life-energy. This is where we have to complete our Selves, ceremonially and symbolically, by bringing our hands together just over the top of our heads, wrists touching the sides of the head, and fingertips contracting so that a sort of triangle is formed. At the same time, we should try to regulate the uneven beating of Chockmah and Binah into a single and absolutely steady note repeated at fairly frequent intervals. As we concentrate on Kether, we must feel the Light above us become brighter and brighter, though not to any unbearable degree. What is so strange about this Ketheric Light is its extraordinary quality of increasing its clarity without increasing intensity. Ordinary light becomes blinding and dazzling as it amplifies its strength. Ketheric Light can clarify to an indefinite degree without raising its intensity any more than needed for cosmic comfort. Ketheric Light could even shine in darkness without disturbing it, yet reveal every secret within that darkness to spiritually sensitive vision. This is indeed the source of Light-life we must follow unto the ends of our entity.

When we have sufficiently "Ketherized" our consciousness, the Concept may be set in its proper position above our heads with the formula:

KETHER

Thy Name is Kether. Be unto me that crowning consciousness creating me the Individual I am in Cosmos.

May I be led to Light infalliby by that special single Spirit guiding me to everlasting good beyond all being.

Now our Tree is fully grown from the seed we planted, but we need some sign of recognition toward the rest of all we are not. Our Non-being, and the quality of Zooic Zero, is termed Ain-Soph-Aur. It is all we need not be in order to become as we ought to be. The infinity of Nil comprehending All. A non-state quite beyond the limits of our appreciation but nevertheless the secret supply-source of everything coming to us in Cosmos. Ain-Soph-Aur should never be confused with Chaos, or deliberate disorder. There is Nothing in Ain-Soph-Aur to become disordered. It is our purest potential of becoming anyone, anywhere, any time, AS WE WILL, IF we Will. If not, then we may rest Eternally in PER-FECT PEACE PROFOUND, which is better than all the being in existence, and clearer than all the consciousness in Creation. Its Being is unbounded, its Light illimitable, its Nil-factor the Equation of everything.

While granting that any symbolic presentation of the Ain-Soph-Aur must necessarily be purely conjectural, the natural gesture here is to raise our arms above our heads as high as we can, bending our heads back and direct attention above us into the Great Unknown with all the faith-force we can summon. Once more we will have opened our Selves out and above our life-level, and this time we realize it is an *ad infinitum* move we shall always make while we exist at all. Now, however, we do not expect a direct answer, for we have only Nothing to grasp. We therefore relate our Selves with Infinite Identity by any means available, including the following formula:

> *Thou which art Not*
> *That I may be*
> *Yet total what*
> *I am as Me.*
> *Be all Thou ought,*
> *My living goal,*
> *I am Thy naught,*
> *Thou art my Whole.*

After which the arms are gently lowered to each side by outward full circling arcs, and the complete Tree of Life in Cosmos is contemplated silently for a short period. The entire ceremony should then be brought to its conclusion by some comprehensive and finalizing formula, such as:

> *As seed is sown*
> *So Tree is grown.*
> *Let this my Tree*
> *Become as Me.*

At the end of all this effort, it may be as well to sit down and think things over quietly and constructively. What have we done with our Selves so far?

Quite a lot. We have created a Cosmos of living energy around us from which to obtain our life-force in calculable and controllable amounts of classified consciousness. We have identified our Selves by means of a magical Name which applies to what we really are as individual entities of living Spirit. Lastly, we have grown up an organized Tree of Life within us consisting of combined principles guaranteed to elevate us from one end of evolution to the other in the best possible states of being. What all this amounts to is that we have created living conditions for our Selves which exist entirely apart from any that confine us only to Earth-life, or bind us into merely material manifestation. We have, in fact, achieved about the most important affair of any life-time: the conscious construction of a Self-state standing for spiritual independence as an immortal Individual living in Light. All else we shall experience in existence develops from this degree of initiation.

In effect, we have associated and arranged our Selves intentionally with powers, principles and personifications which exist and act entirely independently of anything, limited only to the interests and confinements of those concerned purely with the local matters of life applying to this particular planet. With these Keys of consciousness at our command, we need not continue in Creation as no more than little human efforts at living through intervals of incarnation interspersed by sleepy sojourns in semi-spiritual states of Inner awareness. We can Wake Up and become as we should always have intended: real Identities living in immortal states of spiritual Self-hood. So shall we KNOW OUR SELVES at last.

Once we have achieved even a minor degree of this Inner Individual Independence, no power of persuasion, compulsion, or coercion brought to bear upon our Earth-living ends of entity can ever invade us without our consent. Physically and mentally, we may be ill-treated, tortured or murdered in every way devised by human cruelty, but the Spirit in Which we have arranged to live infallibly survives, since it has no associations with such atrocities, and as It lives, so also shall we who are With It. There are actually far more subtle and intelligent ways of interference with our Individuation than misusing our material and incarnate presentations of personality. It is in these Inner areas where a successfully seeded state of Self correctly cosmated is invaluable to the individualizing entity concerned. That is the life-condition leading into ultimate immortality which we shall have gained for our Selves through all our achievements.

For many Selves, of course, the exercises and efforts will amount to a recapitulation of what already was within them in deeper conditions of consciousness. We carry these Self-states from one incarnation to another in essence, but this does not mean we can ever afford to ignore or neglect them. A Self-state calls for care and cultivation like any other living item of existence. Having constructed our Cosmos, named our Nature, and raised our Tree of Life, we may no more abandon this arrangement of Self and lose individual interest in it than we should in the case of our inheriting an entire kingdom (which indeed is an apt simile), for within us lies the Kingdom of Heaven in a very literal, as also a spiritual, sense. Now that we have come into this style of living, the least we should do for our Selves is look after them in the manner to which they are becoming accustomed. Let this be our next, and last, concern in this course of study.

Chapter Nine

Self Systems Are For Living With

Having set up our Self-system, it now needs to be maintained in good order so that we may live in, with, by and through it. Otherwise it gets out of cosmic condition and deteriorates like any other living organism. The same rules apply for keeping a spiritual system healthy as with a physical one. Suitable environment, balanced nutrition, equable stresses, adequate rest periods, sound alimentary and excretory workings and all other factors favoring a good average rate of metabolism. Also important are security, shelter, food, and even the climate. These are translatable into Inner terms, and applied by analogous means.

Physically, we have an Elemental energy exchange via Air (Atmosphere), Fire (Solar radiance), Water (Liquids), and Earth (Solids). There is a connection with the Truth Element in electromagnetic and similar force-fields. We take these in, digest them, convert them to other energies, then excrete what remains. They provide us with muscle and nerve-power, cellular regeneration, and other phenomena concerned with our material forms of manifestation—raw energy taken in from the Elements of life and converted to products of human abilities and behavior. A remarkable change, yet even more wonderful when worked out along corresponding Inner lines of action.

In the Self-system we have been considering, our crude Elemental energies which amount to Inner food, drink, breath and warmth are exchanged with their direct supply-sources via the spiritual Circle-Cross circuits of our Cosmos, then converted into the actions of our cultivated and evolving entities via the Tree of Life pattern. Just as a healthy and fully-functioning basic pattern of metabolism provides the power for trained and accomplished bodily behavior, so does the Circle-Cross of Elemental energy provide the wherewithal for developing our Selves spiritually into the mature and perfect pattern of the Life-Tree, via those qualities it supports, and the relationships between them it outlines. The Cosmic Cross will make us into balanced and effective entities so far as pure energies are concerned, but the Tree of Life allows us to cultivate those energies into what might be described as a more developed cosmic state of civilization. The Self energies are converted to Self-qualities, and this is what makes us the sort of Selves worth cultivating in our turn on higher life-levels. So we use our Cross to grow our Tree.

Since this type of cultivation can only come out of our conscious attention applied by intention, we shall have to maintain our magical procedures if we mean eventually to reap the benefits of our work so well begun. To plant and grow the Tree of Life in our Cosmic Gardens is one thing, but to eat its fruits of immortality is quite another. At least we now know what these fruits are. They are the qualities of Self we need to cultivate and grow in our systems which will make us truly immortal as individual entities. Certainly they are labelled plainly enough—Birth, Breeding, Honor, Devotion, Balance, Discipline, Compassion, Understanding and Will. Given those fruits of our Life-Trees, we can grow our Selves into whoever we intend. Therefore, it is in our own best interests to produce at least specimen samples of our spiritual fructification as soon as we may reasonably expect some token results from our previous efforts.

The only possible way to achieve any degree of success in this direction is to keep the Tree of Life consistently in our consciousness by every practical ritual and other device until we live its pattern into ourselves sufficiently for further developments to follow almost automatically. This happens in just the same way that we acquire any other skill in life, or develop any particular ability. First we have to approach the whole idea with a comprehensive grasp of consciousness, then relate our Selves with it practically piece by piece while we give our entire attention thereto systematically. When we make progress, we shall find our Selves using this new art quite naturally in minor degrees as we apply it to our living-methods more and more normally while we go along with it. Eventually we do things in a relatively free and effortless way as a characteristic of our consciousness employed without any particular strain on our Selves, and directed toward some intended purpose. First we take it in with effort, then we put it out with effect. That is exactly what we must do with our Circle-Cross and Life-Tree Self-system.

Our work along these lines consists mainly of relating our Selves through the system with both our Inner and Outer affairs of life as whole Self-connection with Cosmos. Though this sounds rather grand, it is best approached in deceptively simple ways, associated with the common or garden matters of ordinary mundane existence, almost like the kitchen methods of Brother Lawrence's "Practice of the Presence." The general idea is to link up both ends of our existence so that our physical components are converted into spiritual symbology for the benefit of our Inner being, and our spiritual specialties are brought to bear upon even the most commonplace items of Earth-life in order to enrich and ennoble these areas, not only for our Selves individually but also for other Selves sharing them with us. Thus everyone gains some good out of this operation.

For example, a complete realization of the Cosmic Circle, Inner Identity, and Tree pattern can easily be made while engaged with the very mundane practice of getting up and dressing in the morning. First, while still lying in bed, let ideas be generally awakened by clearly calling the magical Name soundlessly in the center of consciousness. Then, actually out of bed and upright, let the Heaven-Earth contacts of the Circle and Tree be rapidly recognized. Next, either a complete circular turn of this axis, or a swift thought to each Quarter should link in the ideas of the Elemental energies. The same effect can be made while putting on a dressing gown—right sleeve Michael, left sleeve Auriel, back contact Jivrael, front fastening Raphael, cord Savaviel. As simple as that. In our first few moments of the day we have called our Selves into Life and Light by the Name of our true cosmic characters, then connected our Selves consciously with the Elemental energies making such a life practically possible. Quite an achievement from such minor materials, yet why stop there? The Tree of Life pattern has to come next.

Bending down to put on socks and trousers, Malkuth is contacted. With trousers up, fastening the fly takes us to Yesod, and settling at the hips locates Hod and Netzach. The hands momentarily pressed to the epigastric region not only invokes Tiphereth but also encourages colonic activity. With the shirt, Geburah goes on with the right sleeve, Chesed with the left one and, as the buttons are being fastened, the Middle Pillar of the Tree-growth is appreciated. Daath, of course, goes with fastening the tie at the neck of the shirt, and Wisdom and Understanding may come later with the arms of the jacket when we are more awake, or with an upstretching of the arms while fastening the shirt sleeves will take them in. Kether, the Crown, is obviously a hair-combing operation. A final reaching up and swinging down of the arms, accompanied by a sincere hope that the day will be favorable, attaches the Ain-Soph-Aur idea of the Great Unknown to our Self-system. Thus is the Cosmo-Qabalist clothed with consciousness and prepared for another day of life-practice among Earthly environments.

All during the average day of an ordinary human being there will be similar opportunities for combining the materials of Outer life with the construction of the Inner Cosmos to the mutual benefit of both life-states. In the light of what we have learned by means of our magical exercises, we should appreciate how to utilize every possible occasion for the pursuit of our life-purpose. That is one reason why old systems had so many formularies in them concerned with our general and particular human activities—a "rising" prayer, an "eating" prayer, a "sleeping" prayer, and blessing for anything and everything connected with living or dying. Strangely enough there are no records of specific formulations for the two physical functions of sex and excretion, unless one accepts some of the Tantric material associated with sex practices. Yet there is really no valid reason why these very human functional needs should not be treated as indispensable integers of a cosmic life-plan, translatable into spiritual terms and worthy of appropriate magical formulations.

During morning ablutions, for instance, we might try evacuating detritus from our minds and souls as well as from our bodies, then cleanse and freshen our Inner appearance just as we cleanse our physical faces and hands. Why not make this daily occurrence a combined psychophysical operation? It is such an easy thing to do once a little practice is made. An intention of Will, energetically applied through some convenient formulation, and an appreciable effect is sure to be obtained. While engaged with material evacua-

tion, for example, we ought also to direct a determined
effort Inwardly so that we might equally rid our Selves of
the comparable contents of our consciousness. Either previously mentioned formulae may be used, or something of
a general nature like:

> *Leave me without delay*
> *Whatever should not stay.*
> *Away from me proceed*
> *All I no longer need.*
> *Let this release*
> *Cause Inner peace.*

While this or similar formulae are being gone over, a
concentration of consciousness should be directed to deal
with whatever we intend to clear out of our Self-systems,
and Inner expulsive efforts made comparably to those of
the material muscles expelling excreta at the same time. It is
remarkable how well this simple exercise works.

Then again when washing, or making our external
appearance presentable, it is easy to relate this with an
Inner equivalent by some formulated intention such as:

> *Like welcome rain with tree*
> *May water freshen me.*
> *Washing me newly clean*
> *In every way I mean.*

Whether these or other formulae are employed, in no
matter what mundane circumstances, the fundamental
principle of using Outer life to increase Inner Light remains
unchanged. The externals are treated as symbols through
which the forces of our consciousness may be focused in
order to obtain an intended Inner effect.

Very often a great deal of Inner good may come from a
relatively small material symbol, while very little or no
good at all might be had from what seem like more momen-

tous events. It is never safe to estimate the importance of any symbol from its sheer size alone. The significance of symbols can only be calculated by the connections they are likely to make with an Inner Cosmos of someone's Self and the nature of the reactive results ensuing therefrom. Because this factor varies with each individual, it is impossible to be hard and fast in this area. The only practical thing to do is to find out from personal experience what sort of symbol affects which part of a Self-Cosmos or Tree in what particular way, and then live with such symbols so far as possible. Everyone has to discover his own special symbolic sequences.

The great need in the case of the Life-Tree is a swift summative and single symbol which will call it into consciousness as a whole, then a series of other symbols to evoke the separate Spheres in like manner. About the most rapid manual sign of the Tree is to trace with a finger, or follow mentally, the zigzag flash pattern of the Sephiroth from the top to the bottom of the Tree around one's body. This can, of course, be reversed to build the Tree up from the ground. Starting with an indicating finger just above the forehead, this is brought down to a point at Malkuth between the feet. Then the genitals are indicated for Yesod, the right hip for Hod, across to the left hip for Netzach, then up across the body to the right, taking in Tiphereth and turning at Geburah straight across and left to Chesed, up across the throat (Daath) above the right shoulder to Binah, directly back over the left shoulder to Chockmah, up over the forehead to Kether, and then finally back down again to the feet where the circuit is completed. This is more quickly done than described, and if the mind calls up the Spheres as fast as the finger travels, a Life-Tree pattern will appear as rapidly as human consciousness can conceive it.

In a similar way, the Tree pattern may be arranged on the face with a swift series of light touches, as follows: top of head Kether, left temple Chockmah, right temple Binah, above nose Daath, left cheekbone Chesed, right cheekbone Geburah, under nose Tiphereth, left lower cheek Netzach, right lower cheek Hod, center chin Yesod, under chin Malkuth. This is an effective method if accompanied by the Sephirothic realizations on the way, because the sensation of touch on the face persists for quite a little while, leaving a definite impression that something of unusual significance has happened. All sorts of devices and contrivances of such a nature are permissible, providing they result in some sense of connection between the practitioner and the Inner realities represented by the symbolic pattern traced. Another quick way of "tracing a Tree" is by a bare skeletal symbol of it made with our lines at angles in this manner. First the top to bottom center line is drawn, then the Chockmah-Chesed horizontal bar, which produces the long-shafted or Calvary type of Cross. Then two other cross-lines are made along the Geburah-Tiphereth-Netzach and the Chesed-Tiphereth-Hod axes. This results in a design showing the salient points of the Tree in the fewest possible lines, the positions of Yesod and Daath being considered as proportions of the center line. It also produces a glyph very like the Chi-Rho sign, which similarly refers to Humankind on a Tree.

There are many such dodges and "tricks of the trade" in use for summoning up the Tree of Life into service attached to a Self. Most practical Qabalists or Lodges have their specially favored methods which they sometimes consider extremely secret but which are usually available to any intelligently-directed and inventive consciousness. The most elaborate formulae and complicated arrangements of codification are occasionally devised, quite unnecessarily, for the sake of senseless secrecy in Inner areas accessible to even average intelligences intentionally aimed thereat. No one can possibly preserve entire secrecy in open fields of common consciousness, shared among a very high percentage of Humanity, if they care enough to avail them-Selves of it. Yet all of us are entitled to privacy in our spiritual Self-state, and the creation of a Cosmos together with an especial Tree of Life growing therein will provide us with the privilege of possessing our Selves and our souls in a sound state of security. Once we design our particular Keys to this Inner kingdom, we should naturally keep them within the confidence of our own consciousness, but the simpler these personal Keys are made at first, the better. They can always be elaborated upon later, but initially the main objective should be simplicity and efficiency. There is very rarely much need for involved complications on the part of any ordinary Self in the process of spiritual evolution.

The simplest way of summoning the Spheres singly, summatively, and for all they mean to a Self is either by name, number, color or all these together. It must be remembered that although the Sphere concepts are common to the whole of Humanity, each individual Tree consists of what those concepts signify for the Tree grower in particular. Therefore the implication in every case is something like: "This is *my* concept of Wisdom, *my* idea of Understanding, *my* experience of life" etc. Granted, these Trees are grown from spiritual seeds coming from a Life-Tree we all share together, but each of us is responsible for the one we are growing through our own efforts. So the Spheres of those Trees are characteristic of the Self in question. They can be personalized briefly enough by the succinct formula:

I, (code Name) *call forth my* (Sphere-principle) . . .

After which, the Sphere is dealt with, dwelt on, or disposed of as the circumstances require. Once again it may be emphasized that the Spheres should not be thought of as inert globes full of words, but as pulsating frequencies of specific powers all linked up to the living Self through the circuitry of the Tree-pattern, and available for use by means of special switch gear controllable by the Self at Will. We should constantly bear in mind that Sphere-principles are actual *energies* of consciousness concerned with life, even more real than electricity, magnetism or any physical phenomena. We once did, and still could, live without the services of electricity, magnetism, steam or other harnessed forces of nature, but how could we possibly live in any conditions of culture or civilization without the spiritual services of those special life-qualities available on the Tree? They should never be treated merely as words written on a round label to decorate a clever design. When a Self summons, it must definitely feel the frequency of that Sphere in actual awareness. All the various exercises we do with this motive in mind should be calculated to have such an effect. One straightforward formula for calling up the Tree principles as a whole in single sequence is:

O

I AM

WISE   UNDERSTANDING

EXPERIENCED

MERCIFUL   MIGHTY

BEAUTIFULLY BALANCED

VICTORIOUS   GLORIOUS

and
VITALLY
ESTABLISHED

ME
(magical Name)

This can also be applied the other way so as to ascend the Tree. Being an affirmation formula, it has the advantage of promoting a feeling of identity with the qualities invoked.

However much we try to apply our Selves to living out the Tree through ordinary circumstances of our experience, they must still be consistently "charged" from within by means of magical procedures carried out occasionally as opportunity affords and designed for this particular purpose. This demands some degree of ritual regularity and attention, and the only practical way of assuring this is to adopt a minimum of standard formulae to be faithfully followed for the sake of Inner cosmic continuity. Since ritual activities consume Time-Space-Event energies, these have to be allotted according to available supplies. Nevertheless the least to be expected in the way of ritual effort is momentary mental formulations during a day, perhaps a few minutes morning or nightly, with a more elaborate occasion each week, some special event monthly, a quarterly rite with other suitable companions if possible, and a major annual celebration of Self-Cosmos to which no less than a whole day should be devoted if this can conceivably be managed. This program of perfection may sound like rather a lot when taken all together, but it is actually a very small percentage of personal effort spread as economically as possible over an entire life-period. Worked out on approximations of ten minutes per day, twenty minutes per week, one hour per month, two hours per quarter, and one day a year, the total time-bill comes to about five days a year all together—less than two per cent of a lifetime. What other investment on Earth pays such personal dividends?

There are so many ritual activities to choose from that the allotment of them into the various opportunities available may be difficult. For those with a little more than average time to spend there exists an entire "Office of the Holy Tree of Life" (by William Gray, Sangreal Foundation,

Dallas, Texas 1970) which covers the entire Tree of Life, Sphere by Sphere and Path by Path, as a daily exercise of one Path per day. There are invocations for each Sphere and Path which may be used separately, as well as sundry blessings, hymns and other formulae. Although the full Daily Office takes about half an hour if properly carried out, there is no reason why the invocation should not be portioned to suit individual convenience. For instance, a Sphere might be worked in the morning, a Path at midday, and the Sphere of its other end at night. Many possibilities exist for combining standard formulae in accordance with requirements.

A good reliable standby is the Qabalistic Rosary. This is a Path-working bead arrangement by which all the Ten Spheres and twenty-two Paths are counted off in proper order, while reciting short sentences calling each one into the consciousness for consideration. Actual beads are not really necessary, although they make a pleasant accessory. For that matter, an ordinary Christian rosary is easily adapted by substituting a Tree of Life for the crucifix, though both of these symbols may well be combined into a single significance of Humankind and Tree. The Rosary commences with a general invocation which takes in every part of the Tree, thus:

> *O supreme Life SPIRIT, thou alone art cause and CROWN of Cosmos with thy WISDOM and thine UNDERSTANDING.*
>
> *Grant us avoidance of the Great Abyss in our EXPERIENCE of thine existence.*
>
> *Extend thy MERCY unto us with all thy MIGHT that we may realize the blessed BEAUTY of thy being.*
>
> *Let us lovingly ACHIEVE the GLORY of ESTABLISHING our Selves immortally in thy most holy KINGDOM evermore. Amen.*

Then the beads are told off separately for the Spheres:

> V. *Blessed unto us upon the holy Tree of Life be thou the principle and power of . . . (Sphere).*
> R. *Permit and prosper thou we pray, our present purpose with the perfect plan.*

As the Paths come up in order, they are specified in this manner:

> V. *Blessed be the Path of (Path) upon the Holy Tree of Life that links the principles of (Sphere) and (Sphere).*
> R. *May this and every Way within the perfect pattern lead us truthfully toward enlightenment in living evermore.*

Finally a thanksgiving summary is made:

> *Gratitude to thee O greatest SOVEREIGN SPIRIT of supernal WISDOM and omniscient UNDERSTANDING, since we are enlightened by EXPERIENCE of thine existence.*
>
> *Thanks be for MERCIFULLY tempered MIGHT, and blessed be the BEAUTY of ACHIEVING GLORY by ESTABLISHING our living Entities within thine everlasting KINGDOM. Amen.*

The main advantage of a Rosary is that it can so easily be fitted in at odd moments, and taken from any point at all until broken off for whatever reason. It is something to accomplish a bit at a time, which links ordinary living with Inner realities.

The practice known as Path-working consists of confining the consciousness to a specific Path or Paths of the Tree, so that only the associative awareness connected with those categories is dealt with. It is a little more complicated than just meditating on the Spheres, and calls for an ability to focus and define consciousness into very fine concentrations. Each Path of the Tree has its specific frequencies of consciousness, and these are fixed by the nature of the Spheres at each end of a Path. That is to say, every Path is a polarized flow of energy between two Spheres, just as if the Spheres were Pillars and the Path were the balancing connection conjoining them. In this way, all the Paths are different from each other, every one having its characteristic contacts. Sometimes these are symbolized with Tarot trumps by many divergent arrangements, sometimes by letters of the Hebrew, English and other alphabets, or simply by plain numbers. However they are referenced, the various Paths of Life are like Tree-branches which all have to be followed in the complete course of a cosmic existence, and so a symbolic ritualization of them is a useful procedure for any Qabalist of even average ambitions.

Determining which Path-plan to follow often causes much heart searching and confusion among sincere students of the system. Unless any Self is sufficiently instructed to make up its private Path-plan for reasons recognized in its own Self-Circle, the safest thing to do is adopt some suitable scheme used by others until individual determination becomes possible. Since our thinking is in English, it seems most sensible to make use of the Anglo-alphabetical associations if we want our dealings with the Tree to take place in that tongue. Hebrew scholars will naturally prefer Semitic characters.

As regards Tarot associations with Paths, this should be based entirely on the ideological connections of each symbol with the immediate Spheres concerned. Present numerations of the cards should be ignored, since they make little or no sense when applied in that sequence. The Tarots can be distributed among the Paths on an ideological basis, and this has indeed been done at least once. Those disagreeing with it are completely free to set up their own scheme, provided they can show adequate reasons and purpose for every attribution they make.

For calling the Paths into consciousness, there is a rather sing-song chant entitled "Telling of the Tree," which goes all through the Tree-plan point by point while associating each Path with some definite and particular symbol. Since each section is sequentially repetitive, there is no need to quote the whole exercise here, but the first few lines are:

0. *Nil is Zero, Crown comes first*
   The Path of Life between is . . .
11. *Crown is first and Wisdom second*
    The Path of Life between is . . .
12. *Crown is first, Understanding third*
    The Path of Life between is . . .
13. *Crown is first and Beauty sixth*
    The Path of Life between is . . .
14. *Wisdom second, Understanding third,*
    The Path of Life between is . . .

And so on until the end of the 32nd Path. If the raps of each Path are also made by those of the Spheres connected, this is a help.

By and large, the Spheres of the Tree provide the principles of correct cosmic living, and the Paths offer opportunities for practicing those principles in combination with each other. To live entirely, we would have to walk all Paths at once, which may sound incredibly difficult, but at the same time is not an impossibility for an Individual who has grown up with a healthy Tree through its seed, stem, and system. This is what it means to be life-led through the "Paths of Righteousness for Thy Name's sake," or "Becoming Me upon the Tree." We can and should ritualize the Tree in our Cosmos as much as we like in as many ways as we might think of, and those are uncounted, but the inexorable and fundamental purpose of the Tree is for living with, in and through, so as to become the Self we should be, in accordance with our Original Intention, and attain our True Identity thereby. Anyone attempting to grow a Life-Tree for lesser or otherwise unworthy reasons will most certainly fail with such an objective.

It is well to be clear on this point: Our Cosmo-Qabalistic magical Self-system does not confer undeserved or unearned supernatural powers or privileges on anyone. Nor can it guarantee good luck, much money, or material advantages of any description whatever. It positively will bring into its Inner area all the blessings in life which attend a state of spiritually balanced being held by a Self evolving into its ultimate cosmic condition of Entity. Such a Self does not live aimlessly without a sense of purpose extending beyond the ends of one incarnation. Those able to live in larger than human limits of life, with Inner horizons not confined only to Earth-living, will realize what this means. It means that with an adequate Self-system we can begin living as real Individuals with the best part of our Selves, rather than just as poor projections into a Pseudo-Self struggling with an unsatisfactory state of Earth-existence. All Selves know instinctively that physical life is not enough, and without more than material means of living they have no true point or purpose in existing at all. Nothing except a Self-system capable of independent continuity apart from incarnatory limits will satisfy anyone genuinely seeking to Know and Be themSelves, and this acquisition is possible through these methods of Magic. There are others, but they may be dealt with by their exponents elsewhere.

Deep down in himSelf, beyond reach of words in any human language, each human is fundamentally aware of life outside the cosmic confines of one organic body or this one planet; life, which he is entitled to share once he is capable of claiming not his birthright, but his "Being-right."

After many thousands of Earth-years, humans are at last making their first infantile steps toward infinite space. Amazing as this achievement may seem, it is but a feeble effort if human souls are unable to keep pace with their bodies. What is the slightest use of travelling physically around all the planets we can reach if we are unable to extend our Selves the slightest fraction beyond our material bodies? What is the point of keeping those animated masses of moving meat alive by the most spectacular surgery or scientific know-how if we are not able to stay alive in states of Self independent of incarnation? Either we learn how to live as entities existing in cosmic conditions of pure conscious energy, or we miss the whole point of life entirely. The issue involved is as simple as that.

We came up through life as human beings by the long hard way of associating our Selves with organic and biologically reproductive matter, then evolved by those means to our present stage in human history. This may be the maximum we can make with matter, but it is the bare minimum we need for starting to spiritualize our Selves back into better cosmic conditions of life than this Earth—or any other planet—can possibly offer. Sooner or later we shall have to abandon this Earth anyway, when it will no longer support our style of living. Other planets may not prove to be so permissive of our depredations. What applies to the human race as a whole over many millenia also applies to individual entities living among them as single Selves.

There need be little doubt on the point that just as this world is steadily becoming less likely to support a human species engaged in profligate proliferation and perilous power-policies for an indefinite period, so is its Inner atmosphere becoming increasingly inimical for those individualizing Selves depending on more spiritual sustenance for their further development as living entities. In effect, it is becoming harder rather than easier for more highly evolved cosmic life-categories to maintain close contact with consciousness deliberately confined to Earth-events and effects. This also applies to human souls attempting to emancipate themSelves into spiritual states of living. In order to stay here in some sort of spiritual security while necessary Self-developments are being undergone, it is becoming imperative to adopt constructive survival measures for safeguarding those in such advanced states of Self-hood. If it is necessary to construct special cosmic equipment for astronauts to negotiate Outer Space, it is even more vital that Initiates of Inner space be equivalently set up in spiritual dimensions.

A strange but perhaps significant similarity exists between the overall principles of a Space-craft and the Self-system we have been studying. A Space-craft consists of an energizable container with an external surface capable of adapting to conditions of the interplanetary Cosmos and an internal atmosphere and arrangement suitable for supporting the intelligent life-forms steering its course and determining its destination. From their internal positions, these living beings are in conscious communication with the greater life-body to which they belong on Earth, and upon whom they rely for their directions and information concerning their activities during the voyage. Though final decisions in the Space-craft must rest with its commanding intelligence present, these are unlikely to be definitely made without full consultations with the control center on Earth. Similarly, a fully functioning Self-system consists of an external force-framework which adapts to environmental conditions of Time-Space-Event living. Its Elemental energies compare with a Space-craft, and also supply the needed forces for an internal life-economy. The Inner compartment of this cosmic capsule contains a specially suitable atmosphere and arrangement for the satisfactory support of a spiritualizing Self. The circuitry of the Tree keeps the living intelligence responsible for the system in constant communication with its cosmic life-group. Though this individual has a final choice of decision in regard to the conduct and course of its Self-system, such decisions are likely to be made in consultation with other cosmic companions who specialize in the control of whatever spiritual situations any Self-system is likely to encounter. Indeed, one might go on drawing comparisons and parallels between Space-craft and Self-systems *ad infinitum.*

Like astronauts who must live in one atmosphere while dealing with completely different conditions in another, the Self commanding a specialized system while incarnate on Earth is able to live normally and naturally as an integrated spiritual Individual while dealing directly with extraneous conditions which would otherwise be insupportable. Yet a Self in this state of security need in no sense be isolated or cut off from fellow-mortals unless the appropriate switch-out circuits are deliberately used. All the life-affairs available on Earth may be participated in, but only through special sensors which inhibit harmful influences and filter out ill-intentioned forces as far as possible. Providing an initiated intelligence adapts its Self to live via the Tree-system only, and to containing Energy-Cosmos, it is unlikely to sustain any spiritual injury beyond that with which it can adequately cope. Any foolhardy attempt to operate outside such cosmic coverage is simply asking for trouble and well-deserved consequences. An instructed Initiate of Magic learns first and foremost *not* to work beyond the limits of a Self-Circle. This does not mean that he may not take the Circle with him wherever he goes. There is no rule stating that the Circle has to stay in one place.

Once a Self-system of this kind becomes properly organized, the Self so secured cannot be reached or affected except through the qualities specified upon the Tree of

Life. This may not guarantee immunity from every hazard of environmental experience, but it does signify that all such happenings will be converted into terms of the Tree. For instance, we might encounter suffering in some unavoidable circumstances. Though the Self-system would experience suffering, it would do so in a Wise, Understanding, Compassionate and Disciplined fashion instead of aimlessly, painfully, wildly and agonizingly—all to no purpose. The suffering would be turned to useful spiritual account instead of just being miserably and senselessly wasted. Whatever the experience offered, a Self that is spiritually well-organized puts the energies concerned therewith through its system and shows personal profit in the end. That is one of the main distinctions between uninitiated and initiated souls. The former live as life lets them, while the latter live as they let life affect them.

As we progress, we should develop and grow our Self-systems so that we live in them as naturally as in a physical body, and to much better effect. Just as we learn how to reach out with our limbs or control muscles for any particular purpose, so must we activate our Self-systems and extend our faculties of the Tree-principles when they are needed to accomplish specific Inner activities. All those principles have to come under the control of our central consciousness and Will. We must keep practicing and exercising our Inner abilities until we are able to apply any or all of our Elemental energies and Tree-qualities as we Intend and for whatever purpose we Will. This is a spiritual Self-skill which can be acquired and trained like any purely physical competence. Training methods abound through the various schools of the Holy Mysteries, but in the end the most reliable are those which every Self is sure to receive through Inner information becoming available as its spiritual centers of consciousness are opened up by its own efforts in those directions. That is true Qabalah, or "received teaching." Enlightened instruction entering a Self from within, via the contacts connecting that Self with what is sometimes called Superconsciousness, OverSelf, or any other term indicating a superior and independent source of spiritual awareness. In our Self-system being considered here, those contact points are the focalized Concepts we make of the Tree-principles, and that is why they are so important. They link us up with only the very best of "life behind life," and ensure that we evolve into as perfect as possible Identities, providing we live in accordance with their pattern.

Living the Tree by magical means is a fascinating occupation. Almost every day brings new opportunities for invention and application in this field of action. All sorts of interesting suggestions seem to present themselves for investigation or adoption. Ideas appear to come from everywhere as though eagerly demanding attention. Initiated Selves calmly direct these into their correct categories of consciousness so that they will be stored up in their appropriate Spheres for use as required. To obtain any of this typified energy on demand, it is only necessary to invoke or "call up" the code of the requisite Sphere and connect up the intentionally inquiring end of consciousness to it. If, for instance, we specifically need a Compassion contact, we Inwardly invoke a sense of Royal Blueness, quadruple rhythm, or other locational association, then request whatever we intend. By defining the nature of our contact according to whichever level of the Sphere (i.e., Originative, Creative, Formative or Expressive) with which it is linked, very delicate degrees of contact can be maintained, but this demands rather exceptional skill. Those levels of each Sphere are generally codified by God-Names, Archangel titles, Angelic Orders and plain planetary signs. They are all headings under which consciousness is classified and arranged in every conceivable description or degree necessary for the continuance of cosmic life in its finest forms of force. There is no need to worry unduly about these during the initial stages of Tree-growing. They will come at their proper time by themselves, once the Tree grows strong and tall enough to bear them. The main thing is to achieve the ability of "calling the Tree into Cosmos" in an instant, or making it into such an Inner reality that we can awake our awareness to it as and when we Will.

Everyone evolves his own pet formulae for this as a rule, but normally the more concentrated and concise these are, the better. Some we have already considered, but even those may be further condensed for use amid the urgencies of everyday living. Directing the Inner attention accordingly, one might say silently:

> *Heaven, Earth, and cosmic Tree.*
> *Be the way of life for me.*

Or, more simply:

> *I will be*
> *My Cosmo-Tree.*

The chief point to bear in mind, relative to summoning the Self-system into synthesis around us, is that the Circle-Cosmos has to be called before the Tree, and the Tree is not summoned without its containing Cosmos. The reasons for this are simple. First, since the Tree grows out of the energies provided through the power-perimeter of Cosmos, there is no point in expecting a Tree of Life to exist properly without its source-supply of vital force. Second, the Cosmo-Circles create the necessary Inner environment for germinating and growing a Tree as it should stand in spiritual Space. Lacking such protection, a Life-Tree is unlikely to grow well—if at all—for a Self that is unable or unwilling to provide sufficient shelter, at least during the seedling and sapling stages of development.

Another simple summoning symbol is a variation of

the Triple Tau, or "backbone" design. This is no more than a central upright with three equal cross-pieces surrounded by a circle. The proportions of the Triple Tau are those of the Tree, its cross bars being the Wisdom-Understanding, Mercy-Severity, and Victory-Glory equations. Roughly, these amount to a conscious relationship with life being made via the high level of Judgment, the middle level of Justice, and the lowest level of Guesswork. Otherwise one might say conscience, consistency, and convenience, three general grasps of life from low, middle and high viewpoints. The surrounding Circle signifies an associated state of Cosmos, and its edge contacts the Triple Tau at top and bottom. To be effective, the complete symbol has to be applied to a Self so that it becomes "absorbed in" as a life-attitude. Merely looking at it on paper or visualizing it as if appearing in the mind is quite inadequate. The symbol must be literally lived as a Self-arrangement, and this can only be done by moving our Selves metaphysically so as to correspond with whatever principles the symbol presents—like a plan.

To emphasize this very important point, candidates in some of the old initiations were occasionally treated almost traumatically with various physical symbols, so that an impression might be made deeply enough into the underlying state of "unawareness" which had to be awakened. This is not unlike trying to waken a very sound sleeper by shaking him urgently and shouting in his ear at the same time. To awaken Selves from spiritual torpor into states of alert awareness sometimes requires an equivalent treatment. In initiations which try and reach a soul and a Self via material media, a physical shock was often delivered as a means of making contact with much deeper Inner life-levels. For instance, in the case of this particular symbol, it would be constructed, at human height, of solid material, and the candidate marched slowly toward it in time with an appropriate chant containing necessary "seed ideas." Then actual contact was made with the symbol, with considerable pressure. Finally he was bound, or "crucified," with arms outstretched along the center bar, then often left entirely alone for sometimes considerable periods to work out the meaning behind such treatment. If correctly carried out on a properly prepared candidate, and providing Inner contacts were indeed functioning as they should, such an experience could have sufficient spiritual effect to change an Initiate's cosmic course very considerably along an intended direction. To apply precisely the same physical stresses to an unwilling and utterly unprepared soul would only be a cruel, stupid, or even criminal act, causing damage in all directions and serious spiritual consequences for those responsible for it.

Nevertheless, symbols still have to be converted into Self-states if they are to serve any spiritual purpose. It is no good at all simply to stare at them stolidly and assume this to be meditation. Meditation implies going at least half way toward meeting an objective with the mind and then acting mentally on the contact. That is exactly what we are meant to do with symbols encountered in the Holy Mysteries. Treat them as builders treat architectural designs, or as engineers use blueprints. We might say an engineer employs a two-dimensional drawing to produce a three-dimensional machine. Similarly an Initiate will take a three-dimensional symbol as a guide for working with four and more dimensional matters. The principles involved are much the same. In this case a Triple Tau and Circle symbol has to be converted into a conformable arrangement of Self-attitudes expressing the equation as an act of entity.

This effort entails an actual appreciation of being contained in a Circle-Cosmos, connected consciously to Heaven at the top and Earth at the bottom of a median upright axis, then cross-polarized at three points by the highest, lowest and medium markings of ability to grasp life as an experience of existence. These are the minimum essentials of a Cosmic Tree. To achieve some degree of this meditatively, we may start by conceiving the symbol life-sized immediately before us and then bring it into our Self-circles deliberately so that it disappears objectively. Later, we may literally feel our Self-states altering in accordance with the principle of its design, so that we really sense our Selves becoming upright Individuals based on Earth with hopes of Heavenly attainment, reaching out to the Right and Left of ourselves for life with the best, basest, and middle-most motives we can manage. All around us is the circuit of our complete consciousness, which we are able to contact at any point from our position of poise in the spiritual center. It takes a lot of practice and perseverance to change a symbol into a Self-state, but the exercise is a most necessary part of Mystery procedure which has to be mastered quite early in the initiatory stages of spiritual Self-hood.

The fundamentals of this are simply based on the metaphysical mechanics concerning reactive rearrangement of Self-state which is a common feature of consciousness. Say, for instance, that we enter some wonderful environment which tends to bring out all the best in us. That environment is a symbol of the state we shall become, and we react to it accordingly. On much cruder levels, what happens when we react to some very stimulating sex-symbol? This certainly induces a change of Self-state, but the basics are just the same as if it were taking place on far higher parallels of perception. The relation of Self-states to symbols in the Holy Mysteries is just a very refined and spiritually sophisticated development of an ordinary ability transferred to much finer conditions of cosmic capability. It depends mostly on evolutionary advancement and careful training in order to achieve this art with any marked degree, but then, that is what initiation is all about. MAN, KNOW

THY SELF also means MAN, GROW THYSELF.

Growing into an organized state of spiritual Self-hood should be the main motivation behind any system of initiation. The only divergences are differences of opinion and method concerning the same objective, and these variations in turn are due to the many classifications of Self-category. What we have been dealing with in this particular Self-system is a style of Self-arrangement suitable for the stage of evolution that Humanity is approaching, more or less as a whole Entity in the immediate stages of our Inner initiatory status as a life-species. Though it is a universal model, it also becomes exclusively individual for each being building it for themSelves. No matter how many millions or hyper-millions of times its design is used, no unit can ever be absolutely identical to any other. Theoretically, there is only one male and one female human body in existence; all others are copies made in various fashions at different times and places. Similarly, there is only one Great Self alive, and all others have to copy the Individual Idea for themSelves. The better the design we adopt, the nearer we shall come to the Nuclear Self Which exploded everyone into existence. Here, we have been dealing with a basic design of Being which belongs essentially to those heights and depths of life which seem divine to those of us living in these limited conditions of Middle Earth consciousness. If we term the art of our relationships with this incredible Inner Reality "Magic," we shall thereby only be revaluing in a modern way an old Truth-term for something we have been trying to do ever since our Self-beings began.

Despite all the efforts and energies expended over the very prolonged periods it may take consciously to construct this magical Self-system of Cosmos and Tree, those who conscientiously carry it out and succeed with their Self-seeds will realize they have only come to the beginning of a new Inner lifestyle. Nevertheless they will KNOW,

and not merely SUSPECT, the spiritual states of Self awaiting their achievement if they continue in this cosmic course.
Armed with, and aware of this Knowledge, life takes on a
totally different meaning and aspect altogether for a Self in
this actual stage of initiation. Values become based on
spiritual rather than material meanings. Currencies of consciousness change from being purely concerned with the
relatively petty affairs of this mundane world to a sense of
awareness extending far beyond the boundaries of bodily
exigencies. Nor does this increase of Individuality necessarily turn anyone into some remote, disinterested and
disillusioned being unconcerned with the affairs of other
humans. To the contrary, it opens up an Inner ability to
communicate with all living entities in far wider and deeper
ways than previously possible. At the same time we realize
more and more that the truest way to help any other
Individual is by assisting him to help himSelf. The further
our own Inner living is removed from the interference
range of others, the less are we likely to interfere with
theirs, but this does not signify spiritual indifference, only
independence of Identity.

The best way we can serve the spiritual interests of any
other Self is by perfecting our own Selves as far as possible
so that we may benefit others to ever greater degrees
according to their nature necessities. All the energies we
process through the paths of our individual consciousness
eventually pass back to their Inner sources and become
available for use by others in the condition they left our
Self-state. This is rather a serious thought if we consider it
carefully. What it amounts to is that we take into our Self-
states Inner energies which have previously been conditioned by untold numbers of living beings, embodied,
disembodied, or in any life-state imaginable. Having taken
these energies into our Self-states, we make what use we
Will of them, and then put them back into conscious circula-

tion, so to speak. What we have done with them determines the contribution we are making with our consciousness toward the general cosmic welfare in which other Selves are concerned. Moreover, we are reaching a point in our Earth-life evolution when we are becoming increasingly able to affect the common source-supply of consciousness involving all of us alive here. It is thus of proportionately greater importance that more individualizing Selves strive for higher and better standards of Inner living in order to counteract and if possible purify the steady stream of deliberate disintegratives poured into the immediate atmosphere surrounding us in this world.

Just as farsighted and clear-conceiving people have been, and still are, deeply concerned about the end effect of chemical and similar pollutions upon Earth-life and human genetics, so Individuals in both human and other states of Self-hood who have longer life-vision extending into spiritual dimensions are more than anxious to avert the ultimate effects of what might be called consciousness contaminants. These are extremely likely to damage our spiritual genetics, just as their physical counterparts may injure our material genetics. Seeing that both spiritual and physical factors of detriment will probably persist until many of our present generation meet them again in future incarnations, we are really preparing now the seed-states of whatever Hell or Heaven we shall encounter during our coming Earth-lives, unless we become sufficiently developed spiritually to live otherwise elsewhere.

Every Self able to construct its own state of Inner Cosmos so that the Elemental energies it deals with become purified by passage via the Nil-principle, and all consciousness processed through its system is converted into the Ten Terms of the Tree before being re-issued for use by other Selves, is making a maximum possible contribution toward human Self-salvation as an entire life species. It is virtually impossible to over-stress the importance of such individual Initiates in relation to forthcoming human history. Other issues apart, they will provide some of the main facilities for preventing the pressurized consciousness of Humankind from reaching critical mass and blowing itself apart with incalculable effects upon Inner ecology. Each single Self achieving its spiritual independence as an individual Initiate of Truth is a major asset among Humankind. Every one so qualified has far more than a minor part to play in regard to the remainder of human Earth-life, if they so Will. Selves of such a standard cannot be bought, compelled, coerced or influenced by anything except their own intentions in conjunction with what amounts to divine direction. Unless a sufficient proportion of such Selves freely elect to remain in Earth association with their still struggling fellow creatures, life on this particular planet seems unlikely to have a future worth following very far. Fortunately, such Selves usually devote their energies to the best interests of others, unless and until cosmic circumstances make such cooperation virtually impossible. Hard as the lot of Humanity is likely to be on this Earth for future generations, it is certainly not beyond the highest kind of hopes so far as our spiritual chances are concerned. While there is even a single spiritualized Self willing to keep the Inner Way from this world to higher life-states open, no mortal member of the human race need feel abandoned by the Life-Spirit. It is only necessary to seek, ask and knock in order for that Way to be opened for any sincere Self. We have to seek with soul, ask with mind, and knock with activity. So must each Self work out its own way.

There is no end to Self-hood except in Eternal Entity. Meanwhile, we have every problem of personal Self-state to solve, and on the satisfactory solution of those problems depends the whole of our individual and collective cosmic destiny. The best way to start solving any problem lies in giving it a good layout, or presentation. After that point, the application of ingenuity and intention will carry us along considerably. That is precisely what the Cosmo-Tree Self-system should do for those applying it to themSelves—give the best possible and presentable layout of a Self-state for arranging our affairs in steadily perfecting order. Why wait till physical death for a body to be laid out in a peaceful pose, when by laying a Self-system poised around Perfect Peace Profound, we might begin living as real Individuals along the truest Lines of Light toward the finest purpose for anyone in Creation? Ultimate Union of Entity and Identity in a supremely spiritual Self-state. The symbol of this ultra-cosmic condition is LIGHT-LIFE. Just THAT.

To Know our Selves, we have to answer the famous enigma of the Sphinx signifying "What is Man?" The usual version given is not complete. It should read: "What begins on four feet, then two, then three, and finally one?" Physically this can be rendered as an infant's crawl, an adult's walk, an elder with a Staff, and lastly a body lying on the ground. Metaphysically, the meaning expands into much wider areas. Four, 2, 3, 1 equal 10, the decimal scale of Divinity, indicating Humankind's ultimate destiny. It outlines the Tree of Life. It also shows our general relationship with the Four Forces, Two Polarities, Three Principles, and One Life. We might interpret it again as Single Self, faced with Three Ways between Two Pillars on a Fourfold Basis of Being. There are many combinations and connections to choose from here, all of them amounting to much the same conclusion. The sum of Humanity is the Self-equation of its own entity.

Far from the last words on this Self-system having been said, the first few ideas have only been dealt with sufficiently for interested Individuals to make their own start to Inner life. Nor should it be supposed that a single attempt at each exercise is enough to set up the system satisfactorily.

It has to be worked with at all stages, conscientiously and consistently, until the entire Self-state becomes a normality of experience in which the Self simply LIVES while relating to all other contacts of consciousness at any life-level. To attempt a time-estimate with such a program would only be foolish. True, there are constants, insofar as definite degrees of consciousness have to be directed with enough energy in specific styles at definite aims in order to achieve any given condition of a Self-state, but these may be spread over such wide areas with only fractional effects that a Time-factor would be more than difficult to calculate in calendar time. It is certainly possible to organize the system into some sort of sound shape during a few Earth-years, and perhaps obtain a semblance of it in a lesser period, though naturally the more constantly it is worked with, the truer and sounder it becomes. It must be *grown* and not *grabbed*. Any attempts at pushing it past its natural rate of development is only likely to damage its structure beyond hope of rapid repair.

This, or any other Self-system, is only of real value to those who fully intend to become far more than merely mortal and material beings, limited by biological laws to maybe no more than a few embodiments on this one poor little planet. It is designed expressly for Selves meaning to achieve their own Immortal Identity as Individuals and live in that spiritual state of Light. For others with no higher ambition than to remain in relatively helpless heaps of humanity, or who are content to control the activities of those heaps by application of coercive and compulsive cunning, such Self-systems are not only useless but actually dangerous, since to adopt this system would mean abandoning a current way of expending life-energies. None but those with sufficient courage and determination to seek their truest terms of Self and become their own Identities should attempt this, or any similar Self-system. Anyone entertaining unrealistic ideas of trying the system out with hopes of making fortunes, gratifying whims or otherwise obtaining unearned advantages over others for no more than the sake of Pseudo-Self satisfaction should be warned to leave the system severely alone. It will cause them only Pseudo-Self disaster. Where True Self emerges, Pseudo-Self must exit.

For those relatively few individualizing Selves who are becoming aware of an Inner need to extend and expand consciousness in a cosmically controllable way over much wider and finer life-limits than those available on Earth, some organized form of spiritual Self-system is as much, and even more, important than the necessity of a physical body and brain for merely mortal Earth-living. Sooner or later every evolving Self is faced with the decision of synthesizing a system which is capable of cosmic survival into Eternal and Immortal Identity, or simply letting the ordinary currents of living energies carry a supine Self casually down a deteriorating course of circumstances. Either we raise up our Selves spiritually and LIVE, or else we sink our Selves down and expire as entities altogether. The choice is entirely free, and no one can determine it except each one of us for our Selves alone. With or without us as Individuals, life will continue forever, but it is best that most if not all of us will ultimately come into one Self-state together as a Supreme Spiritual Truth of PEACE PROFOUND. Let whosoever desires only darkness and destruction be allowed to end their entities according to their own intentions. Be it unto every Self the way of life it Wills. Who comes toward the life-state of Companionship in Cosmic Light?

STAY IN TOUCH

On the following pages you will find listed, with their current prices, some of the books and tapes now available on related subjects. Your book dealer stocks most of these, and will stock new titles in the Llewellyn series as they become available. We urge your patronage.

To obtain our full catalog, to keep informed of new titles as they are released and to benefit from informative articles and helpful news, write for our bi-monthly news magazine/catalog. A sample copy is free, and it will continue coming to you at no cost as long as you are an active mail customer. Or you may keep it coming for a full year with a donation of $2.00 in U.S.A. ($7.00 for Canada & Mexico, $20.00 overseas, first class mail). Many bookstores also have *The Llewellyn New Times* available.

Stay in touch! In *The Llewellyn New Times'* you will find news and reviews of new books, tapes and services, announcements of meetings and seminars, helpful articles, news of authors, advertising of products and services, special money-making opportunities, and much more.

The Llewellyn New Times
P.O. Box 64383-Dept. 298, St. Paul, MN 55164-0383, U.S.A.

• • •

TO ORDER BOOKS AND TAPES

If your book dealer does not have the books and tapes described on the following pages available, you may order direct from the publisher by sending full price in U.S. funds, plus $2.00 for postage and handling for orders of $10 and under. Orders over $10 require $3.50 postage and handling. There are no postage and handling charges for orders over $100. UPS Delivery: We ship UPS whenever possible. Delivery guaranteed. Provide your street address as UPS does not deliver to P.O. Boxes. UPS to Canada requires a $50 minimum order. Allow 4-6 weeks for delivery. Orders outside the U.S.A and Canada: Airmail—add $5 per book, $3 for each non-book item (tapes, etc.), and $1 per item for surface mail.

FOR GROUP STUDY AND PURCHASE

Because there is a great deal of interest in group discussion and study of the subject matter of this book, we offer a special "quantity" price to group leaders or "agents." Our Special Quantity Price for a minimum order of five copies of *Attainment Through Magic* is $29.85 Cash-With-Order. This price includes U.S. postage and handling. Minnesota residents must add 6% sales tax. For additional quantities, please order in multiples of five. For Canadian and foreign orders, add postage and handling charges as above. Credit Card (VISA, Master Card, American Express) Orders only may be phoned free ($15.00 minimum) within the U.S.A. and Canada by dialing 1-800-THE MOON. Customer Service calls dial 1-612-291-1970. Mail Orders to:

LLEWELLYN PUBLICATIONS
P.O. Box 64383-Dept. 298 / St. Paul, MN 55164-0383, U.S.A.

EVOKING THE PRIMAL GODDESS
by William G. Gray

How can we as individuals find a personal, meaningful, *living* feminine aspect of Deity?

In *Evoking the Primal Goddess*, renowned occultist William G. Gray takes you on a fascinating, insightful journey into the history and significance of the Goddess in human spirituality. For the first time anywhere, he shows that the search for the Holy Grail was actually a movement within the Christian Church to bring back the feminine element into the concept of Deity, and he explains why the Grail is still so vitally important to all who inhabit the Earth today.

Gray provides you with simple techniques, rituals, and prayers that will help you to evoke a personal image of the Mother Ideal, as well as *invoke* her, so that you can join the masculine and the feminine into a spiritual concept of practical power.

0-87542-271-3, 167 pgs., 5¼ x 8, softcover   **$9.95**

BETWEEN GOOD AND EVIL
by William G. Gray

If you are seeking Inner Light, read this important new book. *Between Good and Evil* provides new insight that can help you take the forces of Darkness that naturally exist within us and transform them into spirtual light. This book will help you discover how you can deal constructively, rather than destructively, with the unavoidable problem of Evil. Our lives depend on which way we direct our energy—whether we make the Devil in ourselves serve the God, or the other way around. We must use our Good intentions to understand and exploit the Evil energies that would otherwise prove fatal to us.

In order to confront and control our "demons," Gray has revived a centuries-old magical ritual technique called the *Abramelin Experience:* a practical, step-by-step process in which you call upon your Holy Guardian Angel to assist in converting Evil into Good. By following the richly detailed explanation of this "spiritual alchemy," you will learn how to positively channel your negative energies into a path leading directly to a re-union with Divinity.

The power of altering your future lies in your own hands, and within this unique book you will discover the means to move forward in your spiritual evolution. You will find the principles discussed in this multi-faceted book valuable and insightful.

0-87542-273-X, 304 pgs., 5¼ x 8, softcover   **$9.95**

TEMPLE MAGIC
William Gray
This important book on occultism deals specifically with problems and details you are likely to encounter in temple practice. Learn how a temple should look, how a temple should function, what a ceremonialist should wear, what physical postures best promote the ideal spiritual-mental attitude, and how magic is worked in a temple.

Temple Magic has been written specifically for the instruction and guidance of esoteric ceremonialists by someone who has spent a lifetime in spiritual service to his natural Inner Way. There are few comparable works in existence, and this book in particular deals with up-to-date techniques of constructing and using a workable temple dedicated to the furtherance of the Western Inner Tradition. In simple yet adequate language, it helps any individual understand and promote the spiritual structure of our esoteric inheritance. It is a book by a specialist for those who are intending to be specialists.

0-87542-274-8, 240 pgs., 5¼ x 8, illus., softcover $7.95

THE GOLDEN DAWN
by Israel Regardie
The Original Account of the Teachings, Rites and Ceremonies of the Hermetic Order of the Golden Dawn as revealed by Israel Regardie, with further revision, expansion, and additional notes by Israel Regardie, Cris Monnastre, and others.

Originally published in four bulky volumes of some 1200 pages, this 5th Revised and Enlarged Edition has been entirely reset in modern, less space-consuming type, in half the pages (while retaining the original pagination in marginal notation for reference) for greater ease and use.

Corrections of typographical errors perpetuated in the original and subsequent editions have been made, with further revision and additional text and notes by actual practitioners of the Golden Dawn system of Magick, with an Introduction by the only student ever accepted for personal training by Regardie.

Also included are Initiation Ceremonies, important rituals for consecration and invocation, methods of meditation and magical working based on the Enochian Tablets, studies in the Tarot, and the system of Qabalistic Correspondences that unite the World's religions and magical traditions into a comprehensive and practical whole.

This volume is designed as a study and practice curriculum suited to both group and private practice. Meditation upon, and following with the Active Imagination, the Initiation Ceremonies is fully experiential without need of participation in group or lodge.

0-87542-663-8, 744 pgs., 6 x 9, illus. $19.95

MYSTERIA MAGICA
by Denning and Phillips

For years, Denning and Phillips headed the international occult Order Aurum Solis. In this book they present the magickal system of the order so that you can use it. Here you will find rituals for banishing and invoking plus instructions for proper posture and breathing. You will learn astral projection, rising on the planes, and the magickal works that should be undertaken through astral projection. You will learn the basic principle of ceremonies and how to make sigils and talismans. You will learn practical Enochian magick plus how to create, consecrate and use your magickal tools such as the magickal sword, wand and cup. You will also learn the advanced arts of sphere-working and evocation to visible appearance.

Filled with illustrations, this book is an expanded version of the previous edition. It is now complete in itself and can be the basis of an entire magickal system. You can use the information alone or as the sourcebook for a group. It is volume 3 of **The Magical Philosophy**, the other two books being *The Sword and The Serpent* and *The Foundations of High Magick*. If you want to learn how to do real magick, this is the place you should start.

0-87542-196-2, 480 pgs., 6 x 9, illus., softcover **$15.00**

THE SWORD AND THE SERPENT: The Magical Structure of Cosmos and Psyche
Being a revision and expansion of Books III and IV of the first edition.
by Denning and Phillips

This is the comprehensive guide to the Magical Qabalah with extensive correspondences as well as the techniques for activating the centers, use of images and the psychology of attainment.

In this volume, histories from contemporary life together with references to the works of mystics, poets, artists, philosophers and authorities in psychology are cited to illustrate point by point the action and interaction of the functions of the psyche as identified in Qabalistic teaching.

In this book is set forth clearly the real meaning of adepthood: in relation to this, frequent enigmas of occult literature such as the Abyss, the Knowledge and Conversation of the Holy Guardian Angel, and the supernal attainments, are presented in their true meaning and significance. The natural dignity and potential of life in this world is your birthright. In this volume, its splendor and power are made unmistakably manifest.

0-87542-197-0, 512 pgs., 6 x 9, illus., softcover **$15.00**